The Result Was Revival

The Result Was Revival

How a Renewed Homiletical Theology Contributed to the Effectiveness of the First Great Awakening in the American Colonies

C. STEWART HOLLOWAY

WIPF & STOCK · Eugene, Oregon

THE RESULT WAS REVIVAL
How a Renewed Homiletical Theology Contributed to the Effectiveness of the First Great Awakening in the American Colonies

Wipf & Stock
An Imprint of Wipf and Stock Publishers
199 W. 8th Ave., Suite 3
Eugene, OR 97401

www.wipfandstock.com

PAPERBACK ISBN: 978-1-6667-0700-7
HARDCOVER ISBN: 978-1-6667-0701-4
EBOOK ISBN: 978-1-6667-0702-1

VERSION NUMBER 03/18/26

To my sons, Zachary and Evan Holloway.

May you love Jesus and his church
and may you see awakening in your lifetime.

Contents

Preface

My first encounter with the First Great Awakening came as it does for many people—in a high school English class while reading Jonathan Edwards's famous sermon, "Sinners in the Hands of an Angry God." Ignorant of colonial America and Edwards himself, I read the vivid message as if it were delivered by one of the sweating, big-haired evangelists from my Southern Baptist childhood. I even remember acting out portions of the sermon in "evangelist style" for a friend on our school bus the afternoon we were assigned to read the sermon. Obviously, the vivid imagery employed by Edwards captured my attention! However, it did not impact me as it did the people of Edwards's own day. It was merely a homework assignment that was quickly set aside the next day when our teacher assigned yet another reading. I put Edwards and the First Great Awakening on the shelf for another day.

I glossed over the Awakening in a college course on Christian history. In seminary, however, I dove into the Awakening with great interest through both my church history courses and doctoral seminars in evangelism and preaching. As I learned more about men whose names I recognized, like Jonathan Edwards, George Whitefield, and John and Charles Wesley, and encountered new figures, like Samuel Davies and Gilbert Tennent, my interest in this period of church and American history soared.

Much of my doctoral studies took place while I was pastoring Forestburg Baptist Church, located in a small ranching community of the same name in north Texas. The size of our community was not unlike those in which revival fires sparked centuries before. As I studied the revival events and read of the ministries of these men while sitting in the church's parsonage or my church office, numerous questions burned in my heart and mind. How did awakening happen? How did these mostly Congregationalist and Presbyterian preachers of the mid-eighteenth century ignite sparks of spiritual fervor in their people that resulted in a raging revival fire that swept through the American colonies? Though the Awakening was sweeping and widespread, it was not felt in all denominations or even all Congregational and Presbyterian churches. So, did these preachers do something different than some of their co-laborers? Was there something about these revivalists that I could adopt as a young pastor and perhaps see revival come to my own church and community?

I was learning from my studies that all awakening begins with prayer, so I assumed people had been praying for revival to come, and I discovered that was true. I began to focus on the role of prayer in ministry. However, I was also learning that the sparks of the First Great Awakening were fanned into flame by the preaching of local pastors and the traveling preachers like George Whitefield. As I studied the stories and read the sermons of these preachers, my question became, "What made their preaching unique? Why might God have used it to fan the flames?"

As my study continued, I decided to point my doctoral dissertation to seeking an answer to this question. I initially considered studying how what these men believed about preaching—their homiletical theology—impacted the results of their preaching—specifically, the revival. I focused on three of the preachers, one for each major section of the colonies, and was off to the library! As I got deeper into the dissertation, however, my supervisor and I ultimately decided the dissertation had to have a narrower focus. Therefore, we concentrated only on the homiletical theology of the men.

Nevertheless, my research still provided some answers to my initial questions. I wrote a chapter that brought together my conclusions on the impact the homiletical theology of these men could have had on the revival but did not include it in the dissertation. Instead, I held onto the chapter, hoping to one day bring all my thoughts back together into a book. Seventeen years later, this is that book.

The time seems right for this work on the impact of preaching on awakening. The stirring at Asbury University and other colleges in early 2023 raised people's awareness of and longing for awakening. The conflict that erupted in Israel in late 2023 and the continual unrest in the Middle East has people wondering what is going on in our world. Mass shootings, prolific sexual sin, political scandals, and more have caused many people to realize our nation and world need another widespread, great awakening. Pastors are searching for ways to penetrate the darkness and reach the hearts of their listeners and communities in a new era of culture. As we watch fewer people in each succeeding generation in the United States identify as a Christian, we know something drastic needs to happen to shift our nation back to the Lord in the coming generations.

It is easy to become despairing when we see declining statistics and shuttered churches. But thankfully, we have been here before. Thankfully? Yes, thankfully! Because we have been here before, we can learn from the past!

Nearly three hundred years ago, in the days just before the First Great Awakening, things were no better than they are today. In fact, they may have been far worse! Though our modern world is far different from colonial America, people are not. We tend to think of the colonial citizens as saintly individuals who attended church weekly and said their prayers daily. The truth is those people struggled with sin and their commitment to God as anyone does today. In the days before the revival, sin was rampant, church attendance was declining, and many preachers and church members were not even regenerate followers of Jesus Christ! Within that colonial culture, God raised up one pastor after another through whom he brought about revival. In so doing, God dropped sparks of awakening that eventually united to form a raging fire that burned across the colonies, changing everything in America for a generation and laying the foundation for the Second Great Awakening in the next generation.

It is my prayer that such a movement will happen once again. We have attempted to bring change through politics and policies, methodologies and technologies, but none of those have resulted in lasting change. Perhaps it is time we go back to the basics—back to a preacher empowered by the Spirit of God prayerfully heralding forth the word of God to the people of God. Sound too simple? It probably did in the 1700s as well, but it worked then and it will work now.

I propose that what these men believed about preaching influenced what they preached and how they preached. *The result was revival.* While awakening is purely the work of the Holy Spirit, there are certain things we can do to make conditions amenable to a new work of God in our day. While we can never force God's hand, we can make our hearts and hands ready to receive his work in his time.

Because this book is a revamp and slight expansion of my doctoral dissertation, it is somewhat scholarly in presentation. There are numerous quotes from scholars and block quotes from the eighteenth-century preachers themselves. You may find portions of the book rather wooden and even dull! I encourage you to press on through those sections because they lay the groundwork for the other parts of the book that you will find more beneficial and applicable to your own church and ministry. In the end, all the pieces work to inform the whole.

Certainly pastors will get the most benefit from this book because it speaks to their primary task of preaching. However, I encourage church members to read this book as well. The sparks of awakening will typically come from a preacher through whom God speaks. However, congregations are the kindling upon which the sparks of revival will fall! In fact, as you will find, one part of a homiletical theology is the role as a listener! Therefore, this book is also for church members.

The saints of God should pray for two things. First, they should pray that they will be ready to be ignited by a fresh move of the Spirit of God. If they will, they will be far more likely to see awakening in their church. Second, church members should pray for their pastor to have a heart for preaching similar to these eighteenth-century revivalists. If they will, the pastor will be more likely to be renewed by the Spirit of God and, consequently, so will their church.

May God bring revival to our land and may it begin in me.

Stewart Holloway
Pineville, Louisiana
January 2026

Acknowledgments

IT HAS BEEN REWARDING to dust off the research from my dissertation and rework it into a, hopefully, more reader-friendly work. Since this book began with my doctoral dissertation, it would not have been possible without the support of many people over the last twenty years. First, I must mention my parents. Mom and Dad paid for my education and supported and encouraged me in every way possible. Unfortunately, Dad went to heaven a year and a half before I graduated with my PhD. Therefore, he has not been present for most of my life as a pastor and father. However, since Hebrews tells us we are surrounded by a great cloud of witnesses, perhaps Dad has had the best seat of anyone. Mom has blessed Rebecca and me as "Super Gram" to our boys and is a constant help and encourager to us in life and ministry. Never would I have imagined that she would be a member of my church and get to be such an integral part of our lives. We are grateful.

My professors at Southwestern Baptist Theological Seminary in Fort Worth, Texas, gave me a love for homiletics and the First Great Awakening. I could never adequately express my appreciation for Grant Lovejoy, Al Fasol, Steven Smith, and Roy Fish, especially. These men impacted countless ministers and missionaries who sat in their classes, read their books, or heard them preach. I am grateful to have been one student who was afforded a little extra time with these great men. Any strengths of this work are owed to them while any weaknesses are due to my own frailties. Though he was not my professor, David Allen was an encourager and has remained one since my time at Southwestern.

It is said that a church makes a pastor. If that is so, I have been blessed far more than I deserve by three loving and encouraging congregations in Forestburg, Texas; Pineville, Louisiana; and Lecompte, Louisiana. My part-time seminary church where I served on staff, Bellevue Baptist Church (now Pipeline Church) in Hurst, Texas, was also vital for support and training for most of my seminary experience. I am grateful for these churches who have made this pastor.

Of course, this book would not be possible without my wife, Rebecca. She is my greatest encourager and an excellent mother to our boys. This book would not be possible without her love and support.

I began reworking this book near the end of the worldwide COVID-19 shutdown. As things began opening back up and our church had to quickly pivot and then keep on pivoting because of new rules and possibilities, I shelved my work on this book once again. The last several years have been beyond hectic as ministry has been in full swing. I am grateful to my publisher, Wipf and Stock, for their patience, understanding, and encouragement through these challenging years. A sabbatical afforded me by our church gave me the time to make more progress. For that time of writing, rest, and renewal, I am forever grateful.

Ultimately, my gratitude goes to the Lord Jesus Christ. May people be changed by his name in another great awakening.

Introduction

I WAS A SENIOR in high school listening to my pastor deliver his morning message when I began wondering, "I guess they teach you how to preach in college and seminary?" The previous summer I had responded to God's call to ministry, and my whole life of preaching, pastoring, and whatever else God had in store was ahead of me. However, I had no idea what I was getting into as a future pastor/preacher. I knew I wanted to be effective. I knew I wanted to see God move. But how could that happen? Certainly preaching would play a great role. But was preparing a sermon basically like what I did for my essays or papers for English class each week? Or was there something more to it? What really is preaching anyway? I began paying greater attention to the sermons I heard at church, listened to on the radio, or watched on television. I listened for content, but I also listened with a curiosity of what made preaching different from every other talk or speech. I would soon learn that there was much to preaching—and, yes, when done correctly, it goes far beyond preparing a weekly essay for the congregation.

As I completed my master's degree in seminary, I began turning my attention to the focus for a PhD. However, I faced a dilemma—I knew my Greek and Hebrew were not good enough for Old or New Testament studies, I didn't want to memorize names and dates for a church history degree, and I wasn't smart enough to hang with the theologians and philosophers! Besides, I knew my calling was to pastor, and I wanted my PhD to further prepare me for what I would spend the rest of my life doing. While sitting in preaching class one day, I realized that preaching brings every other discipline together from study to theology to delivery! Even better, the study of preaching fit my calling and passion as a pastor!

I entered my PhD studies without a clue as to all they would involve. I soon learned that my field had a fancy name: *homiletics*, the official name for the study of preaching.

The field of homiletics covers such topics as the biblical basis for preaching, the history of preaching, the theology behind preaching, as well as the more widely known areas of methodologies for preaching. Most introductory preaching classes in seminaries necessarily place most of their emphasis on methodology and mechanics. This is understandable as a seminary's purpose is largely to prepare ministers for effective ministry in the local church. Preachers need to know how to prepare and preach a message because Sunday is always coming, not to mention Sunday night and Wednesday in many churches! Therefore, introductory preaching classes teach the preacher how to study a Bible passage and then present a message grounded in that passage to the people. The focus is largely on defining a central idea for the message that will drive to a specific objective and then developing relatable introductions, conclusions, explanations, illustrations, and applications to communicate the biblical truth to the congregation.

It is typically only in more advanced homiletical studies, such as upper-level electives or doctoral studies, that a seminary student will delve into other areas of homiletics, such as the history of preaching or specific topics related to the task of preaching. These studies add a level of depth to a preacher's understanding of his task. They also provide a great deal of inspiration, especially when one studies preachers of old and the spiritual power God has granted his heralds.

One of the important areas of the field of preaching treated in these more advanced studies is homiletical theology. There is a difference between the more familiar homiletical methodology and the lesser-known homiletical theology. Homiletical methodology concerns such issues as the construction and delivery of the sermon and is mostly interested in the *how* of preaching. In contrast, homiletical theology describes the theological beliefs that drive one's preaching and is mostly interested in the *what* and *why* of preaching. Considerations of the role of the preacher, the role of Scripture, the role of the Holy Spirit, the role of the listener, and the aim of preaching are included in a homiletical theology. For variation, the terms *homiletical theology* and *theology of preaching* will be used interchangeably in this book.

The foundational issues of preaching are the prominent emphasis of a homiletical theology. By penetrating beyond the *how* of preaching, a homiletical theology goes deeper to discover the *who*, *what*, *why*, and *where* that help empower such a "foolish" thing as preaching (1 Cor 1:21). It recognizes with Paul that the power is not in the wise and persuasive words of the preacher, one's methodology, but in something deeper—namely, the Spirit's power working in and through the preacher as he carries out the God-anointed practice of preaching (1 Cor 2:4–5).

David Greenhaw, retired president and professor of preaching at Eden Theological Seminary in St. Louis, Missouri, states, "Theology of preaching is concerned with the role and place of preaching in the life of the Christian church" and "what the church is doing when it preaches."[1] Greenhaw suggests that the major issues within a homiletical theology include the authority of the preacher and the relationship of preaching to Scripture, as well as the historical, cultural, and liturgical contexts of preaching.

A study of these foundational issues causes us to realize that effective preaching is not the result of homiletical methodology alone but homiletical theology as well. Further, while a good methodology is vital, I would suggest that homiletical theology sways the effectiveness of preaching more than does methodology since theology is the foundation of preaching. If one does not have a strong homiletical theology, then his carefully developed, creative methodology will matter little. However, preaching that emanates from a strong theology of preaching will find an effective methodology and produce lasting positive spiritual effects upon the preacher's hearers and culture. As homiletician Paul Scott Wilson observes, "All preaching tries to make a difference in people's lives. That is why Christ commissioned people to do it."[2] The preacher who possesses a strong theology of preaching will be more likely to develop an effective methodology of preaching and thus see positive spiritual effects in his hearers than one who does not.

This dynamic relationship between homiletical theology and positive spiritual effects is illustrated during the First Great Awakening in the

1. Greenhaw, "Theology of Preaching," 477.

2. Wilson, *Preaching and Homiletical Theory*, 66.

American colonies[3] (ca. 1726–1776).[4] This book will identify and explore the homiletical theology of Jonathan Edwards (1703–1758), Gilbert Tennent (1703–1764), and Samuel Davies (1723–1761) and how this homiletical theology impacted the First Great Awakening. Correlations will be made between what the revivalists believed about preaching and the resulting revival.

3. Bumsted and Van de Wetering provide a helpful summary of the geography and population of the American colonies. The population of the colonies in the 1740s was approximately 840,000. Massachusetts and Virginia (150,000 inhabitants each) were the two largest colonies. Regional characteristics divided the colonies into distinctly different areas, regardless of population.

"Most contemporary observers divide the British colonies into three distinct sections: New England, dominated by the province of Massachusetts Bay; the Middle Colonies, dominated by Pennsylvania; and the South, dominated by Virginia. The New England colonies—New Hampshire, Massachusetts, Connecticut, Rhode Island, and perhaps Nova Scotia—were a region of small subsistence farms and coastal maritime/commercial activity, relatively homogeneous ethnically and religiously. The Middle Colonies—New York, New Jersey, Pennsylvania, the Pennsylvania Lower Counties (now Delaware)—contained several large centers of commercial and industrial activity and a sizeable number of market farms, . . . and were already characterized by a religio-ethnic diversity which served as the prototype for the American melting pot. The South—Virginia, Maryland, the Carolinas, Georgia—had large-scale farms (usually called plantations), based on the labor of African slaves, and small family farms." Bumsted and Van de Wetering, *What Must I Do*, 3–4.

4. The Awakening is difficult to date. Some limit it to the years 1735–1742, but evidence suggests that the general work came in various movements over the course of several decades in three primary regions (New England, Middle, and Southern Colonies). Armstrong, "Editor's Introduction," 9. This study dates the Awakening in the American colonies beginning with the ministry of Frelinghuysen in the Middle Colonies and ending with the Revolutionary War. For more, see Maxson, *Great Awakening in the Middle Colonies*, 141, and Kidd, *Great Awakening*, xix.

CHAPTER I

Why These Men? Why This Study?

WHO WERE THESE MEN? WHY ARE THEY SIGNIFICANT?

EDWARDS, TENNENT, AND DAVIES possessed a theology of preaching that allowed them to be effective in advancing the gospel within the American colonies during the First Great Awakening. Each of these three men was the leading preacher in his colonial region and each man's preaching was decidedly different from the mainstream preaching of his day.[1]

In the history of preaching, all three men maintain honored places of importance. Edwards was the great apologist[2] of the Awakening and pastor of one of the most famous and influential churches of the New England revival, the Northampton Congregational Church in Northampton,

1. In popular and scholarly writings, George Whitefield and John Wesley are mentioned frequently and accurately as great preachers of this period. Wesley was the leader of the Evangelical Awakening in Britain. Whitefield was the great unifier of the revivals on both sides of the Atlantic and is widely recognized as the most popular preacher. While both men were important to the Awakening, this book is concerned with those preachers whose ministries were primarily in the American colonies. Further, this book's focus on Edwards, Tennent, Davies, and thus the Congregational and Presbyterian denominations, may seem to diminish or exclude the role of numerous other preachers and their denominations. This is not the intention since the author's own tradition gained much energy from the Awakening. The scope of this work simply demanded exclusion of many worthy subjects.

2. Noll, *History of Christianity*, 95.

Massachusetts. Through his writings and preaching, Edwards helped fan revival's flame throughout the New England colonies.[3]

Gilbert Tennent was one of the first preachers in the colonies to experience awakening. In the early 1700s, Tennent arrived to pastor a church in central New Jersey; a church he found to be spiritually dead. Despite meeting hostility when he preached on personal faith, Tennent pressed on and, in 1727, saw revival break out. Tennent was later used to carry the revival to other areas throughout the colonies but was especially effective in the Middle Colonies of Delaware, Pennsylvania, New York, and New Jersey. Leading Tennent expert, Milton Coalter Jr., states that before the American Revolution, Tennent published more than any other clergyman in the Middle Colonies and, during the Awakening, "he maintained close relations with numerous New England ministers and practically all of the major middle colony awakeners."[4]

Samuel Davies was a brilliant combination of statesman, preacher, poet, and humanitarian. As such, he was able to unify Presbyterians and provide a doctrinal basis for the revival in the Southern Colonies. Though he was opposed by some Virginia Anglicans because he emptied their churches, Davies maintained a careful balance between boldness and gentility, refusing to attack Anglicanism, yet expressing appall at their lack of concern for religion.[5] George William Pilcher, the leading Davies expert, states, "Davies was a major leader of the Great Awakening in the American colonies and perhaps was unsurpassed as a pulpit orator either in Great Britain or in America."[6]

Edwards, Tennent, and Davies were remarkably effective in both reaching their culture through preaching and leading their culture to revival through preaching. These three preachers saw their congregations spiritually mature, their churches' attendance numerically increase, and their culture change as the result of preaching.

3. Revival most certainly would have occurred without Edwards, "but he became the primary apologist for, and defender of appropriate revival methods as legitimate tools of the church in performing its task." Holland, *Preaching Tradition*, 56.

4. Coalter, *Gilbert Tennent*, xvi.

5. Pilcher, *Samuel Davies*, 14–15.

6. Pilcher, *Samuel Davies*, viii. Heimert and Miller call Davies "the leading instrument of the southern revival." Heimert and Miller, *Great Awakening*, 376.

DOES THIS STUDY MATTER?

While numerous studies have emphasized the impact of the revivalists' homiletical methodology, largely emphasizing the influence of the sermonic flamboyance of Whitefield, few, if any, have gone deeper to determine the homiletical theology that drove such impassioned preaching.[7] Further, while previous studies have rightly shown the influence of Whitefield and the change of methodology that occurred in eighteenth-century preaching, they have often failed to realize that not everyone employed the same methodologies. As will be demonstrated, Edwards, Tennent, and Davies employed slightly different homiletical methodologies. However, their homiletical *theologies* were remarkably similar. Such historical examples from a period of enormous cultural and homiletical transformation can help preachers in similar periods remain biblically grounded and culturally relevant as they watch their preaching affect change in their hearers and culture. These men were remarkably effective preachers. This book posits that their ministries may be used to help contemporary preachers answer the question, "What homiletical theology is fundamental to effective preaching?"

Contemporary Questions

Homiletics is concerned with effectiveness in preaching. The discussions concerning preparation, hermeneutics, form, content, style, history, culture, theology, etc., are an attempt to answer the question, "How does one preach effectively?"

In recent decades, answers to this question have focused upon methodology, specifically in terms of sermon form, style, and creativity in delivery. Such an emphasis has led to numerous discussions and publications concerning these issues. Certainly, many of the works published during these discussions will be enduringly helpful. However, in lingering so long on methodology, homileticians have often neglected their homiletical theology. In turn, they have allowed, perhaps unknowingly, an errant perspective of the basis for effective preaching to become prevalent.

The result of this methodological emphasis has sometimes caused young church leaders through each generation to claim that preaching is

7. See Stout, *Divine Dramatist*; Stout, *New England Soul*. Histories of preaching also emphasize methodology.

broken. Though most of these leaders emerge from an evangelical background that values preaching, they insist that preaching is broken because the church often fails to take seriously the cultural shifts of each generation.

In some ways, these leaders are correct. First, preachers have at times failed to take cultural shifts seriously, feeling they will soon go the way of other pop-culture crazes. Confident that these shifts are only subcultural and will eventually die out, ministers continue to preach as they always have, largely ignoring the cultural shifts. However, as Craig Loscalzo states, "Only a pulpit that identifies with the milieu of the time will be heard over the babble of other voices demanding people's attention."[8]

Second, the church leaders are correct to point out a persistence of the familiar in preaching. As it appears in many churches, preaching is not effective because it is always there, and it is always the same. In his young days of ministry, Ed Young, Pastor of Fellowship Church in Dallas, Texas, said, "People get bored with seeing and hearing the same old thing week after week. When they know what's coming, they tune it out; the higher the predictability, the lower the communication."[9] Much of the purported sameness of preaching results from the model preachers follow. Loscalzo notes that preachers are using a modern model in a postmodern world. He explains,

> The modern pulpit was steeped in a reasoned homiletic, marked by point-making sermons, alliterated outlines, and third-person descriptive logic. Sermons of the modern era often talked about God, about the Bible, about life, viewing these matters like specimens under a microscope.[10]

While such a model can still be effective in the postmodern era, a preacher who becomes caught in a routine of comfortable sameness in this or any model, can find his preaching falling short of its intended goal. Sadly, despite the hard work preachers may put forth in crafting their outlines, their listeners often depart the services having learned little, having experienced nothing, and having left the sermon at the pulpit with the preacher.

Contemporary church leaders are correct in raising awareness of these issues. Preachers must learn to address their culture. However, the common reaction is to dismiss the old and develop something new. Thus, depending on their own era, pastors sometimes redefine preaching by replacing the sermon with a spontaneous monologue or dialogue, talk

8. Loscalzo, *Apologetic Preaching*, 20.

9. Young and Stanley, *Can We Do That*, 151.

10. Loscalzo, *Apologetic Preaching*, 21.

shows, films, interviews, art, or dramas.[11] Some change their dress in order to connect with a modern audience. Others redesign the platform from which they speak, replacing the pulpit with a bistro table or nothing at all. While there is nothing inherently wrong with some of these changes, they are mere changes to methodology. The attitude seems to be: "Preaching is broken; therefore, I must replace it. And I will do so with a new or renewed methodology."

While these and other methods are helpful and powerful communication vehicles and may accompany preaching at times, they cannot be defined as "preaching." Preaching is helping people hear from God for the purposes of edification and evangelism through the oral proclamation of God's truth, revealed in Scripture, by a person called of God, affected by the message of God, and empowered by the Spirit of God. Talk shows, movies, pictures, etc., are not primarily oral proclamation and many are not proclaiming truths revealed in Scripture. Nor do they involve the human element of a person who is called by God, affected by the message of God, and empowered by the Spirit of God. While they may be beneficial in a church, they should not be identified as "preaching."

Whereas some church leaders rightly encourage preachers to use a variety of creative forms in preaching, they often fail to realize that the problem is not with methodology alone and certainly not with preaching itself. Preaching is not broken. Since the beginning of the church, the proclamation of the word of God has been central, effective, and mandated.

Jesus Commissioned the Church to Preach

The act of proclamation is central to the tasks of evangelism and discipleship commanded in Christ's commission to the church (Matt 28:19–20). As the apostle Paul planted churches and equipped men for ministry, he placed emphasis upon the centrality of preaching. In 1 Timothy, Paul wrote, "Give attention to the public reading of Scripture, to exhortation and teaching" (1 Tim 4:13). In 2 Timothy, Paul said, "Preach the word; be ready in season and out of season; reprove, rebuke, exhort, with great patience and instruction" (2 Tim 4:2). And to Titus, Paul charged, "But as for you,

11. For example, Kimball says, "Through various experiential elements as well as through the space itself, we can actually preach biblical truth. Art preaches. Scripture preaches. Music preaches. Even silence preaches." Kimball, *Emerging Church*, 186.

speak the things which are fitting for sound doctrine" (Titus 2:1). Certainly, preaching is central to the task of the church.

It is likely that over three billion sermons have been preached since Pentecost.[12] The New Testament makes clear that the church's growth was largely due to preaching. Luke records, "And the word of God kept on spreading; and the number of the disciples continued to increase greatly in Jerusalem" (Acts 6:7). Peter reminded his readers that they had been "born again not of seed which is perishable but imperishable, that is, through the living and abiding word of God" (1 Pet 1:23). This word was the one *preached* to them (1 Pet 1:25). Paul wrote to the Corinthians, "We preach Christ crucified, to Jews a stumbling block, and to Gentiles foolishness, but to those who are the called, both Jews and Greeks, Christ the power of God and the wisdom of God" (1 Cor 1:23–24). Paul realized that there is an indelible power in preaching that does not exist in other communication forms. To the Romans he wrote, "I am eager to preach the gospel to you also who are in Rome" (Rom 1:15). Though he was writing to them, he longed to preach to them. According to Haddon Robinson, "A power comes through the preached word that even the written word cannot replace."[13]

Preaching has always been important for the church's advancement. P. T. Forsyth, one of the heralded thinkers in British theological history, was correct when he said, "With its preaching Christianity stands or falls."[14] Former Yale theologian Leander Keck claims, "Every renewal of Christianity has been accompanied by a renewal of preaching."[15] Preaching has always been important and will continue to be important because, as Michael Quicke asserts, "preaching echoes through the millennia sometimes fortissimo, often pianissimo, but always vital for the church's life. . . . Preaching at its best has always accompanied church life at its best."[16]

Preaching Has Always Allowed Creative Methodologies

Preaching has been presented through a variety of methods throughout the history of God's revelation of himself to humanity. It has been and still can be creative. Some of today's church leaders have missed the fact that both

12. Buttrick, *Mystery and the Passion*, 1.
13. Robinson, *Biblical Preaching*, 19.
14. Forsyth, *Positive Preaching*, 1.
15. Keck, *Bible in the Pulpit*, 11.
16. Quicke, *360-Degree Preaching*, 29.

the prophetic examples of preaching and the numerous New Testament references to Christian preaching provide freedom of variety in methodology. There are manifold methodologies revealed in the way preaching is described in the Bible. These range in type from prophecy to heralding to explaining to defending to conversing as indicated in table 1.

Table 1: Selected Descriptions of Preaching in the Bible[17]

Methodology	**Reference (selected examples)**
To give the sense or meaning	Neh 8:7–8
To announce as a prophet	Deut 13:1; 18:20; Jer 23:21
To announce glad tidings	Isa 61:1; Ps 40:9
To call out	Isa 61:1
To herald	Rom 10:14–15; 1 Cor 1:21–23; 2 Tim 4:2
To announce joyful news	Luke 4:1
To unfold the meaning of, to expound	Luke 24:27–32
To reason, to discuss, to converse	Acts 17:2–3
To place alongside (like in Jesus's parables)	Matt 13:31
To declare	Luke 9:60
To proclaim	Acts 4:2; 13:5
To preach, to speak boldly	Acts 9:27–29
To expose, to correct, to convict, to reprove	2 Tim 4:2; Titus 1:9; 2:15
To rebuke or warn seriously	2 Tim 4:2
To encourage, to defend	2 Tim 4:2
To affirm solemnly, to give a witness	Acts 20:21
To agree with; to profess	1 Tim 6:12
Converse	Acts 20:11
To speak	Mark 2:2
To teach	Acts 5:42
To explain	2 Pet 1:20
To discuss, to dispute	Acts 9:29
To give a defense	Acts 22:1; 1 Pet 3:15; Phil 1:7, 16; 2 Tim 4:16
To share the gospel as a gift	1 Thess 2:8

17. This table is adapted from two provided by Bryan Chappell. For a more extensive treatment with Hebrew and Greek words included, see Chapell, *Christ-Centered Preaching*, 89–91.

This list is not exhaustive, but it indicates that varying and creative methodology is natural to preaching. Though preachers do not always utilize such variety, methodology alone is not the problem. And, certainly, preaching is not broken.

Preachers Must Possess a Strong Homiletical Theology

If preaching is not broken, what is? The answer lies much deeper than methodology. There must be something more, something at preaching's core.

The Unending Cycle of Methodology Must Be Broken

In the 1970s Clyde Fant delineated a cycle in which preaching participates. Though over fifty years have passed since Fant described this cycle, the passing decades have only confirmed his accuracy.

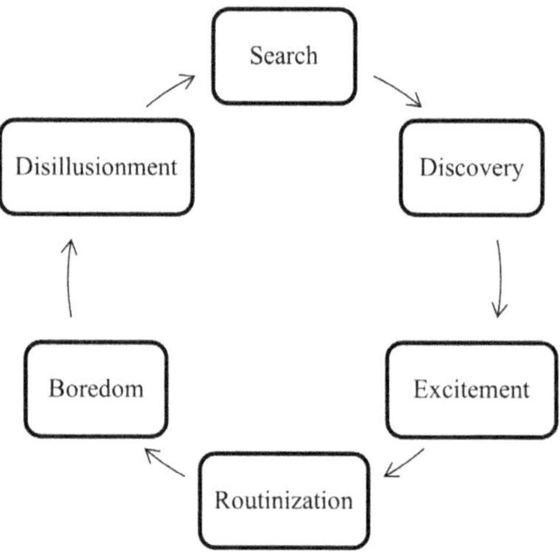

Clyde Fant's Preaching Cycle

Preaching has always been important for the church's expansion, but it has not always enjoyed the same level of prominence and practice. At times, as in the early medieval period (500–1000), the church's preaching suffered under a dark climate. At other times, as in the later medieval period (1100–1300), the church experienced a revival of preaching. Fant states:

> With respect to the proclamation of the gospel, a definite cycle can be observed for two thousand years: *search, discovery, excitement, routinization, boredom, disillusionment, search.* Naturally, this order is not mechanically reproduced in every generation, but the broad outlines are plainly discernible in Christian history. Further, there are smaller waves of this effect going on within the larger cycle. The church as a whole might be at one point, while individual locales might be at an altogether different stage of development.[18]

Fant explains that during the period of *search*, homiletical scholars and practitioners "search for an adequate means of conveying the Word." The search then leads to *discovery*: "discovery of words for the realities it has grasped, however imperfectly, and of means for expressing these words to its age." During the discovery period new forms and methods of preaching are promoted. With such refreshing breakthroughs, "great *excitement*" arises as an increasing number of preachers "seize upon the words and means which have been found faithful servants of the Word." With so many people joining the homiletical march, a process of *routinization* follows, "wherein that which was spontaneously done in its beginnings is made the common practice and eventually the official program for proclaiming the faith." As a result, "*boredom* quickly sets in as the church suffers from the deadening routine of 'the right way to do it.'" Soon, "*disillusionment* follows, as more and more of the faithful discover that the standard routine does not work any longer, that the words and means that were once strong and honest servants have now become tottering and powerless tyrants." The old systems soon suffer from critique and cynicism as a new group emerges that sets out to *search* for another meaningful methodology for its day and age. Soon the cycle repeats.[19]

Fant concludes that "when someone, somewhere, in this process realizes that these efforts are no more than updated versions of the same mistake that has held the Word captive all along, and waits in humility to listen until it speaks fresh words to him, then the Word becomes flesh again and discovery begins."[20]

Fant's cycle reveals the continuing emphasis upon methodology and the cyclical pattern it produces. While Fant himself did not say one could break out of this cycle, it seems that if one could, he might find an answer

18. Fant, *Preaching for Today*, 10–11.

19. Fant, *Preaching for Today*, 11.

20. Fant, *Preaching for Today*, 12.

to so-called "broken preaching." By breaking out of the cycle of methodology and delving into the deeper foundations and stimuli for preaching, one could unearth enduring, effective preaching. Instead of merely discovering (or rediscovering or readapting) the same methodologies that have been around since biblical times, the preacher would go deeper to find why the word is so powerful when it becomes flesh, what makes it become flesh, where does it become flesh, and, whose flesh does it become?

Preachers Must Establish Their Homiletical Theology

Graeme Goldsworthy, author of *Preaching the Whole Bible as Christian Scripture*, writes,

> We have to ask about the stimulus for this activity through which multitudes have been converted to Christ. Can it really be simply a passing phenomenon destined to become outdated as we enter a more technologically oriented age of electronic communication media?[21]

The answer is no. However foolish it may seem, preaching is the act through which God has chosen to spread his word (1 Cor 1:21). The stimulus for this activity is much more than methodology, which shifts with time. The stimulus for truly effective and enduring preaching is a strong theology of preaching. Discussions on methodology have "held the Word captive."[22] A strong theology of preaching sets the word free.

What is really "broken" is not preaching. Rather, what is broken is the homiletical theology of some preachers. In the preface to his theology of preaching, originally delivered as the 1993 Moore College Lectures, Peter Adam states,

> We . . . need a theology of preaching because the practice of preaching suffers nowadays from an uncertain theological base. Changes over recent years in our theology of God's revelation, of the Bible, of Christian formation, of communication, of community and of ecclesiology have tended to undermine preaching. In such a situation it is not wise to continue a ministry without a deep conviction about its sound theological base.[23]

21. Goldsworthy, "What Is Preaching," 46.
22. Fant, *Preaching for Today*, 12.
23. Adam, *Speaking God's Words*, 9.

In his seminal homiletical text *Between Two Worlds*, John R. W. Stott insists that the essential secret to perseverance and effectiveness in preaching "is not mastering certain techniques but being mastered by certain convictions."[24] The convictions of a preacher's homiletical theology drive his homiletical methodology. Fant points out, "The divorce between theology and practical homiletics is a primary reason for the parish minister's ongoing frustrations with preaching."[25] When a preacher is totally mastered by certain convictions and preaching, his preaching will be effective.

Effective Preaching Will Result from Strong Homiletical Theology

What is effective preaching? How can one know he is effective? Fred Craddock provided part of the answer in his groundbreaking text *As One Without Authority*. He asserts that a powerful, effective pulpit "effects transformation in the lives of people and in the structures of society."[26] Graham Johnston appropriately adds, "Effectiveness must be understood in terms of bringing the listener to a clear appreciation of the biblical message."[27] As Chapell says, "Applications of biblical truth are not complete until the preacher explains how to plug in to the power that God provides."[28] Ramesh Richard condenses effective preaching into three statements that deal with the intellectual, affective, and volitional components of the Christian experience: inform the mind, instruct the heart, influence behavior.[29] Changed people who appreciate the biblical message and thus affect change on society are the results of effective preaching. Such were the results of the preaching of Edwards, Tennent, and Davies, and the preaching of the First Great Awakening as a whole.

24. Stott, *Between Two Worlds*, 92.
25. Fant, *Preaching for Today*, xi.
26. Craddock, *As One Without Authority*, 19–20.
27. Johnston, *Preaching to a Postmodern World*, 62.
28. Chapell, *Christ-Centered Preaching*, 309.
29. Richard, *Preparing Expository Sermons*, 24–25.

CHAPTER II

Historical Context of the First Great Awakening

THE FIRST GREAT AWAKENING

THOUGH JON BUTLER HAS argued that the Awakening was an "interpretive fiction" invented by nineteenth-century Christian historians and amounted to "a short-lived Calvinist revival in the early 1740s," numerous scholars still affirm that a general awakening did take place in the mid-eighteenth century.[1] For example, Thomas Kidd takes issue with Butler, saying, "No doubt the eighteenth-century awakenings were centered in New England, but over time they came to influence parts of all the colonies." Kidd asserts that the revivals brought about "a major alteration of global Christian history."[2]

Before the Awakening: Declining Spirituality

On the surface, colonial America may seem like an especially religious place. Religion of some type was everywhere. "By the 1730s, colonial America teemed with an abundance of European religious groups."[3] Anglicans and

1. Butler, "Enthusiasm Described and Decried," 309.

2. Kidd, *Great Awakening*, xviii.

3. Butler, *Religion in Colonial America*, 7. For a discussion of the developing pluralism and religious diversity in the colonies, see Butler, *Religion in Colonial America*, 7–73.

Dissenters, Catholics and Protestants, Christians and heathens, all lived side by side in a religious melting pot. But such diversity and pluralism often allowed true spirituality to wane and religious interest to decline. The decline began during the closing years of the seventeenth century and continued into the first three decades of the eighteenth. It was not confined to America, "for the same was true of England, Scotland, Wales, and continental Europe."[4]

While the state of religion prior to the Awakening may not have been as decrepit as often described, "still," Mark Noll states, "even objective evaluators have recognized that confident religious life, persuasive preaching of the gospel, and effective Christian pastoring were in relatively short supply during the first decades of the eighteenth century."[5] The climate created by the depletion of these three elements set the stage for the Awakening as well as influenced the homiletical theology of its leaders. The depleted nature of the elements as supplied by Noll will now be treated.

Lack of Confident Religious Life

Though Christianity enjoyed great prestige, "it failed to capture popular enthusiasm. In every section the vast majority of the population was outside of the membership of the churches."[6] Even as late as the 1690s, New England was universally regarded as the best churched section; still, even for the Puritan establishment, attendance had greatly declined.[7] Further, many of those who were members lacked religious fervor.[8]

In 1733, Massachusetts Congregational pastor Samuel Wigglesworth (1688–1768) delivered an election sermon portraying the lack of spiritual interest and fervor in New England. Wigglesworth proclaimed,

4. Webber, *History of Preaching*, 67.

5. Noll, *Rise of Evangelicalism*, 38.

6. Smith et al., *American Christianity*, 1:311.

7. Bonomi, *Under the Cope*, 90. Membership in Puritan churches that had been as high as 80 percent of the population in the 1630s and 1640s plunged to half those rates by the 1670s. Butler, *Religion in Colonial America*, 42. See also Holifield, *God's Ambassadors*, 57.

8. While the worship of God may have been the primary motive for many who attended church, attendance also served non-spiritual needs. Churches in both country and town were vital centers for community life and places for the dissemination of information. Government proclamations were broadcast from the pulpit and news exchanged in the churchyard. Bonomi, *Under the Cope*, 87.

> It is a Truth, that we have a *goodly exterior Form of Religion*; Our *Doctrine Worship* and *Sacraments* are *Orthodox*, *Scriptural*, and *Divine*. There is an external Honour paid to the *Sabbath*; and a professional veneration for Christ's *Ambassadors* for the sake of their Lord. We set up and maintain the *Publick Worship* of God, and the Voice of the Multitude saying, *Let us go in to the House of the Lord*, is yet heard in our Land.
>
> Moreover *Practical Religion* is not quite extirpated among us, and there are, it is to be hoped, a considerable number of serious and vigorous Christians in our Churches, whose *Piety* is acknowledged and respected by their Neighbours. . . . Whilst on the other hand, the *prophane and wicked Person* is generally abhor'd; and the more deformed Vices seek the retreats of Darkness to hide their detestable heads.
>
> And yet with what sorrow must we speak, that these things are but the *Remains* of what we *Once* might show; the shadow of past and vanish'd Glory![9]

The motions of worship were happening in New England, but spirituality was declining. Such was the case throughout the colonies.

For example, in the Anglican-dominated South, though religion fared well in the 1620s and early 1630s, as congregations tried to maintain vigorous worship and moral discipline,[10] "by the 1680s, the Virginia and Maryland colonies had become remarkably indifferent in matters of religion. Though churches were the important centers for community assembly, settlers seldom participated in public Christian worship, and many children grew to adulthood without Christian baptism."[11] The problem of congregational drift was exacerbated as the colonies experienced a geographical migration away from religious practice. As waves of immigrants landed in the colonies and moved off the coast in search of arable land, they quickly outran the reach of the Anglican parish system. Likewise, many of those who may have brought piety with them to the colonies abandoned it as they settled new land.

9. Wigglesworth, "Essay for Reviving Religion," 4. Election sermons provided annual opportunities to expound political theory, assess local conditions, and even propose policies to the legislature. Heimert and Miller, *Great Awakening*, 3.

10. Butler, *Religion in Colonial America*, 46.

11. For example, "Some 85 percent of children born in Charles Parish, VA, between 1649 and 1680 never received baptism in the Church of England, and since no dissenting Protestants were active in the parish, it is doubtful they were baptized anywhere else." Butler, *Religion in Colonial America*, 49.

Ineffective Christian Pastoring

When we look at the ministers of the period, the decline in spirituality is understandable. F. R. Webber points out that most of America's great church leaders were dead and the new generation "lacked the emphatic religious zeal of their fathers."[12]

In many religious groups, academic training became a more important prerequisite for ordination than piety; sometimes it was the *only* prerequisite.[13] The result was a large number of ministers who had "intellectual competence but spiritual incompetence."[14] The absence of colonial education facilities and the necessity of journeying to Europe to gain formal ordination and training led to the importation of ministers from Europe. Some of these ministers had left Europe because they had proven to be ineffective.[15] As the population continued to expand,[16] would-be colonial clergymen found professional advancement in other areas of the prosperous society. Such a deficit of ministers caused churches, especially in New England, to hire men who were in no position to assert leadership.[17]

12. Webber, *History of Preaching*, 67. Roger Williams died in 1638. John Eliot, the first person to print a Bible in America, died in 1690. Increase Mather died in 1723. Justus Falckner, the first Lutheran pastor ordained in America, died in 1723. Cotton Mather died in 1728, and Solomon Stoddard died in 1729.

13. Conrad, "Importance of Preaching," 119.

14. Conrad, "Importance of Preaching," 119. In America, a lack of spiritual zeal led to an absence of evangelical preaching. Webber, *History of Preaching*, 67–68.

15. Old states, "The Anglicanism of Virginia tended to preach an abstract sort of moralism, cooked up in the theological leisure of Oxford and Cambridge and served lukewarm by clergymen who for one reason or another were unable to get 'a good church' back in England." Old, *Moderatism, Pietism, and Awakening*, 156.

16. Noll reports colonial population growth as follows (all figures in thousands): New England (92 in 1700; 360 in 1750; 1,233 in 1800), Middle Colonies (51 in 1700; 268 in 1750; 1,454 in 1800), Southern Colonies (107 in 1700; 542 in 1750; 2,621 in 1800). The population multiplied by more than twenty times in the eighteenth century. Noll, *Rise of Evangelicalism*, 31–32.

17. Bumsted and Van de Wetering, *What Must I Do*, 57. For more on the challenges the lack of educational training brought to the ministry, see Holifield, *God's Ambassadors*, 80–88. Such ineffective pastoring caused some congregations to view their ministers with indifference as well as hostility. Gaustad, *Great Awakening*, 3. Laymen sometimes took control for political and societal prestige. Bumsted and Van de Wetering, *What Must I Do*, 56–57. Holifield reminds us that clergymen have never had unlimited authority: "Their effectiveness has always depended on responses of congregants." Holifield, *God's Ambassadors*, 5.

While numerous ministers called for change, Gilbert Tennent is most famous for addressing the problem of ineffective pastoring in his sermon "The Danger of an Unconverted Ministry" on March 8, 1740.[18] During a visit to a pastorless Presbyterian congregation in Nottingham, Pennsylvania, Tennent expressed anger over carnal ministers and encouraged the congregation to seek a revival minister to fill their pulpit. In this most scathing attack on unconverted ministers, Tennent likened ministers to "Pharisee-shepherds" and "Pharisee-teachers" and pitied the congregations who suffered under their service. Tennent concluded his sermon by inviting his listeners to leave their unconverted ministers and seek churches where godly men gave profitable teaching.

Melancholy ministry was a serious problem in many areas. One Boston Anglican pastor, Jonathan Mayhew (1720–1766), revealed his own flat spirituality by ridiculing the practice of having Anglican missionaries sent to New England. The very thought was appalling to Mayhew. He insisted worship was regularly held, and the word and sacraments were administered. What more was needed? Such an attitude suggests that many Anglicans "were not interested in converting the ignorant and heathen to

18. In Heimert and Miller, *Great Awakening*, 71–99. On September 24, 1740, Whitefield wrote a similar thought: "The Lord enabled me to open my mouth boldly against unconverted ministers; for, I am persuaded, the generality of preachers talk of an unknown and unfelt Christ. The reason why congregations have been so dead is, because they had dead men preaching to them." Quoted in Bushman, *Great Awakening*, 30. Samuel Finley, who eventually became president of the College of New Jersey, added his own condemnation (1741). Proclaiming that revival came when it was desperately needed, Finley described the state of the church saying, "The Lives of Professors careless, unholy, unguarded; Ordinances attended, Duties performed, Sermons preached, without Life or Power, and as little Success. Was not worldly discourse our mutual Entertainment at our solemn Assemblies on Holy-days? Thus in Darkness and Security were we: And *like People, like Priest*." Finley, "Christ Triumphing and Satan Raging," 72. Joseph Tracy concludes that the number of unconverted ministers "were probably fewer than these men supposed, especially in New England. Still, it is useless to deny their existence. . . . There can be no doubt, that a considerable number of ministers were converted during the revival." Tracy, *Great Awakening*, 393. Tracy's work was first published in 1842.

Christianity but only in subverting the orderly and established New England Way."[19] Similar scenes played out in other colonies.[20]

Short Supply of Persuasive Preaching of the Gospel

Preaching "had firm and conscious ties with secular society. Politics, education, philosophy, and literature all made demands upon, and in turn created demands for, sermons."[21] Therefore, the sermon was the natural way to address the problem of declined spirituality. Sadly, many colonial ministers attempted to address the declining piety through ethical or moralistic preaching.[22] While legitimate for the times, the moralistic tone "failed to move people to grand eternal realities of the Gospel."[23] The church seemed to become "a society for the reformation of manners."[24] Preaching on such topics as sin, salvation, and eternal punishment seemed to belong to a past age. F. L. Chapell states, "People heard scarcely anything in many cases from

19. Gaustad, *Religious History of America*, 61. Many Anglican priests were "men who wanted genteel status and a good annual income rather than men who felt a genuine calling." Stretched too thin by sprawling parishes and focused on material wealth as opposed to spiritual edification, these priests "failed to move the emotions of the well-fed gentry . . . or the servants and farm tenants who came to church only to please their masters. It failed to preach at all to many far-flung communities of workers." Olsen, *Daily Life*, 281.

20. Hugh Jones taught mathematics at the College of William and Mary in Williamsburg from 1716 to 1721. After returning to England, he wrote an account of his time in the colony. Speaking of his own colonial Anglican brothers, Jones writes, "It is an opinion as erroneous as common, that any sort of clergymen will serve in Virginia; for persons of immoral lives, or weak parts and mean learning, not only expose themselves but do great prejudice to the propagation of the gospel there; and by bad arguments or worse example, instead of promoting religion, become encouragers of vice, profaneness, and immorality. . . . Neither do they want quarrelsome and litigious ministers, who would differ with their parishioners about insignificant trifles, who had better stay at home and wrangle with their own parishes. . . . Neither would they have mere scholars and stoics, or zealots too rigid in outward appearance, as they would be without loose and licentious profligates; these do damage to themselves, to others, and to religion. And as in words and actions they should be neither too reserved nor too extravagant; so in principles they should be neither too high nor too low." Jones, *Present State of Virginia*, 96.

21. Downey, *Eighteenth Century Pulpit*, 10.

22. Bumsted and Van de Wetering, *What Must I Do*, 58.

23. Armstrong, "Editor's Introduction," 11.

24. Downey, *Eighteenth Century Pulpit*, 10. Dargan, *From the Close*, 290–91. See also, Alexander, *Biographical Sketches*, 17.

the pulpit that was at all searching, for a dead ministry, must, of course, preach dead sermons."[25]

Such moralistic preaching was unable to satisfy the spiritual needs of the masses.[26] In 1723, Solomon Stoddard wrote, "It is notoriously known by those that are acquainted with the state of the Christian World, that tho' there be many eminent Truths taught, yet there is a great want of good Preaching."[27] Stoddard concluded his message stating the reason for the great want of good preaching: there was so little conversion and "many men that make an high Profession, lead Unsanctified Lives."[28]

As the eighteenth century began, a lack of confident religious life was evident. Ministers were often spiritually weak, and powerful preaching was a relic of the past. Too many churches had wandered from the path of personal piety. Some three generations of spiritual decline made the colonies a tinderbox for one of two effects: atheistic despair or spiritual revival. Thankfully, it would be revival that burned with the more effectual heat in the American colonies.

The Spark of Revival[29]

Church historians note that "outbreaks of spiritual concern and sudden upsurges in church attendance were common throughout the American

25. Chapell, *Great Awakening of 1740*, 10.

26. Downey, *Eighteenth Century Pulpit*, 19. The changes in preaching content were originally meant to help, not to hurt. In fact, Crawford writes, "Much in the new preaching resulted from the attempt to defend Christianity against the deistic attack by demonstrating the reasonableness of the Christian religion. Thus, sermons became rational discourses." Crawford, *Seasons of Grace*, 53–54.

27. Stoddard, *Defects of Preachers Reproved*, 6–7. In this message, Stoddard calls for increased clerical piety and delineates the features of good preaching. These include helping people be conscious of their time of conversion, teaching that humiliation is necessary for faith, preaching on the danger of damnation, giving proper account of the nature of justifying faith, and providing accurate signs of godliness.

28. Stoddard, *Defects of Preachers Reproved*, 18.

29. Numerous pastors and itinerant preachers were involved in the Awakening. Emphasis in this summary, however, will be placed upon Tennent, Edwards, and Davies. Justice cannot be done in only a few pages to the movement that became the First Great Awakening. For this, one must turn to the major works on the revival such as those listed in footnotes below by authors such as J. M. Bumsted and John E. Van de Wetering, Edwin Gaustad, Thomas S. Kidd, Charles Maxson, Malcolm McDow and Alvin Reid, Joseph Tracy, Wesley Gewehr, along with many others.

colonies before 1740."[30] But these sporadic revivals "were either connected with the successful activities of individual pastors or with external events—usually natural catastrophes—which wreaked temporary fear in the hearts of the public."[31]

God finally brought widespread revival to the colonies through the anointed preaching of both faithful pastors and itinerant preachers. The Awakening moved along three primary fronts. The Middle Colonies saw the first revival of religion. New England soon followed under the leadership of Jonathan Edwards. The Southern Colonies were the last to experience manifestations of the Spirit. George Whitefield is credited with uniting all three fronts.

Middle Colony Revival

The first sparks of a general revival occurred in 1726 in the Middle Colonies in four Dutch Reformed churches pastored by Theodore Jackobus Frelinghuysen (1691–1747/8). By preaching pietism[32] as well as experiential

30. Bumsted and Van de Wetering, *What Must I Do*, 61. For example, Edwards states that Stoddard (d. 1728/9) "had five harvests, as he called them: the first was about 57 years ago; the second about 53 years; the third about 40; the fourth about 24; the fifth and last about 18 years ago." Edwards, *Faithful Narrative*, in *Works of Jonathan Edwards*, 4:146.

31. Bumsted and Van de Wetering, *What Must I Do*, 61. The most famous of these was an earthquake that occurred on October 29, 1727, in New England. Crawford has documented at least fifteen spiritual harvests in New England, mostly in towns along the Connecticut River, between 1712 and 1732. Crawford, *Seasons of Grace*, 108.

32. Pietism arose from the confluence of various streams of spiritual renewal within the Lutheran and Reformed state churches of Central Europe during the second half of the seventeenth century. These tributaries came to a head water in the 1650 manifesto published by Philip Jakob Spener, *Pia Desideria* (*The Piety We Desire*). Spener believed spiritual and ecclesiastical vitality were the direct result of each individual Christian's pursuit of the simple and spiritual disciples of personal piety. His work called for six proposals for reform: (1) intensive Bible study, (2) the priesthood of all believers, (3) the outward practice of faith, (4) an end to destructive theological controversies, (5) universities as the key institution for the spiritual reform of the clergy, and (6) enriched preaching.

faith,[33] Frelinghuysen saw revival fire catch in 1726 and began to itinerate widely to spread the revival.[34]

When in 1726 revival fire reached the Presbyterians in New Jersey, the young Tennent was a tinderbox, and Frelinghuysen had the opportunity to encourage and influence the preacher.[35] In a letter to Thomas Prince of Boston published on August 24, 1744, in *Christian History*, a newspaper published to promote revival, Tennent wrote,

> When I came [to New Brunswick], . . . I had the pleasure of seeing much of the fruits of [Rev. Mr. Felinghuysen's] ministry; divers of his hearers, with whom I had the opportunity of conversing, appeared to be converted persons, by their soundness in principle, Christian experience, and pious practice; and these persons declared that the ministrations of the aforesaid gentleman were the means thereof. This, together with a kind letter which he sent me . . . excited me to greater earnestness in ministerial labours.[36]

Frelinghuysen made a strong impression upon young Tennent.

It was not Frelinghuysen alone who influenced the Middle Colony revival. Tennent's father William Tennent (1673–1746) had already laid the foundation. William trained his four sons in biblical languages, logic, and theology, as any formal theological training of the time would, but he also went a step farther. McDow and Reid note, "Most importantly, however, he instilled in each student a passion for evangelism, for a devotional life, and for the Word of God."[37]

Soon, other young men aspiring to the Presbyterian ministry sought training from William. Consequently, he built a small log building for this purpose. Named The Log College by critics and historians alike, this school

33. Experiential faith had its foundation in Dutch Calvinism. Experiential faith began with an obvious personal conversion experience. Frelinghuysen further organized his congregation into small groups for study and prayer, urged private and public extemporaneous prayer, and reserved communion for those who could make a convincing profession of faith.

34. In 1739 Whitefield called Frelinghuysen "the beginner of the great work which I trust the Lord is carrying on in these parts." Whitefield, *Journals*, 352. For more on Frelinghuysen see Maxson, *Great Awakening*, and Tanis, *Dutch Calvinistic Pietism*.

35. Coalter suggests Tennent's association with Frelinghuysen "altered the theology, preaching and quite likely the personality of the Presbyterian." Coalter, *Gilbert Tennent*, 18.

36. Quoted in Alexander, *Biographical Sketches*, 71.

37. McDow and Reid, *Firefall*, 208.

produced several revival leaders[38] and in time led to a succession of other log colleges that were operated by Presbyterian ministers as they followed the advancing frontier.[39] Though many ministers were launched from the Log College and the schools it influenced, it was Gilbert Tennent who emerged as "the principal exhorter of the fiery New Jersey revival."[40]

After suffering from a serious illness that caused him to become aware of deficiencies in his ministry and to cling more securely to God, Tennent arose "determined to endeavor to promote [God's] Kingdom with all my Might at all Adventures."[41] Tennent soon experienced "sweet meltings" among his flock, and "New Brunswick did then look like a field the Lord had blessed."[42]

In 1739–1740, the revival was greatly accelerated in the Middle Colonies by the first preaching tour of George Whitefield. Almost immediately, Whitefield experienced success.[43] Tennent and his Presbyterian colleagues welcomed the Anglican as a co-laborer. When Whitefield arrived in Tennent's charge, he found him to be a "worthy brother and fellow-labourer."[44] Though Tennent was ten years Whitefield's senior, "the two men quickly discovered that their theological and pastoral interests were hardly distinguishable."[45] After hearing Tennent preach, Whitefield recorded that he "never before heard such a searching sermon. . . . Hypocrites must either soon be converted or enraged at his preaching. He is a son of thunder and does not fear the faces of men."[46] Tennent offered to guide Whitefield

38. Whitefield, *Journals*, 354.

39. The school ultimately led to the establishment of the College of New Jersey, later Princeton University. For more on the Log College and the other schools that were birthed from it, see Alexander, *Biographical Sketches*; Coalter, *Gilbert Tennent*, 1–26; Miller, *Revolutionary College*; and Murphy, *Presbytery of the Log College*.

40. May, *Enlightenment in America*, 52. Even though Tennent completed his education before the Log College was built, he may still appropriately be classified among the pupils of the school. Alexander, *Biographical Sketches*, 24–25.

41. Alexander, *Biographical Sketches*, 72.

42. Alexander, *Biographical Sketches*, 72–73.

43. "Soon churches could not hold the crowds that came to hear him, and he took his ministry out-of-doors." Stout, "Heavenly Comet."

44. Whitefield, *Journals*, 347.

45. Coalter, *Gilbert Tennent*, 59.

46. Whitefield, *Journals*, 347–48.

through the Middle Colonies. Whitefield accepted the offer. As a result of the tour, revival's fire accelerated.[47]

New England Revival

The New England colonies were the next to be caught up in the broader revival. In 1733, awakening began in the Northampton Congregational Church under its relatively new pastor Jonathan Edwards. The Spirit began to move among the young people as "there began to be a sensible amendment of . . . evils."[48] Around the fall of 1734, Edwards preached a series of sermons on justification by faith alone that "was most evidently attended with a very remarkable blessing of heaven to the souls of the people in this town." He notes,

> And then it was . . . that the Spirit of God began extraordinarily to set in, and wonderfully to work amongst us; and there were, very suddenly, one after another, five or six persons who were to all appearance savingly converted, and some of them wrought upon in a very remarkable manner.[49]

From that fall and through the following spring, more than three hundred people were converted in the town of eleven hundred.

These mass conversions generated a spiritual revolution in Northampton. By 1735, the citizens were increasingly anxious about irreligion. Edwards reports,

> There was scarcely a single person in town, either old or young, that was left unconcerned about the great things of the eternal world. Those that were wont to be the vainest and loosest, and those that had been most disposed to think and speak slightly of vital and experimental religion, were now generally subject to great awakenings. And the work of conversion was carried on in a most astonishing manner, and increased more and more; souls did as it were come by flocks to Jesus Christ. From day to day, for many months together, might be seen evident instances of sinners brought out of darkness into marvelous light. . . . This work of God, as it was carried on, and the number of true saints multiplied, soon

47. Whitefield made an even more successful second tour of the Middle Colonies in the spring of 1740.

48. Edwards, *Faithful Narrative*, 147.

49. Edwards, *Faithful Narrative*, 149.

> made a glorious alteration in the town; so that in the spring and summer following, . . . [it] seemed to be full of the presence of God: it never was so full of love, nor so full of joy.[50]

The congregation was "alive" and had a burden for their own salvation and devotion for that of their friends and relatives. Every hearer was "eager to drink in the words of the minister," some being "in tears while the Word was preached; some weeping with sorrow and distress, others with joy and love, others with pity and concern for the souls of their neighbors."[51]

News of the religious events quickly spread throughout the Connecticut River Valley, ultimately affecting one hundred communities.[52] As travelers came for business in Northampton[53] and as peddlers roamed the valley in pursuit of their trade, revival spread northward in Massachusetts and southward to Connecticut.[54]

In 1737, the world became aware of the events in and around Northampton through the publication of Edwards's letter (November 6, 1736) to Benjamin Colman (1673–1747), the respected pastor of Brattle Street Church in Boston. The letter, titled *A Faithful Narrative of the Surprising Work of God, in the Conversion of Souls in Northampton and Neighboring Towns and Villages in New England*, was Edwards's attempt to correct any false impressions about the revival. In it, Edwards sought to be historical, scientific, detailed, reflective, and restrained. *A Faithful Narrative*, along with other stories of regional revivals, caused many ministers to recognize that a general revival might be a solution to the problems in their churches.

As the fall of 1740 approached, the red, orange, and yellow leaves were a subtle hint of the revival fires that would soon burn across New England. On September 14, 1740, Whitefield came, "bristling, crackling,

50. Edwards, *Faithful Narrative*, 150–51.

51. Edwards, *Faithful Narrative*, 150–51.

52. Lescelius, "Great Awakening," 30. By 1736 more than twenty Connecticut churches had felt its impact. Schmitt, "Preparation for the Great Awakening," 439.

53. Northampton was an important center. "The regions round about were tributary to [Northampton] and took their impressions from it. Its church was a kind of authority for all the churches in that vicinity at least, and its influence was felt more or less all over New England. Probably no place except Boston stood before Northampton in general influence at this time." Chapell, *Great Awakening of 1740*, 47.

54. Stearns, *Great Awakening*, 22.

and thundering."[55] As he had in the Middle Colonies, Whitefield fanned revival's embers into a raging fire, generating a broad and general awakening.

In his thirty-nine-day tour of New England, Whitefield met unprecedented success. From the moment Whitefield stood to preach his first sermon, the people were attentive. After touring northward into Maine, Whitefield returned to Boston where thousands were saved, including twenty ministers.[56]

Upon leaving Boston, Whitefield turned westward. He preached in many small towns before arriving in Northampton on October 17. The word of the Northampton revival of some five years previous had reached Whitefield as had the reputation of Edwards. After meeting Edwards, the impression was only greater. Whitefield wrote, "Mr. Edwards is a solid, excellent Christian. . . . I think I have not seen his fellow in all New England."[57] The breath of Whitefield upon the embers of Northampton helped awakening to flame. On Sunday, he reported:

> Preached this morning, and good Mr. Edwards wept during the whole time of exercise. The people were equally affected; and, in the afternoon, the power increased yet more. . . . I have not seen four such gracious meetings together since my arrival. Oh, that my soul may be refreshed with the joyful news, that Northampton people have recovered their first love; that the Lord has revived His work in their souls, and caused them to do their first works![58]

The fire would continue as the Awakening became a continental movement.[59]

By October 29, Whitefield's tour of New England was ended. As he left New England, Whitefield felt that much was unfinished and untouched. Such a feeling prompted his encouragement of Tennent to preach through the area in 1740 as well as his own return to the region twice more in

55. Gaustad, *Great Awakening*, 25.

56. The revival in Boston would continue for some time. Benjamin Colman, the most influential minister in Boston and a promoter of the revival, reported to Whitefield in 1742 that even Harvard was touched. Gaustad, *Great Awakening*, 51.

57. Whitefield, *Journals*, 476. Edwards, hearing of Whitefield's upcoming tour of New England, had requested the evangelist make this stop in Northampton. See Edwards, *Letters and Personal Writings*, 79–81.

58. Whitefield, *Journals*, 477.

59. In the December following, Edwards reported that the state of religion had "been gradually reviving and prevailing more and more, ever since you was here." Edwards, *Letters and Personal Writings*, 87.

subsequent years. As in the Middle Colonies, the revival reached its climax under Whitefield's itinerant ministry.

Southern Colony Revival

Revival came to the Southern Colonies later than it did to the other two regions. Because of this, the southern revival benefited from the work of quickly growing denominations such as the Presbyterians and Baptists, as well as the fledgling Methodist movement. The revival burned first through the Presbyterians, encouraged by Davies, continued to the Separate Baptists, guided by Shubal Stearns (1706–1771) and the Sandy Creek Baptist Church (November 22, 1755), and concluded with the Anglican-Methodists led by George Shadford (1739–1816).

The sparks of the Awakening in the Southern Colonies were set by Whitefield.[60] Unlike in the other colonies, however, it was not his mass preaching services that set them. Instead, it was his ministry of publication. One of the most famous revival fires set by Whitefield's publications occurred in Hanover, Virginia.

In Hanover, layman Samuel Morris (n.d.) and several friends dissented from the Anglican Church due to "a dislike of the doctrines generally delivered from the pulpit, as not savouring of experimental piety nor suitably intermingled with the glorious peculiarities of the religion of Jesus."[61] In 1740, Morris began reading to this group Whitefield's published sermons, Martin Luther's (1483–1546) *Commentary on Galatians*, the writings of John Bunyan (1628–1688), sermons of several seventeenth-century Puritan preachers, and similar materials.

Whitefield's published sermons were the initial factor in the conversion of Morris and his friends. Morris said, "The plainness and fervency of these discourses being attended with the power of the Lord, many were convinced of their undone condition, and constrained to seek deliverance."[62] Three years later, the southern awakening shifted from reading to preaching with the arrival of William Robinson (b. ca. 1722) in Hanover, Virginia.

60. Whereas the Southern Colonies were the last region to be caught up in the general awakening, they were the first to encounter Whitefield. In 1738, Whitefield arrived in Savannah. After nearly four months in Georgia and the Carolinas, Whitefield headed back to England with great vision for all the colonies. Whitefield, *Journals*, 165.

61. Davies, "Dissent in Virginia," 162.

62. Alexander, *Biographical Sketches*, 221.

Robinson was already a well-known minister when the Hanover group invited him to preach for them. Beginning on July 6, 1743, Robinson preached four sermons to the congregation, which was overwhelmed with the unexpected goodness of God. Few appeared unaffected. Morris said, "There was as much good done by these four sermons as by all the sermons preached in these parts before or since."[63] As gratitude for his work, the Hanover group presented Robinson with a large sum of money, which he refused. Nevertheless, the people insisted. Therefore, Robinson offered a solution. He would take the money and apply it to the training of a ministerial student. That student was Samuel Davies.

In April 1747, Davies arrived to supply for a few weeks in Hanover. Though the congregation had been discouraged by a recent government proclamation prohibiting and suppressing itinerant preachers, they were greatly encouraged when Davies arrived to preach. Davies ministered in and around Hanover for about a month. By his own admission, his labors were not blessed with success equal to those of his fellow itinerants, yet he records, "I have reason to hope they were of service in several instances."[64] Perhaps the congregation's aggressive attempts to secure Davies as their permanent pastor were the reason for his optimism. Yet, in spite of the congregation's attempts, Davies denied the call and spent a year at home.[65]

By the spring of 1748, Davies's health was improving. When a messenger from Hanover arrived in April with a renewed call, Davies accepted their call and in May became the first resident dissenting pastor in this area of Virginia.[66] Davies envisioned his ministry would be one of preparation for a more useful successor. The reality of his ministry was much different. With Davies's arrival, Presbyterianism entered a new period in eastern

63. Alexander, *Biographical Sketches*, 223.

64. Davies's letter to Bellamy, quoted in Alexander, *Biographical Sketches*, 226.

65. Pilcher, *Samuel Davies*, 13. Reasons for his denial included a desire for more experience, his poor health, and the death of his wife. Davies was married less than a year. Apparently, his wife died during childbirth or a serious miscarriage. The child, a son, was described as "abortive." Davies remarried on October 4, 1748. He married Jane Holt, who was a member of a well-known Anglican family in Williamsburg. Pilcher suggests that much of Davies's success in an Anglican-dominated county may have come from this union. Despite his health, Davies traveled tirelessly, preaching throughout Pennsylvania, New Jersey, and Maryland.

66. Scharpff, *History of Evangelism*, 62. "Not a single organized Presbyterian church was to be found in the older settled parts of Virginia, nor was there any other minister of his denomination within two hundred miles of Davies." Gewehr, *Great Awakening in Virginia*, 70. See also Davies, "Dissent in Virginia," 164.

Virginia. Gewehr writes, "The Log College missionaries had done their work in laying the foundation well, and now the master builder was at hand to complete the structure."[67]

After arriving in Hanover, Davies says, "It would have been my choice to confine myself wholly to one meeting-house," yet considering that hardly half of the people could come to one meetinghouse and the extreme deficit of Presbyterian ministers in the area, he concluded "to take pastoral care of them all, and to divide my labours at the sundry meetinghouses."[68] Davies later petitioned the colonial court for licensing for additional meetinghouses in new neighborhoods. Despite the court's disfavor of dissenting groups, Davies obtained licenses for three additional meetinghouses, expanding his influence to seven areas in five counties. Revival continued and spread.

In addition to preaching at his seven satellite congregations, Davies regularly published sermons, poems, and essays, and took frequent journeys to attend to courts of the church and made many missionary excursions into other parts of the region. Davies would preach to families and land owners as well as their slaves, bringing many from each group to saving faith in Christ. As he itinerated beyond his own congregations, Davies also worked to fill vacant pulpits with ministers from the northern Presbyteries.

The story of Davies's revival work includes few exciting tales of balconies breaking, people rapturous in ecstatic expressions, or the like. In fact, the revival in Virginia as a whole was free from the emotional excess that brought disrepute to the awakening in both the Middle Colonies and New England. Davies's revivalism was of a moderate sort. Though he was criticized at times for inspiring tears, faintings, and tremblings, such criticisms fell on deaf ears because such displays were infrequent.[69] In correspondence with Edwards, Davies asserted that a proper preacher must not be a "fiery, superficial" pulpit orator, but rather "a popular preacher, of ready utterance, good delivery, solid judgment, free from enthusiastic freaks, and of ardent zeal."[70] Such conviction allowed Davies to attract increasingly large numbers of frustrated Anglicans[71] as well as people from all levels of society.

67. Gewehr, *Great Awakening in Virginia*, 59.

68. Bushman, *Great Awakening*, 164.

69. Pilcher, *Samuel Davies*, 59–60.

70. Davies, "Letter to Bellamy, 4 July 1751," 513.

71. Davies was careful not to proselytize Anglicans or directly challenge the establishment. In his letter to the Bishop of London, Davies writes, "In all the sermons I have

Near the end of his pastorate, Davies was known as one of the best spokesmen for the Awakening. Thus, he was asked to travel with Tennent to Great Britain to raise money for the College of New Jersey. During this journey, Davies and his older associate became friends and achieved enormous success.

Unfortunately, during Davies's absence, the New Lights[72] cooled. But upon his return in 1755, they caught fire again. The four years following were a time of expansion and consolidation for Virginia Presbyterianism. With the increased number of ministers and the broader interpretations of the Toleration Act, the years 1755 and 1756 were marked by a considerable extension of the Awakening and a great increase in the number of Presbyterians.

Repercussions of the Awakening

The awakening that resulted from the combined regional revivals is termed *great* because of its vast, sweeping impact. The intensity and power of the revival can be felt in the words of evangelism scholars Malcolm McDowell and Alvin Reid:

> The colonies were touched from north to south to east to west. Multitudes professed to changed lives. Churches were established or strengthened. Missions enterprises were birthed. Theological convictions hammered out on the anvil of the Reformation were renewed and given fresh vigor. The importance of Christian experience, when yoked with doctrinal fidelity, was affirmed. Institutions were founded ranging from orphanages to colleges.[73]

Patricia Bonomi explains that in the closing years of the revival, the skylines of the eastern cities of the colonies

---

preached in Virginia, I have not wasted one minute in exclaiming or reasoning against the peculiarities of the established church; nor so much as assigned the reasons of my own non-conformity. I have not exhausted my zeal in railing against their imperfections, in exposing their imperfections, some of which lie naked to my view, or in depreciating their characters. No, my lord, I have matters of infinitely greater importance to exert my zeal and spend my time and strength upon—To preach repentance towards God, and faith towards our Lord Jesus Christ." Davies, "Dissent in Virginia," 165.

72. Revival promoters were generally called "New Lights" whereas revival opponents were called "Old Lights." Like most labels, the distinctions were not always clear.

73. McDow and Reid, *Firefall*, 203.

> were in their way just as striking as they are now, perhaps more so. But what drew the eye then, and gave the horizon its definition, was a very different sort of edifice from those that mark it today—not skyscrapers but church spires—and beneath that contrast lies a fundamental shift in the spiritual perspective of the American population during the more than two centuries that have intervened. The seaboard cities of colonial America, though relatively small, were amply supplied with places of worship. You walked no distance at all, in any of them, without passing a meetinghouse, and you were never beyond the earshot of church bells. The sights and sounds of today's cities are not primarily symbolic of religion. But in eighteenth-century America—in city, village, and countryside—the idiom of religion penetrated all discourse, underlay all thought, marked all observances, gave meaning to every . . . crisis.[74]

The awakening, along with a growing population, contributed to this ecclesiastical growth. Congregations and ministers alike were finally revived.

As fires of revival burned through the colonies, key leaders rose as fanners of the flame. In New England, Edwards gained prominence due to his brilliant mind and his auspicious position as pastor in Northampton. In the Middle Colonies, Tennent gained prominence as an outspoken and fiery successor to Whitefield. In the Southern Colonies, Davies soared on the wings of his well-fashioned oratory and impenetrable character.

As these men led their congregations and regions to and through revival's fire, answered critics, endured opposition, and experienced the remarkable grace of God at work in their midst, their homiletical theology matured and began to express itself in their preaching. The next chapter will narrow the focus to their preaching ministries.

74. Bonomi, *Under the Cope*, 3.

CHAPTER III

The Preaching Ministries of Edwards, Tennent, and Davies

PREACHING THE GOSPEL: THE POWER USED BY GOD TO PROPEL AWAKENING

The eighteenth-century artist William Hogarth (1697–1764) immortalized preaching in his century in two masterpieces. While both engravings are caricatures of eighteenth-century preaching, they convey the dynamic difference between two extremes that existed between the two major forms of eighteenth-century preaching.

The first engraving, titled *The Sleeping Congregation* (1736), depicts a minister reading his manuscript to a congregation who have long lost interest.

The Sleeping Congregation

The only interested congregational member is a fellow clergyman who shows interest not in the sermon but in the curves of a nearby young maiden. The rest of the congregation is fast asleep, some apparently snoring. The engraving depicts the deplorable state of affairs in churches of the day. One might argue, however, that the congregation has applied the preacher's text perfectly, for one can clearly read what the preacher is saying, "Come unto me all ye who are weary and heavy laden, and I will give you rest" (Matt 11:28).

The second engraving, titled *Credulity, Superstition, and Fanaticism* (1762), depicts the extremes to which the awakening could be taken.

Credulity, Superstition, and Fanaticism

The engraving is replete with caricatures. The preacher terrorizes his congregation with a pair of puppets. The text beside him is open to a page reading, "I speak as a fool." A religious thermometer registers the level of excitement that is likened to sexual arousal. The faces of the congregation display terror and agony at the words of the preacher. This is a far different congregation from *The Sleeping Congregation* of nearly thirty years previous.

Whatever Hogarth's intended messages, these engravings portray in graphic detail two extremes of eighteenth-century preaching—though admittedly grotesque in their exaggeration. While all congregations were not asleep prior to the revival and all awakened congregations did not suffer from hyper-charismatic extremes after the revival, major changes did take place. The comparison of pre-awakening and post-awakening preaching is nearly as drastic, though not as fantastic, as Hogarth's engravings suggest.

Preaching Prior to the Awakening

Prior to the awakening, preaching was long and boring. In the spiritually parched days before the revival, sermons were dissertations read to blank-faced congregations. Leslie Conrad notes, "The sermon sometimes measured four hours in length, and the cruel intensity of it may have been a substitute for heat in the meetinghouse. The form of worship was simple. The elements were prayer, praise, the Scriptures, and the sermon."[1] Likewise, these sermons "were preached with little feeling, and they were heard with an emotional response proportionate to the stimulus."[2] Due to the influence of the Enlightenment, preaching "had firm and conscious ties with secular society. Politics, education, philosophy, and literature all made demands upon, and in turn created demands for, sermons."[3] Moral, ethical preaching became the norm, and the church seemed to become "a society for the reformation of manners."[4] Furthermore, some ministers were as much politicians as they were preachers.[5] Preaching on such topics as sin, salvation, and eternal punishment seemed to belong to a past, less enlightened age. Many preachers addressed their congregations "as though they were all pious, and only needed instruction and confirmation."[6] Not surprisingly, such preaching was unable to satisfy the spiritual needs of the masses. In 1723, Solomon Stoddard wrote, "It is notoriously known by those that are acquainted with the state of the Christian World, that tho' there be many eminent Truths taught, yet there is a great want of good Preaching."[7] In this message, Stoddard called for increased piety among the clergy and delineated a number of features of good preaching.[8] He concluded his message stating the reason for the great want of good preaching: there was so little conversion and many ministers led unsanctified lives. Preaching before the awakening was in a deplorable state.

1. Conrad, "Importance of Preaching," 111.
2. Conrad, "Importance of Preaching," 111.
3. Downey, *Eighteenth Century Pulpit*, 10.
4. Downey, *Eighteenth Century Pulpit*, 10.
5. Downey, *Eighteenth Century Pulpit*, 18.
6. Alexander, *Biographical Sketches*, 17.
7. Stoddard, *Defects of Preachers Reproved*, 6–7.
8. These included helping people be conscious of their time of conversion, teaching that humiliation is necessary for faith, preaching on the danger of damnation, giving proper account of the nature of justifying faith, and providing accurate signs of godliness. Stoddard also deplored the practice of reading sermons.

Awakened Preaching

Two forms of communication contributed to the widespread influence of the First Great Awakening: printing and preaching. Both forms of communication were effective; however, preaching enjoyed the blessing of Almighty God.

Printing

New England was the most literate society in the world; therefore, many of the revival events and sermons[9] were recounted in print. Perhaps the most recognizable print source was the *Christian History* of Thomas Prince Jr. This paper appeared as a weekly periodical from March 5, 1743 through February 23, 1745 and included accounts of the revival submitted by various persons. Whitefield published his journals and sermons for distribution and used print media in innovative ways, but it was John Wesley (1703–1791), publishing approximately 250 books and tracts, who earned the title "Father of the Religious Paperback."[10]

Edwards, Tennent, and Davies also benefited from print media. Edwards gained international fame through his *A Faithful Narrative* and then was able to publish more works. The massive collection of his life works is a testament to his publishing. Tennent also used the print media to further his preaching ministry. The publication of his sermon of condemnation upon unconverted ministers brought him ever-increasing popularity among friend and foe alike. Davies's brother-in-law John Holt supplied him with books and information and served as his publisher and adviser. Through Holt, Davies regularly published sermons, poems, and essays, most of which appeared in the *Virginia Gazette* or as separate publications. Davies also is distinguished as America's first important writer of original hymns.[11]

Throughout the time of awakening, revivalists used publications to kindle and continue the revival's fire. However, the awakeners' purposes for using print media seem to have been directly related to preaching. Print

9. Publishing sermons increased in popularity during the eighteenth century. Witham states, "Published sermons outnumbered almanacs, newspapers, and political pamphlets by four to one." Witham, *City Upon a Hill*, 23.

10. McDow and Reid, *Firefall*, 194 and 200.

11. Pilcher, *Samuel Davies*, 49.

media was most often used to promote upcoming preaching, to give testimony of the results of previous preaching, or to put a sermon in print, whether a transcript or a manuscript. Therefore, the real power behind the awakening was not printing; it was preaching.

Preaching

Colonial America was familiar with the sermon as a communication form. In addition to religious instruction, congregations also heard the latest news from the pulpit. Sermons were nothing new. However, "a large measure of the Great Awakening's sudden success lay in the absence of dullness in the preaching styles of its leaders."[12] Even the masses were able to note the difference in the Awakened preachers and their preaching. Homiletical historian Hughes Oliphant Old explains that these preachers had much more than a renewed style:

> [They] had had a profound experience of the presence of God. They had entered into the holy of holies and heard the seraphic song. They knew they were men of unclean lips dwelling in the midst of a people of unclean lips, and yet their guilt had been taken away. Their lips had been touched with glowing coals from the altar, and therefore they preached.[13]

Such preaching was so new, so fresh, and so relevant that people gathered in coastal and frontier areas, rural and urban areas, meetinghouses, churches, and outside, to hear whatever preacher came. Awakened preaching's success also lay in its appeal to the oral culture of the day. Social bases such as African slaves, Native Americans, illiterate frontiersmen, and other primarily oral groups were reached through the revival's emphasis on the spoken rather than the written word.[14]

Local pastors and itinerants alike canvassed the colonies, proclaiming their good news. Not everyone liked this, especially some of the established clergy, because some of the itinerants, unfortunately, left a mess in the areas they ministered.[15] Soon, "the neat and orderly pattern of one church

12. Conrad, "Importance of Preaching," 111.

13. Old, *Moderatism, Pietism, and Awakening*, 156.

14. Bonomi, *Under the Cope*, 124.

15. Perhaps most notorious was James Davenport. Gaustad calls Davenport the "archfanatic of the Great Awakening." Gaustad, *Great Awakening*, 36. After becoming acquainted with Whitefield and Tennent in 1740, Davenport set out for his own itinerant

in one town with one minister solemnly appointed thereto found itself threatened by noisy and critical itinerants who preached where they had not been invited," and who often left in their wake "angry ministers and divided towns."[16] Nevertheless, the best awakeners were like lightening on a dry prairie, igniting a raging wildfire that spread uninhibited from town to town, county to county, and colony to colony. After hearing the sermons, the people carried the message back to their homes and villages, recounting what they heard. Thus, revival spread.

People responded to the preaching of the revivalists; consequently, revivalists increasingly used preaching to spread revival. "No strategy-feature received more attention; no human gift or ability was more highly prized. Even the results of the Great Awakening—whether present or future, temporary or permanent, direct or indirect—could be traced to the effectiveness of preaching."[17]

Revival authority Richard Owen Roberts asserts that "ordinary preaching produces ordinary results," but "revival is always extraordinary." Whether a preacher practices mouth-to-ear preaching, with its aim of speaking well and sounding good; head-to-head preaching, with its aim of stimulating thinking and affecting the minds of one's listeners; or soul-to-soul preaching, with its aim of leading people to higher spiritual ground; Roberts says a preacher is still only producing ordinary preaching with ordinary results.[18] Yet, the preaching of Edwards, Tennent, and Davies yielded extraordinary results including numerous conversions and changed communities.

---

preaching tour of Connecticut and Rhode Island. Though he achieved some converts, he made even more enemies. Friends of revival such as Edwards and opponents of the revival such as Chauncy agreed that Davenport was a problem. Only a small circle of radical New Lights considered Davenport anything but a villain, but these, too, were eventually betrayed by him. Brockway, "Significance of James Davenport," 86.

16. Gaustad, *Religious History of America*, 60.

17. Conrad, "Importance of Preaching," 118.

18. Roberts, *Revival*, 16–18.

THE PREACHING OF JONATHAN EDWARDS IN NEW ENGLAND

Religion in New England

Puritanism and Congregationalism

Since Puritan settlers began worshiping in Plymouth Plantation (est. 1620),[19] New England had been a stronghold for Puritan ideals. Though the Puritans initially thought of themselves as purely a reforming sect of the Church of England, they soon became so distinctive that their movement became independent and developed a new name: Congregationalism. It is in the writings of John Cotton (1584–1652), an earlier Boston clergyman, that the beginnings of Congregationalism become evident.

By the seventeenth century, Congregationalism had become the state church of New England and probably "enjoyed the loyalty of the larger proportion of the local population than any other established church in the [British] empire."[20] Because the church was the chief institution in every village, even the state was subservient. "Everyone was in some way connected with the church and conversant with its doctrines. These doctrines were the staple mental pabulum of the people. Newspapers were rare, but sermons were thick, and long too."[21]

Congregational Preaching

In the early days of the Congregational establishment, however, "thick" sermons were expected. The ministry of the word in New England had a unique supremacy. In his preeminent work, *The New England Soul*, Stout demonstrates that never before or since has a society so earnestly and intently listened to so many sermons, supported so many educated and conscientious preachers, or taken the reading and the preaching of the Scriptures so seriously.[22] New England Puritanism and Congregationalism held to the exposition of the word of God. Worship was to be fixed in accordance with the Bible and only the Bible. "One came to church to praise God

19. Plimoth Plantation was the site of the first permanent European settlement in New England. "Plimoth" is the old spelling.

20. Noll, *Rise of Evangelicalism*, 36.

21. Chapell, *Great Awakening of 1740*, 41.

22. Stout, *New England Soul*.

from the heart, to hear the Word expounded and interpreted, not ritually intoned or read without comment."[23] Preaching was worship, and preaching took a great deal of the time given to worship. Old explains the intense interest in the sermon on the part of the congregation:

> The sermon would take at least an hour. Anything less the congregation would have considered inadequate. If the hourglass was turned a second time, the congregation more than likely admired the faithfulness of their pastor in providing for them such an abundant feast of the Word. . . . They delighted in ministers who had thoroughly explored the Scriptures, and they gladly listened to the fruit of their minister's labors. They regularly took notes during the sermon and then returned home to study those notes, discuss them with family and friends, and rehearse them with their children. . . . [Ministers] knew their congregations longed to hear the Word, and this was a constant inspiration to them.[24]

The typical New England Congregational Church of the early seventeenth century was nothing like Hogarth's *The Sleeping Congregation*.

Declining Spiritual State

Regrettably, a century later things had changed, and New England's Puritan tradition weakened. While its politico-religious system remained strong, Congregationalism's spiritual strength was weakening. Signs of weakness included ministers outside of Boston worrying about the construction of elegant church buildings and the general lust for luxury in the city, while nearly everyone struggled with the decline of the once great and respected office of preaching. In his pastorate Edwards was concerned that Arminian ideas were beginning to influence the biblical expositions of his fellow pastors. Though direct preaching for conversion and intense longing to live for God did wax and wane throughout the course of New England's history, by "the early eighteenth century such vital concerns were on a gradually declining course."[25] Psalm singing had lost its earlier vigor, and "some ministers' exhortations against sin were as likely to put the congregation to sleep as to promote piety."[26] By 1730, things may have become, as Old

23. Gaustad, *Religious History of America*, 59.
24. Old, *Moderatism, Pietism, and Awakening*, 175.
25. Noll, *Rise of Evangelicalism*, 71.
26. Bonomi, *Under the Cope*, 67.

states, "a bit dry, or a bit tedious."[27] The movement was more than a century old, and it is rare that enthusiasm for any kind of movement could remain at high pitch for such a long period.

As New England approached the middle of the eighteenth century, Congregationalism was facing a problem. "The problem was not that the pews were empty . . . but that those who sat there, all quite steadfastly enough, were falling asleep."[28] Hogarth's engraving was becoming reality.

Thankfully, "the Puritan sense of duty as well as the Puritan sense of living under the first inspection of God left New England a religiously tender place."[29] In this environment, God would use Edwards to awaken the sleeping congregations of New England and bring revival to the land. "By 1740, Congregationalists had well over four hundred churches concentrated largely in Massachusetts, Connecticut, and southeastern New Hampshire,"[30] many of which would be awakened out of their spiritual slumber.

Jonathan Edwards: Preacher of Personal Intensity

Jonathan was born on October 5, 1703 to Timothy (1669–1758) and Esther (1672–1770) Edwards. The only son of eleven children, Jonathan distinguished himself as a prodigy at an early age by reading Latin by age six, writing remarkable treatises as a middle-school boy, and entering Yale at age thirteen. While at Yale, he benefited greatly from the library where he "devoured everything from natural philosophy to polite literature. . . . Like many men of his time, Jonathan was determined to know everything and how it all fit together in God's universe."[31] At age sixteen, Jonathan graduated as valedictorian of Yale.

Jonathan marked the beginning of his spiritual life to the time of revival in his father's parish (1712–1713). In his *Personal Narrative*, he states that when he was a boy "at a time of remarkable awakening" in his father's congregation, he was "concerned about the things of religion," his "soul's salvation," and was "abundant in duties." He prayed "five times a day in secret" and spent "much time in religious talk with other boys" and prayed

27. Old, *Moderatism, Pietism, and Awakening*, 253.

28. Old, *Moderatism, Pietism, and Awakening*, 253.

29. Noll, *Rise of Evangelicalism*, 47.

30. Gaustad, *Religious History of America*, 60.

31. Marsden, *Jonathan Edwards*, 62.

with them as well. Whereas young boys usually build forts in the woods, Jonathan and his friends built a prayer booth in their forest. His affections seemed "to be lively and easily moved," and he felt he was in his "element when engaged in religious duties."[32] In time, however, Jonathan "went on in ways of sin."[33] Several years later, during his last year of college, Jonathan was brought to another point of conviction. While he soon fell into his "old ways of sin," this time he "had great and violent inward struggles." Such struggling caused him to break off his "former wicked ways" and to make seeking his salvation "the main business" of his life.[34] From this time on, Jonathan's sense of "divine things gradually increased, and became more and more lively, and had more of that inward sweetness."[35]

As Jonathan grew spiritually and educationally mature in college, he struggled to make sense of the new philosophies that he found in his reading and the old religion under which he had been raised. In time, Jonathan became convinced "that he stood at a pivotal point in New England's history."[36] Little did Jonathan know, however, that not only did he stand within a pivotal point in time in New England's history, but he himself was to be a pivot of this historical shift.

Preaching Ministry

Edwards's call as successor to his famed and powerful grandfather in Northampton placed him in this position. Though Edwards was only the third pastor of the church, his predecessors had been respectable leaders. The first pastor was Eleazer Mather (1637–1669), the brother of Increase Mather (1639–1723) of Boston. The second was Solomon Stoddard, who was the son of the town's founder and the minister of the church for nearly sixty years.

Stoddard's shadow fell long over Northampton. To step onto Stoddard's stage and into Stoddard's pulpit would have been intimidating for anyone, but for a grandson who personally knew the larger-than-life persona of Stoddard better than anyone, it must have been especially foreboding.

32. Edwards, *Letters and Personal Writings*, 790–91.

33. Edwards, *Letters and Personal Writings*, 791.

34. Edwards, *Letters and Personal Writings*, 791.

35. Edwards, *Letters and Personal Writings*, 793.

36. Marsden, *Jonathan Edwards*, 63.

Nevertheless, as Edwards began his ministry to the thirteen hundred people of Northampton, he met the challenge with confidence.

In the Puritan style, he preached on Sunday and lectured on Thursdays. Always the scholar, Edwards averaged thirteen hours daily in his study, a practice that did not allow him much time as pastor to his people and yet one that sets him apart as a preacher of awakening. Whereas Whitefield's extemporaneous and emotional methodology was popular and characteristic of much of the itinerant preaching he influenced, many of the leaders of the movement were not particularly emotive. Some leaders, like Edwards, were scholars. The goal was not emotional worship services "but rather a single experience that would lead each believer to greater devotion and more conscientious study of Scripture."[37]

In fact, Edwards's homiletical methodology was nothing like that of Whitefield. Yet his preaching was still effective. Through his "calm, rational, highly intellectual approach plus his considerable gift for the pictorial world," Edwards incredibly could move people to repentance and faith.[38] An exegetical preacher in the Puritan tradition, Edwards had the ability of making the members of his congregation feel singled out as sinners. Conrad notes,

> In [Edwards's] sermonic applications, he was bold enough to call the roll of the town's sins, making it appear that he was actually walking up and down the village street, pointing his accusing finger at one house after another, unearthing secret sins and holding them up for all to see.[39]

Edwards's scholarship gave him great gifts, such as logic, which he used in combating the Enlightenment, checking the spread of deism and Arminianism, and catching his congregation in his web of arguments. "He had read everything the 'modernists' of the eighteenth century had to offer—in order to refute it—and had learned from John Locke that ideas are imparted through the senses. He wished to reach man's emotions, to present in vivid form these religious ideas he thought essential."[40] Marsden notes, "Whereas Stoddard's preaching was sometimes blunt in getting directly to the point, Edwards's was intricate, extremely clear, logical, and relentless."[41]

37. Gonzalez, *Reformation to the Present Day*, 229.
38. Stearns, *Great Awakening*, 34.
39. Conrad, "Importance of Preaching," 113.
40. Gewehr et al., *American Civilization*, 42.
41. Marsden, *Jonathan Edwards*, 128.

In the delivery of his sermons, Edwards was nothing less than unsensational. His voice was neither loud nor strong. Holding his four-inch-by-six-inch, finely penned manuscript close to his face with his left hand, his elbow resting on the Bible and his right rarely raised but to turn the page of his copy, Edwards proclaimed the word of God.[42] After Whitefield's visit to Northampton, Edwards did move away from his manuscript and began employing an outline. However, his pulpit delivery still could not compare to the dramatic delivery of the English revivalist. One would think Edwards's preaching would be ineffective, yet, Edwards's church was filled with listeners, hundreds who were converted, and its pastor became a leading preacher of awakening.

Even though Edwards's preaching was unremarkable in delivery, other parishes often called upon him to preach for them. It was in Enfield, Connecticut, on July 8, 1741, that he preached his most famous, though not characteristic, sermon, "Sinners in the Hands of an Angry God." In New Haven during that same year, he delivered "The Distinguishing Marks of the Spirit of God." This sermon placed him at the head of the revival apologists and served as a model for other proponents.[43]

What caused Edwards's preaching—though it may have lacked spark in delivery—to catch fire? Certainly it was not his methodology. Any preaching professor would harangue his sermon delivery. The cause for such fire was Edwards's homiletical theology, that strong belief in the power of preaching as the chosen vessel of God to affect change upon the lives and hearts of listeners. Though he used little nonverbal communication and his eyes were often either buried in his notes or fixed upon the bell-rope at the back of the meetinghouse, Edwards's "personal intensity could hold audiences spellbound."[44] His sheer passion generated emotion. In Edwards's *Some Thoughts Concerning the Present Revival of Religion in New England*, one finds a revealing statement on the nature of good preaching. Critics of awakening complained that the frequency of sermons in the awakening period produced no effect because one sermon tended to thrust out another.[45] Edwards countered, "The main benefit that is obtained by preaching is by impression made upon the mind in the time of it and not by an effect that

42. Holland, *Preaching in American History*, 102.

43. Gaustad, *Great Awakening*, 48.

44. Marsden, *Jonathan Edwards*, 206.

45. Edwards, *Great Awakening*, 397.

arises afterwards by a remembrance of what was delivered."[46] There was power in the preaching moment. Edwards believed preaching that touched the affections would create change in the hearers, a change that would last even if they heard another sermon soon thereafter. A sermon that was consistent with reason and Scripture could accomplish such effects whether or not the preacher employed an emotive methodology.

Certainly, Edwards was effective in bringing about change in his culture. Though the people of Northampton eventually rejected him, his ministry among them had awakened them to the wonders of the gospel, led them deeper in discipleship, and caused them to become a leading force in the New England awakening. As homiletical historian F. R. Webber notes, "His lasting fame is but proof that greatness rests upon foundations more enduring than merely a fine voice, dramatic ability, and a pleasant personality."[47]

THE PREACHING OF GILBERT TENNENT IN THE MIDDLE COLONIES

Religion in the Middle Colonies

Plurality of Churches

Whereas New England had long been a stronghold for Congregationalism, the Middle Colonies "somehow managed to get along without any established churches at all."[48] These colonies were well supplied with churches, but with churches of many different kinds. "By the early eighteenth century, the possibility of establishing one state-church in these colonies was ruled out by the simple sweep of events that brought into this region Anglicans, Quakers, Roman Catholics, Jews, Presbyterians, Congregationalists, Dutch Reformed, Mennonites, Moravians, German Reformed, and smaller numbers of several other religious bodies."[49] New Jersey provides a snapshot example of the religious diversity. West Jersey had a degree of uniformity, being a haven for Quakers, though religious hegemony was not complete. East Jersey, however, from the start was made up of a wide diversity of social

46. Edwards, *Great Awakening*, 397.
47. Webber, *History of Preaching*, 89.
48. Noll, *Rise of Evangelicalism*, 37.
49. Noll, *Rise of Evangelicalism*, 37.

and religious groups—English, Scots, Irish, Welsh, French Huguenots, Dutch Reformed, Presbyterians, Congregationalists, Baptists, German Lutherans, Moravians, and more.[50] In settled regions, the numerous existing denominations competed against one another. In spite of the amount of religious influence in the Middle Colonies, churches struggled to meet the needs of the growing population that was extending westward into the wilderness.

Presbyterianism

One of the denominations that emerged as a strong influence in both the wilderness and established areas alike was Presbyterianism. In the early eighteenth century, the Presbyterian church of the Middle Colonies was unlike its sister denomination Congregationalism. Whereas Congregationalism was old, strong, well-established, and equipped, Presbyterianism was new, weak, and lacking in homogeneity. The first Presbyterian church in the American colonies, established in Philadelphia, had only been around since 1703.

Though it was young, Presbyterianism still had its share of divisions and spiritual problems. Such problems have been discussed previously. Nevertheless, after suffering a bitter split (1741) followed by an amicable reunion (1758), by 1780 Presbyterianism had grown to nearly five hundred churches.[51] The awakening was a major factor in the split, reunion, and phenomenal growth of the denomination, and Gilbert Tennent was a major factor in the awakening's influence on Presbyterianism.

Gilbert Tennent: Son of Thunder

Born in the county of Armagh, Ireland, on October 5, 1703, the eldest son of William Tennent Sr., Gilbert was barely a teenager when his family immigrated to the colonies. Near the time of immigration, young Gilbert became seriously concerned about his salvation. This concern continued for several years until he finally found peace. During his years of struggle, he pursued the field of medicine, thinking himself unworthy of being a minister. However, as Alexander explains, "about this time it pleased God

50. Jamison, *Religion in New Jersey*, 3.

51. Presbyterians had approximately ninety-five congregations in 1740. Balmer and Fitzmier, *Presbyterians*, 31.

to reveal himself to him with so much clearness and comfort, that all his doubts and sorrows and fears were dispelled."[52] After experiencing this confirmation in his spirit, Gilbert wasted no time pursuing his calling. He committed to study and preparation, building upon the education he had received from his father by completing an MA at Yale College in 1725. With the necessary training behind him, Gilbert presented himself in the usual manner as a candidate to the Presbytery of Philadelphia. Gilbert passed his trials before the presbytery and received a license to preach in May 1726. After preaching several weeks in New Castle on the Delaware River and declining a call to the church there, he soon accepted the charge of planting a Presbyterian church in New Brunswick, New Jersey. In the autumn of 1726, the Presbytery of New Brunswick ordained Tennent.

Preaching Ministry

The expansive reach of Tennent's preaching ministry is evident from the previous chapter. Seen even in his earliest works, Tennent's preaching was "unusual"[53] and "popular and attractive with all classes of hearers."[54] The reasons for this popularity were numerous. Alexander notes that Tennent "possessed uncommon advantages as a preacher" that included a taller-than-common and well-proportioned stature, a venerable appearance, a clear and commanding voice, and an exceedingly earnest and impressive manner in the pulpit.[55]

Personal charisma, voice, and communication abilities can only take a preacher so far. Many a man with such enviable traits has seen his effectiveness fizzle before its time because the ministry was built on the traits of the man and little more. There must be something deeper that makes a preacher truly great. As John the Baptist declared, "He must increase, but I must decrease" (John 3:30). Gilbert Tennent allowed Christ to increase. In fact, despite his "uncommon advantages," the historical record makes clear that many people, both supporters and opponents alike, were sometimes unimpressed with Tennent's abilities as a preacher. Opponents such as Timothy Cutler, an Anglican missionary in Boston, recalled Tennent

52. Alexander, *Biographical Sketches*, 26.
53. Macartney, *Sons of Thunder*, 193.
54. Alexander, *Biographical Sketches*, 27.
55. Alexander, *Biographical Sketches*, 27.

was a noisy "monster."[56] Likewise, vocal revival opponent Charles Chauncy described Tennent as

> A Man of no great Parts of Learning; his preaching was in the extemporaneous Way, with much Noise and little Connection. If he had taken suitable Care to prepare his Sermons, and followed Nature in the Delivery of them, he might have acquitted himself as a middling Preacher, but as he preached, he was an awkward Imitator of Mr. Whitefield, and too often turned off his Hearers with mere Stuff, which he uttered with a Spirit more bitter and uncharitable than you can easily imagine.[57]

One would expect these opponents of Tennent to say such things. However, Jonathan Parsons, a New England pastor and promoter of revival, was also rather unimpressed with Tennent's abilities. Parsons recalled for the *Christian History* Tennent's visit to his church during Tennent's New England tour. He writes,

> Mr. Tennent came thro' this Place, and preached *two Sermons* among us: The first was in the *Evening*, from *Ezek*. 37.9. But he seem'd to be very dull; and, I tho't, several Times, he wou'd have had nothing, almost to say. Yet he got thro', and, I believe, he preached the Truth, tho' with no Freedom; nor had the People in general much Sense of what was deliver'd according to the best Observations I cou'd make; yet it was not wholly in vain: one of our Communion was convinced of Sin, which after some Days, issu'd, I trust in saving Conversion to God.—The next Morning he preached again from *Luke* 13.24 to a very attentive and deeply affected Auditory. Many that I heard lamented their own Folly immediately after Sermon, spake as one wou'd expect those to do that had the Arrows of Conviction shot deep into their Hearts.[58]

The difference in Parson's perception and that of revival opponents was Parsons noted the unique work of God through Tennent. Though at times his sermons were "very dull" and seemed to have "nothing, almost to say," people were converted and the effects of the sermon lingered for days. Thomas Prince Sr. of Boston noted that Tennent "did not . . . at first come

56. Timothy Cutler to Zachary Grey, September 24, 1743, quoted in Coalter, *Gilbert Tennent*, 74.

57. Chauncy, *A Letter from a Gentleman in Boston*, quoted in Coalter, *Gilbert Tennent*, 74.

58. Parsons, "Account of the Revival at Lyme," quoted in Heimert and Miller, *Great Awakening*, 196.

up to my Expectations; but, afterwards, exceeded it. . . . His Preaching was as *searching* and moving as ever I heard."[59]

Though sometimes unimpressive externally, Tennent's messages were, no doubt, impressive internally. Tennent might have been unimpressive at times, but the work of Christ through him was impressive all the time. F. L. Chapell notes,

> A curious fact of his preaching was that in many places his sermons did not seem to produce any immediate marked result in the way of sudden awakenings or conversions, which were then so common. But in a few days after he was gone, those who had listened to him would be struck under conviction. And a blessed work would be the result.[60]

Such a fact indicates that it was much more than methodology that set apart a man like Tennent. Hearers may have forgotten the messenger, but they could not forget the message. His preaching was more than a carefully executed technique to gain results.[61] There was something more that made his preaching effective and him great. That "something" was his strong, homiletical theology revealed in his passion for preaching. While pastoring in New Brunswick, Tennent "came to understand conversion as the chief purpose of preaching to be brought about by preaching the terrors which awaited those who were unconverted and then by applying the balm of the gospel."[62]

One anonymous admirer described this passion shortly after Tennent's tour of New England. Seeking to describe both Tennent's manner and method of preaching, this admirer penned verses that likened Tennent to a farmer, warrior, and surgeon:

> We bless the Man sent by the Spirit of Grace
> To turn poor Sinners into Wisdom's Ways;
> To plow the barr'n and break the fallow Ground,
> Dissect the Heart and shew the mortal Wound.
> There's few like him that ever we have seen,
> Since lovely *Whitefield*—O! how sharp and keen.
> He wields GOD's Law—the Holy Spirit's Sword,
> And wound the Heart at almost every Word,

59. Quoted in Coalter, *Gilbert Tennent*, 74.
60. Chapell, *Great Awakening of 1740*, 85.
61. McDow and Reid, *Firefall*, 209.
62. Old, *Moderatism, Pietism, and Awakening*, 107.

A *Boanerges* sometimes he'l appear,
And then a sweet and lovely Comforter.
So skilful Surgeons first rip up the Wound,
Then ply their Medicines 'til the Patient's sound.[63]

The poet notes the uniqueness of both Tennent and other evangelists, i.e., Whitefield, in their focus on the new birth. As farmer, warrior, and surgeon, Tennent worked to prepare the souls of his listeners for the work of the Holy Spirit. As Prince had observed, Tennent's preaching was "searching and moving." His preaching was apparently much different than what the anonymous poet and others experienced elsewhere, for Tennent stood out among professors, formalists, and other religious leaders as he defeated them with the word of God and won numerous souls to Christ. As the poet admirer chimed,

The false Professor's by him tri'd and cast,
He shows the Doom they're sure to have at last.
The formalists he searches to the Root,
And shews they bring forth nought but rotten Fruit.
The Hypocrites he doth anatomize,
Shews they're made up of sordid Falicies.
When he sounds forth the Thunders of the Law,
He strikes the Soul with Trembling and with Awe.
And when the Gospel Charms he doth display,
On Wings of Faith believing Souls away.
They mount, they fly unto the blest Abode.
Where Jesus reigns the great incarnate GOD.
While he sets forth the great Redeemer's Charms,
They soar aloft into his blessed Arms.[64]

Such was the experience of a young Samuel Hopkins in March 1741 at Yale College in New Haven. Recounting the major awakening of spiritual concern Tennent affected among the students, Hopkins declared, "When I heard Mr. Tennent, I thought he was the greatest and best man, and the best preacher, that I had ever seen or heard. His words were to me, 'like apples of gold in pictures of silver.'"[65] Tennent biographer Milton Coalter concludes,

63. "On the Reverend Mr. Gilbert Tennent's Powerful and Successful Preaching in Boston," in Heimert and Miller, *Great Awakening*, 192–93.

64. "On the Reverend Mr. Gilbert Tennent's Powerful and Successful Preaching in Boston," in Heimert and Miller, *Great Awakening*, 193.

65. Quoted in Coalter, *Gilbert Tennent*, 75.

> Similar plaudits were recorded by ministers in most of the towns on Tennent's itinerary. In those places where Whitefield had preceded Tennent, the New Jersey pastor was credited with bringing home the Awakening message with a force greater than that witnessed during Whitefield's stay, and in regions untouched by the Anglican evangelist's ministry, Tennent was recognized as the source of a resurging religious piety.[66]

Tennent was effective as a preacher and contributed to the Awakening's successful penetration of culture and transformation of lives within the American colonies.

Though his methodology may have been similar to Whitefield, though not so nearly beloved, it was his homiletical theology that set him apart. Tennent himself realized as much. A female admirer once asked Tennent "what there was in the matter of manner of his addresses . . . that produced such a wonderful and irresistible effect." The question was obviously one of homiletical methodology. However, Tennent replied with a response of homiletical theology specifically of the role of God in preaching. "Madam," he said, "I had very little to do with it. I did not preach better than common and perhaps not so well: for I was often much fatigued with traveling, and had little time to collect or arrange my thoughts. But I went into the pulpit and spoke as well as I could, and God taught the people."[67] As the poet had penned,

> I'll hear the Call the lovely *Tennent* brings,
> Because I know it's from the King of Kings.[68]

Would that listeners to all preachers could say the same.

THE PREACHING OF SAMUEL DAVIES IN THE SOUTHERN COLONIES

Religion in the Southern Colonies

In ecclesiastical structure, the Southern Colonies were more like New England than the Middle Colonies. The colonies of Virginia, Maryland,

66. Coalter, *Gilbert Tennent*, 75.

67. "Biography [of Gilbert Tennent]," *Evangelical Intelligencer* 3 (1807–1808) 244–45, quoted in Coalter, *Gilbert Tennent*, 75.

68. "On the Reverend Mr. Gilbert Tennent's Powerful and Successful Preaching in Boston," in Heimert and Miller, *Great Awakening*, 193.

Georgia, and the Carolinas were dominated by the Church of England, or Anglicanism, by the middle of the eighteenth century. Such dominance was achieved only after years of struggle, but, by the time awakening began to enter the Southern Colonies, Anglicanism was strongly established in the majority of the Southern Colonies. For the purposes of this work, Anglicanism in Virginia is of particular importance.

Anglicanism

During the early to mid-eighteenth century, Anglicanism had the strongest grounding and control in Virginia. Rys Isaac explains the Anglican churches were

> the important centers for community assembly dispersed at frequent intervals in the countryside. The parishes of the established religion were sometimes, in the western part of the colony, coterminous with counties, but usually they were considerably smaller.[69]

Unfortunately, Anglican churches had become little more than important centers for community assembly. Gewehr quotes early nineteenth-century Virginia historian John Cooke, who graphically paints the picture of a sleepy congregation:

> The planter and his family came in their coach, and the parson read his homily; and then all went back to their week-day pursuits but slightly edified. It was very much of a Drowsyland, and a trumpet blast was necessary to arouse the sleepers.[70]

Two problems contributed to the drowsiness: spiritually dead priests and ineffective preaching. Many of the Anglican priests were "men who wanted genteel status and a good annual income rather than men who felt a genuine calling."[71] Such priests were spiritually detached from their flocks. The fact that there were too few churches for the population exacerbated the problem. Stretched too thin by sprawling parishes and focused on material wealth as opposed to spiritual edification, Anglican priests "failed to move the emotions of the well-fed gentry who came late to services and left early

69. Isaac, *Transformation of Virginia*, 58.

70. Cooke, *Virginia: A History of the People*, 334, quoted in Gewehr, *Great Awakening in Virginia*, 33.

71. Olsen, *Daily Life*, 281.

or the servants and farm tenants who came to church only to please their masters. It failed to preach at all to many far-flung communities of workers who later proved all too receptive to Methodism."[72] Though many who came to Anglican services were not particularly there for anything more than social connections, some colonists, especially in the western frontiers, needed real answers to the real problems they faced each day. Weather, disease, crop failure, Indian attack, or any of England's covetous neighbors kept the reality of death—and the prospect of heaven or hell—before the colonists. Still, Anglican priests largely ignored the real problems of life in their sermons. Instead, as Old states, "The Anglicanism of Virginia tended to preach an abstract sort of moralism, cooked up in the theological leisure of Oxford and Cambridge and served lukewarm by clergymen who for one reason or another were unable to get 'a good church' back in England."[73] Spiritually dead priests cannot help but produce ineffective preaching. Ineffective preaching often produces dead spirituality among parishioners.

Need for Awakening

Though it was unconsciously contributing to the spiritual lethargy of the Southern Colonies, the Anglican Church was not unconscious of the spiritual lethargy. In fact, Anglicans bemoaned the deplorable state of religion in the South. They were not innately anti-revival—Whitefield himself was an Anglican along with John Wesley (1703–1791) and Charles Wesley (1707–1788) in England. Most of the Anglican clergy who longed for revival, however, saw themselves as the only potential solution to a problem that was largely their own making. Therefore, they prayed for a spiritual awakening as long as it was an Anglican awakening. They could not contemplate a transdenominational revival. Through the Society for the Propagation of the Gospel, Anglican leaders sought to spread Anglicanism throughout the colonies. In some places this was successful; in others, as in North Carolina, the project was a failure.

As New Light preachers brought their message into the Anglican establishment and provided real answers to real-life problems, Anglican

72. Olsen, *Daily Life*, 281.

73. Old, *Moderatism, Pietism, and Awakening*, 156. Pilcher agrees, saying that such preaching "was bound to arouse even more dissatisfaction in the colonies where it lacked the vitality demanded by the necessities of precarious semi-frontier conditions." Pilcher, *Samuel Davies*, 63.

churches began to feel the heat of revival. "As long as the laity remained loyal to the Church of England, however, resentment on the part of the ministers toward their employers only smoked and smoldered. When at mid-century the gentry began to join the Dissenters, clerical anger burst into flame."[74] Anglicans fiercely defended their rights as the established church even more so than they did in the mother country.

Into this religious imperialism came the twenty-four-year-old Samuel Davies, a Presbyterian preacher with real answers to real problems, a new religion of sorts, divested of formalism, and infused with relevance and spiritual power. In the next thirteen years of his short life, Davies would become the first great non-Anglican leader in Virginia.

Samuel Davies: Preacher of Fiery Eloquence

Old declares, "Samuel Davies was the most well balanced, the most literate, the most popular in his appeal, and, at the same time, the most theologically cogent American preacher of the eighteenth century."[75] Samuel was born near Summit Ridge in New Castle County, Delaware,[76] November 3, 1723, to David (b. 1680) and Martha Davis.[77] His parents were of Welsh Baptist descent. Samuel's grandfather, Morgan David (d. 1695), immigrated to Pennsylvania in 1684 from the Welsh town of Lantwidvoryde in Glamorganshire. Both parents possessed Christian character and were known for their integrity. Samuel was the only child his parents bore, and the name his mother gave him "was at once a token of her faith and her dedication of her son to the service of the Lord."[78]

Martha Davies, endowed with intellectual abilities, sought for her son the best manner of education that the family's humble circumstances permitted. Early on, Martha likely educated Samuel herself, but she soon sent Samuel to study under Abel Morgan, the local Baptist minister. Samuel rapidly progressed in his studies under Morgan until his mother was cast out of the congregation for rebelling against Baptist doctrine. Martha

74. Old, *Moderatism, Pietism, and Awakening*, 204.

75. Old, *Moderatism, Pietism, and Awakening*, 154.

76. At that time, this county was part of Pennsylvania.

77. David Davis was originally David David. He and his brother began to use Davis or Davies after purchasing land together in Delaware. Pilcher, *Samuel Davies*, 4.

78. Macartney, *Sons of Thunder*, 205. More is known about Davies's mother than his father.

immediately united with the Presbyterian Church, finding "a greater degree of spiritual satisfaction" in their view of things.[79]

Rev. William Robinson served as itinerant pastor of the Presbyterian Church at St. Georges, Delaware, which Martha joined. Like many ministers of his day, Robinson conducted a classical school, and it appears Samuel became his pupil. During his initial time with Robinson, Samuel made enormous academic progress but negligible spiritual progress. Around the age of twelve, however, Samuel experienced salvation, though he did not make a public profession of his faith until he was fifteen. By the time of this profession in 1738, the need for a classical academy became apparent. Robinson decided to send the maturing Davies to Fagg's Manor to the new school opened by Log College graduate Samuel Blair. Such a decision proved formative in young Davies's life and influenced him as a preacher.

By the spring of 1746, Davies was prepared to go forth as a preacher of the New Light. On July 30, the Presbytery of New Castle licensed him for the customary probationary period of six months. After successfully completing his probationary period, he was ordained on February 19, 1747, as an evangelist "to all congregations without pastors in Virginia, but especially the one in Hanover County, the center of New Light strength in a colony that had no settled New Light preacher."[80]

Preaching Ministry

In the year before his return to Hanover, Davies grew in popularity as a preacher, "putting in long hours of study and almost constantly traveling on horseback to increasingly numerous preaching assignments."[81] The congregation immediately accepted him, and the beloved preacher became a beloved pastor.[82] Until Davies was called to the College of New Jersey,

79. Pilcher, *Samuel Davies*, 6.

80. Pilcher, *Samuel Davies*, 13.

81. Pilcher, *Samuel Davies*, vii.

82. It is frequently noted, as Pilcher states, that Davies was "a minister who saw his duties in a much larger perspective than merely preaching." Pilcher, *Samuel Davies*, ix. He was not confined to the pulpit or his study, but served his people as a devoted pastor. "Though he had so many congregations to care for, and his charge was spread over so wide a territory, he had his eye, as far as possible, upon the spiritual needs of all; and none ever wanted for suitable counsel, or consolation, or help, whom his pastoral attentions could reach." Sprague, "Memoir of President Davies," quoted in Davies, *Sermons*, 1:29.

the Hanover congregations were the center of the southern Presbyterian awakening.[83]

Within a year of settling in Hanover, Davies became one of the most sought-after preachers in the Presbyterian Church. People listened to his preaching "with profound attention and admiration."[84] His church, which accommodated about five hundred persons, was still too small for the throngs who came to hear him preach. Therefore, he often held services in an adjoining forest. Nearby Anglicans attended Davies weekday sermons, other Virginians traveled miles to hear him speak, and other ministers desired to host him in their pulpits. Much of Davies's attraction stemmed from his meritorious character, but such extensive demand was related to his role as a New Light preacher and the only one permanently settled in the county for many years. Gewehr offers additional insight:

> While Davies's success . . . depended wholly on his own efforts, the times favored him. The Established Church had reached a low ebb. . . . As a body the clergy had lost all influence over the mass of the people and were considered as the mere parasites of the rich and the great. The Hanover revival showed how eager people were to hear the gospel, whether read from pious books or preached by the itinerant evangelists. It was Davies's good fortune to come into a community where the soil had already been prepared and where a large number of the people were open to conviction and easily impressed by evangelical preaching.[85]

While the soil was prepared, the preacher still had to plant, water, and harvest. And this Davies did with expert skill. Old says that though he was a settled pastor, "he saw himself as an evangelist preaching to people who had never heard the gospel."[86]

83. Davies was increasingly stretched thin as he traveled among his seven satellite congregations as well as his various itinerant opportunities. He pleaded with the synod to send additional assistants. They did so and throughout the years an increasing number of New Light preachers settled in the areas. Davies also sought help from another colleague outside Presbyterianism. After hearing of Jonathan Edwards's dismissal from Northampton, Davies invited Edwards to join him as his coworker in the southern revival movement. Unfortunately, the message arrived too late, and Edwards was unable to come. It seems that he would have had the invitation arrived sooner. One can only imagine what wonders would have taken place had these two giants of awakening been working alongside one another. See Pilcher, *Samuel Davies*, 94–95.

84. Sprague, "Memoir of President Davies," quoted in Davies, *Sermons*, 1:13.

85. Gewehr, *Great Awakening in Virginia*, 71.

86. Old, *Moderatism, Pietism, and Awakening*, 157.

The people of the western portion of the southern colonies were looking for real answers to the real questions they faced on the frontier. Therefore, Davies made the uncertainty of frontier life one of the chief emphases in his preaching. "His message was one of preparation, so that his listeners would be better able to face death should it suddenly confront them."[87] Surely Davies was the perfect man to deliver such a message. Having lost his first wife and child, he could empathize with those in his congregations who had lost loved ones to the frontier's harshness. Further, since he was always burdened with illness, Davies faced the imminence of his own death. He lived out the words of Richard Baxter (1615–1691), "I preach . . . as a dying man to dying men."[88]

Davies was also popular with the elites of society. For example, on his fundraising journey with Tennent to England, Davies commanded the highest respect. His "fine social qualities and eminent Christian character" helped him gain a hearing, and his "great powers of pulpit eloquence" impressed his listeners. A famous story is told of Davies preaching before King George II (1683–1760). In the midst of his sermon, Davies noticed the king speaking several times to the people sitting near him. Shocked at such irreverence, Davies stopped his message, looked in the direction of the king, and said, "When the lion roars, the beasts of the forest all tremble, and when King Jesus speaks, the princes of the earth keep silent." The king bowed and remained quiet for the remainder of the message. The story goes that the king had been so impressed with Davies that he was commenting about this to those who sat near him. Unfortunately, Davies provides no reference to this incident in his diary; therefore, it is regarded by most scholars as apocryphal. However, as Macartney says, "Whether apocryphal or not, it is a clear intimation of the sway, power, and reputation of Davies as a preacher."[89]

Much of Davies's attraction and success came from his intense preparation for the preaching event. He loved his Hanover study, and there he exegeted and meditated upon the Scriptures, considering nothing a sermon unless it was the product of at least four days of hard study. The result of such careful, reflective preparation was sermons that were theologically sound, but even more importantly, theologically perceptive.[90]

87. Pilcher, *Samuel Davies*, 65.

88. Baxter, *Poetical Fragments*, 35.

89. Macartney, *Sons of Thunder*, 208.

90. Old, *Moderatism, Pietism, and Awakening*, 154.

Davies's methodology in the pulpit was in keeping with his Welsh background. Exhibiting the "fervent Celtic eloquence for which the Welsh pulpit has always been distinguished,"[91] Davies's preaching combined "the highest graces of rhetoric and elocution with the most luminous, simple, and forcible exhibition of divine truth."[92] In this, Davies was unlike some of his evangelical colleagues. He believed a preacher should not be fiery and superficial in order to gain a congregation's attention; rather, he needed to be "of ready utterance, good delivery, solid judgment," and "free from enthusiastic freaks and of ardent zeal."[93] No matter his intensity of delivery, Davies maintained his dignity. This may have been due to his careful and effective use of a sermon manuscript. Unlike many of his colleagues, Davies wrote out his sermons and then memorized the manuscript. However, in the course of the sermon he extemporized from the manuscript, allowing him to be extemporaneous in delivery and genuine in presentation.[94] In his sermon occasioned by the death of Davies, Samuel Finley, Davies's successor as president of the College of New Jersey, affirms that Davies was truly genuine:

> In the sacred desk, zeal for God, and love to men, animated his addresses, and made them tender, solemn, pungent, and persuasive; while at the same time there were ingenious, accurate, and oratorical. A certain dignity of sentiment and style, a venerable presence, a commanding voice, and emphatic delivery, concurred both to charm his audience, and overawe them into silence and attention.[95]

Such fiery eloquence allowed Davies to remain a consummate orator, yet never a rabble-rouser, and to gain a "broad acceptance among a broad spectrum of the population in Great Britain as well as in the American colonies."[96]

Davies's preaching, though known for its fiery eloquence in the pulpit, was fueled by something behind and beyond the man in the pulpit. That something was his homiletical theology. Davies knew his orations

91. Macartney, *Sons of Thunder*, 205.

92. Sprague, "Memoir of President Davies," quoted in Davies, *Sermons*, 1:13. Heimert notes, "Samuel Davies was especially noted for the warmth of his voice and the use of a variety of sounds in his sermon delivery." Heimert, *Religion and the American Mind*, 231.

93. Davies in a letter to Bellamy, quote in Pilcher, *Samuel Davies*, 54.

94. Old, *Moderatism, Pietism, and Awakening*, 165.

95. Finley, quoted in Davies, *Sermons*, 1:43.

96. Pilcher, *Samuel Davies*, 67.

were nothing without the Spirit of God working in and through him in the preaching event. In his sermon "The Success of the Ministry of the Gospel, Owing to a Divine Influence," Davies's belief of the role of God in preaching, one portion of his homiletical theology, is clear:

> One may attempt to convert sinners to Christianity, and the other to build them up in faith, but they are both nothing, as to the success of their labors, unless God gives the increase: that is, unless he affords the influence of his grace to render their attempts successful in begetting and cherishing living religion in the hearts of men.[97]

Such a strong homiletical theology helped Davies and the southern awakening to be effective. Impressively, "his reputation, unlike that of some of his contemporaries, did not diminish upon his death but continued to grow."[98]

Commenting on the values and results of revivals, F. L. Chapell says,

> The chief value of a revival of religion is seen in its permanent results that live on long after the first excitement has passed away. God has promised that his spirit "shall come down like rain upon the mown grass." Now the value of the rain is not merely in the freshness which it sheds abroad while it is falling, but in the springing growth and maturity of the vegetation that results therefrom.[99]

One might also say this about one's preaching at any time, whether during a great awakening or not. The preaching of Edwards, Tennent, and Davies in their homiletical contexts produced permanent results. Though their churches may not have reached the spiritual heights to which their pastors called them, still, permanent results followed Edwards, Tennent, and Davies. The sparks begun by Edwards and Tennent were fanned and united through the work of Whitefield, and this raging fire burned into the South where Davies was able to lead one of the first revived groups toward a general awakening.

Though they employed different methodologies, Edwards, Tennent, and Davies were all gifted communicators of God's word. Edwards, though scholarly and stiff, possessed a personal intensity that drew his hearers in and wrapped them in a web of logical conclusions, causing them to be

97. Davies, *Sermons on Important Subjects*, 2:523–24.

98. Pilcher, *Samuel Davies*, 68.

99. Chapell, *Great Awakening of 1740*, 126–27.

captured by the gospel. Fiery and outspoken, Tennent was able to ring loud the call of the King of kings, causing his hearers to answer that call. Scholarly and eloquent, Davies impressed people with his oratory, earning the respect of many learned Anglicans, while strongly impacting frontiersmen as he answered the needs of the people. Each man was effective, but each man was different methodologically. Therefore, it could not be their homiletical methodology alone that was the common link in their effectiveness. It had to be something deeper. That something was their homiletical theology. Though influenced by their personal theologies, the homiletical theology transcended denomination and allowed God to use these men to transform lives.

CHAPTER IV

The Homiletical Theology of Edwards, Tennent, and Davies

The homiletical theologies of Edwards, Tennent, and Davies did not develop in a vacuum but were likely influenced by the historical circumstances of the day. With the historical context of the First Great Awakening established and the homiletical ministries and significance of Edwards, Tennent, and Davies described, it is now possible to identify and explore the homiletical theology of these men. While these men may have differed methodologically in their preaching, they were remarkably similar in their homiletical theologies.

THE ORIGIN OF THE HOMILETICAL THEOLOGY

Sermon writing was the workbench of the eighteenth-century theologian. In the act of sermon writing, preachers shaped their theology, attached concept to concept, and fine-tuned their interpretation of the Scriptures. In fact, as Old states, "It is rather typical of eighteenth-century religious leaders that often their most important writing took the literary form of the sermon rather than the theological treatise."[1] Certainly, this was the case for the three pastor-preachers we are considering. For example, Old claims that Samuel Davies's three volumes of sermons "were regarded as

1. Old, "Gilbert Tennent," 133. Old links Edwards, Tennent, and Davies as key thinkers who helped the Great Awakening become a "cohesive spiritual force."

one of the most literate expressions of American religious thought" up to the Civil War.[2]

Edwards, Tennent, and Davies were keen thinkers who worked long hours at their sermonic workbenches constructing homiletical masterpieces that the Holy Spirit used to engage and change numerous congregants. Thus, these sermons are excellent sources for clarifying not only what these preachers believed about God but also what they believed about preaching as well. In some sermons, especially in ordination sermons or in the farewell sermons to their congregations, the preachers clearly state elements of their theology of preaching. In other sermons, they demonstrate this homiletical theology in their praxis. This chapter will rely primarily on the previous.

ISSUES COVERED IN A HOMILETICAL THEOLOGY: A PARADIGM FOR STUDY

The study of a homiletical theology is, as Dietrich Ritschl says, "A study in the basic Biblical and dogmatical questions which . . . will inevitably come to every responsible preacher when he begins to think seriously about the proclamation of the Church in which he and his congregation has a part."[3]

The paradigm I use to discuss the homiletical theology of Edwards, Tennent, and Davies in this chapter finds its origins in David Greenhaw's work.[4] However, it has been further informed by other homileticians and consequently modified. This modification is explained below.

Greenhaw says, "Theology of preaching is concerned with the role and place of preaching in the life of the Christian church" and "what the church is doing when it preaches."[5] Greenhaw demonstrates that a preacher's understanding of preaching and expectations for preaching often influence his preaching. In addition, differing core theologies often lead to differing expectations of preaching. Greenhaw concludes his article stating, "Exactly what is being done [in preaching], how it is being done, and to what end it is done remain the areas of lively debate in the theology of preaching."[6]

2. Old, "Gilbert Tennent," 133.
3. Ritschl, *Theology of Proclamation*, 7.
4. Greenhaw, "Theology of Preaching."
5. Greenhaw, "Theology of Preaching," 477.
6. Greenhaw, "Theology of Preaching," 482.

Explanation of the Paradigm

The core issues of a homiletical theology as identified by Greenhaw are the preacher, the relationship of the Bible to preaching, and the historical, social, and liturgical contexts of preaching. The church's ultimate aim in preaching is also valued. These are similar issues that are identified by other homileticians. For example, Peter Adam constructs his theology of preaching around two major categories.[7] Adam first discusses three biblical foundations of preaching that include the core beliefs that God has spoken, the Bible is God's written word, and that the church is to preach that word. One might see in this Greenhaw's ultimate aim in preaching as well as the relationship of the Bible to preaching. The second major category in Adam's homiletical theology is the preacher's task. Here, Adam covers such topics as preaching as the ministry of the word, the preacher's Bible, and the preacher's purpose, as well as the demands of preaching. Within this, one can see the same issues being addressed as found in Greenhaw's authority of the preacher and contextual section.

A brief and representative survey of other homiletical theologies indicates that other homileticians organize their words around similar themes as Greenhaw. Ritschl develops his theology of proclamation around first, the word to the church and the word from the church; second, worship and the office of proclamation; and, finally, the sermon itself.[8] Roman Catholic homiletician Domenico Grasso arranges his theology of preaching according to the object of preaching, the principal subject of preaching (God), the mediation of the human word, the mystery of preaching, man's response to preaching, and the various dimensions of preaching.[9] Richard Lischer endeavors to show how theology informs preaching and how preaching, as an oral, practical activity, informs theology and brings it to its final form of expression.[10] Lischer speaks to the issues of the source of power in preaching, how law and gospel work in preaching, preaching as the word of God, and how preaching can be effectively communicated to and received by sinful human beings. E. Eugene Hall and James Heflin organize their book on preaching by exploring the basis of preaching from different angles that include the theological, personal, social, logical, inventive, ideational,

7. Adam, *Speaking God's Words*, 5.

8. Ritschl, *Theology of Proclamation*, 11.

9. Grasso, *Proclaiming God's Message*, vii.

10. Lischer, *Theology of Preaching*.

structural, expressive, and communicative basis of preaching.[11] Donald English says his 1996 work, *An Evangelical Theology of Preaching*, is "a book about why anyone would want to preach in the first place."[12] English gives a basis for evangelical preaching by exploring such topics as the uniting of reason and faith, making the gospel public, and developing the preacher, as well as many others. Princeton professor Charles Bartow develops his homiletical theology around such issues as hearing the word of the Lord and what the preacher and listeners should do with Sunday's sermon. Bartow states the kerygmatic expectation as follows: "In Christ Jesus God takes us as we are and presses us into the service of what he would have us to be."[13] In *The Imperative of Preaching*, John Carrick develops his theology of "sacred rhetoric" around the "crucial role of the Holy Spirit" and the "crucial role of means."[14] Johnson Lim, in *Power in Preaching*, developed his homiletical theology because "many homiletical books are long on the outward aspect of preaching but short on the inward aspect."[15] He treats such issues as who the preacher should be, what preaching is all about, some basic axioms of all preaching, and how the preacher should relate to the text before turning to more practical issues such as how to craft and deliver a sermon.

Though these authors approach the subject of a homiletical theology from slightly differing angles and are influenced by their own ecclesiastical traditions and theologies, each homiletician deals with most if not all of the key components in a homiletical theology as suggested by Greenhaw. Therefore, taking the wider breadth of homiletical studies into account, I extend Greenhaw's issues as follows: the role of the preacher, the role of Scripture, the role of the Holy Spirit, the role of the listener, and the ultimate aim of preaching. Organizing the thoughts under similar headings according to role provides cohesive labeling and allows us to consider homiletical theology as something influenced by many different factors. Table 3 demonstrates how these issues relate to Greenhaw's classifications.

Table 3: Relation of Issues in Homiletical Theology: Greenhaw to Holloway

11. Hall and Heflin, *Proclaim the Word*.
12. English, *Evangelical Theology of Preaching*, 11.
13. Bartow, *God's Human Speech*, 53.
14. Carrick, *Imperative of Preaching*, 6.
15. Lim, *Power in Preaching*, vii.

<table>
<tr><th>Greenhaw</th><th>Holloway</th><th></th></tr>
<tr><td>Authority of the preacher</td><td>Role of the preacher</td><td rowspan="3">Ultimate aim of preaching</td></tr>
<tr><td>Relationship of the Bible to preaching</td><td>Role of Scripture</td></tr>
<tr><td>Historical, social, and liturgical contexts of preaching</td><td>Role of Holy Spirit
Role of the listener</td></tr>
</table>

Further explanation of this paradigm as well as how it has been informed by other homileticians is provided in the subsequent sections.

Role of the Preacher

As was sometimes evidenced during the Awakening, Lim states, "Some preachers by their preaching give the impression that it is a job to be done rather than a calling to be fulfilled. It then becomes more of a fulfillment of some contractual obligation to the Church rather than a ministry."[16] Homiletical theologies treat the role of the preacher to avoid such misunderstanding. Who the preacher is, how he is equipped and qualified, and what he is to do in preaching are just some of the basic questions we can consider when assessing the role of the preacher. All of these questions speak to the preacher's authority in approaching the sacred desk. The section below concerning the role of the preacher will deal with the revivalists' view of the preacher as the servant of God and authoritative messenger of his word.

Role of Scripture

Greenhaw says a homiletical theology is interested in the Bible's relationship to preaching. I will treat this subject under "The Role of Scripture." Lischer rightly emphasizes, "People listen to preaching only when they are convinced that it is the Word of God."[17] The relationship of the written word of God and the preached word of God is vital in one's homiletical theology. The section on the role of Scripture will treat how the revivalists viewed Scripture's relationship to preaching.

16. Lim, *Power in Preaching*, 1.

17. Lischer, *Theology of Preaching*, 66.

Role of the Holy Spirit

Greenhaw's third element of a homiletical theology casts a wide net covering such broad issues as the historical, cultural, and liturgical contexts of preaching. Because the historical, cultural, and liturgical contexts in which the revivalists ministered have already been discussed in the second and third chapters, the research paradigm focuses the discussion on two elements that are at work in any context. These elements are the role of the Holy Spirit and the role of the listener, the two primary participants in any context of preaching other than the preacher himself.

Since revival is brought by the Holy Spirit and any spiritual impact in preaching is affected by the Holy Spirit, the Spirit is part of one's preaching context and a necessary component of one's homiletical theology. In *Theology of Proclamation*, Ritschl asks, "Do we not depend utterly on God's promise that He will surprise us and will do in the assembled congregation what we could never do?"[18] The Awakening was a time when this happened. Therefore, how the revivalists expressed the Spirit's role in their preaching is of keen interest.

Role of the Listener

While it is "far easier to reach and instruct students and ministers than to teach and to persuade church members," still there is a need to teach people "how to read their Bible, to understand the sermon, and to share in the responsibility of the minister."[19] Accomplishing such biblical engagement is rather difficult; nevertheless, it should be a consideration in anyone's homiletical theology. As has been shown, the revivalists ministered in a time when sermons were prevalent but not always penetrating. In contrast, their preaching seems to have been life-transforming. Greg Heisler is convicted "that the Spirit of God and the Word of God come together in the heart and mind of the preacher to produce the substantive and compelling sermons that transform the lives of listeners."[20]

18. Ritschl, *Theology of Proclamation*, 15.
19. Ritschl, *Theology of Proclamation*, 18.
20. Heisler, *Spirit-Led Preaching*, 10.

The Ultimate Aim of Preaching

A homiletical theology is not only concerned "with the Biblical understanding of preaching but also with the Biblical concept of the Church, its worship, and its mission in the world."[21] The homiletical theology of Edwards, Tennent, and Davies will conclude with a discussion of their ultimate aim in preaching. Such a discussion will give their answer to the question suggested by Greenhaw, "What is the church doing when it preaches?"[22]

In the sections below, the classifications discussed above will serve as headings for a discussion of the revivalists' homiletical theology. Under each heading, first a summary of that portion of the homiletical theology will be given. Second, the revivalists' thoughts concerning this subject will be demonstrated and explored.

THE ROLE OF THE PREACHER

Because Edwards, Tennent, and Davies were preachers from whom others sought wisdom and guidance, much remains of what these men had to say regarding the role of the preacher in preaching. In fact, it seems that more remains of what these men had to say about the role of the preacher than any other part of their homiletical theology.

Edwards, Tennent, and Davies believed the office of the preacher was a high calling from God to men whom he specifically equipped for the task. Therefore, preachers should be savingly converted and practice piety in their personal and public lives. Likewise, because preachers participate in the great work of redemption through their preaching, they are to be well-studied in the Scriptures. Still, ministers are not to be noisy gongs or clanging cymbals but are to speak the redemptive word of God to listeners with whom they have a relationship and with whom God desires a relationship.

The Office of Preacher: A High Calling

Awakeners believed preachers should be consumed by their calling. Whereas many eighteenth-century preachers merely performed an *occupation*,

21. Ritschl, *Theology of Proclamation*, 7.

22. Greenhaw, "Theology of Preaching," 477. Ritschl shares a common question. He writes, "I . . . tried to rethink and formulate *why* the Church is called to preach and *what* we are actually doing when we preach." Ritschl, *Theology of Proclamation*, 8.

revivalists expected true preachers to fulfill a *vocation*. The distinction between the terms *occupation* and *vocation* is simply demonstrated. Merriam-Webster defines an *occupation* as "an activity in which one engages" or "the work in which a person is employed."[23] The word often describes how a person makes a monetary living. Webster's defines a *vocation*, however, as "a summons or strong inclination to a particular state or course of action; *especially*: a divine call to the religious life."[24] Edwards, Tennent, and Davies insisted that the office of preacher was a vocation, not an occupation.

To those of us living in the twenty-first century, the attraction of the ministry as an occupation may seem odd. However, in colonial America, the office of preacher was highly esteemed and privileged. Preachers were usually respected by the public, were frequently the most educated persons in a city, and were typically guaranteed a salary by the government if they were part of the regional, established church. For some men, the ministry may have seemed an easy means of gaining respect and supporting a family. Further, if the community knew no better, and often even if they did, the minister could fall slack in his duties with little or no repercussion.

As was shown in chapter 2, by the time of the Awakening, the plague of an ineffective Christian pastorate and its inattention to the need for persuasive preaching of the gospel had infected nearly every major denomination in the colonies. Too many pastors held their positions as an occupation rather than a vocation. The consequential demise of their churches was also discussed in previous chapters.

Awakeners believed a man seeking ministry for purposes of self-advancement and prosperity demonstrated an un-Christian aspiration for wealth and lordly status and an indifference to the welfare of others. In one ordination sermon, Davies eloquently challenges such ministers:

> I have now nothing to do with those unhappy creatures, who desire and catch at the sacred office as a post of honour, profit, or ease; or as the last shift for a livelihood, when other expedients have failed. Such deserve to be exposed in severer terms than I am disposed to use; and I cannot but tremble to think what account they will be able to give to the great Bishop of souls, and Judge of the universe. But, as to those honest souls, who engage in it with

23. Merriam-Webster, s.v. "occupation."

24. Merriam-Webster, s.v. "vocation."

> proper motives and views, they are generally determined to it after many hard conflicts and reluctations.[25]

A few years later, in his farewell sermon to his Hanover congregation on July 1, 1759, Davies analyzes his ministry and concludes that he has maintained proper motives. He says, "I hope I understand my office better than to make a money-business of it, or a trade to acquire an estate. Or if it has been my design, I would have chosen some other place than Hanover to carry on the trade."[26] Each of the revivalists believed that a minister must be committed to his vocation regardless of position or reward in order to be effectively used by God. Therefore, the revivalists taught that preaching was a high calling and that ministers must be committed to the requirements of the vocation.

In his sermon "The Office of Bishop a Good Work" based on 1 Tim 3:1, occasioned by an ordination in Hanover on June 5, 1757, Davies reflects upon the meaning of Paul's description of the ministry as a "good work," or high calling, by comparing the work of a minister to the work of the most prestigious and life-affecting offices of the world. Davies proclaims,

> To be the minister of Jesus Christ, the King of kings, and the Lord of lords, is a greater honour than to be prime minister to the most illustrious monarch upon earth. To save souls from death, is a more heroic exploit, than to rescue enslaved nations from oppression and ruin. To make a multitude of wretched, perishing souls rich with the unsearchable treasures of Christ, is a more generous charity, than to clothe the naked, or feed the hungry. To refine depraved spirits, and improve into a fitness for the exalted employments and enjoyments of heaven, is a higher pitch of patriotism, than to civilize and polish barbarous nations, by introducing the arts and sciences, and a good form of government among them. To negotiate a peace between God and man . . . is a more benevolent and important service than to negotiate a peace between contending nations.[27]

Few life endeavors could achieve such glowing accolades. But then, few endeavors have such a glow about them. As Edwards emphasizes in

25. Davies, *Sermons*, 3:543.

26. Davies, *Sermons*, 3:639.

27. Davies, *Sermons*, 3:558.

an ordination sermon from August 30, 1744, the ministry is an honorable work because preachers are set to be lights in the spiritual world.[28]

It is through ministers that God continues his great work. In another ordination message, preached in Portsmouth on June 28, 1749, Edwards confirms God's work through men, saying, "So it is by the ministration of men, that the Scriptures are given; they were the penmen of the holy Bible; and by them the gospel is preached to the world: by them ordinances are administered, and, through their ministrations, especially, souls are converted."[29] Tennent likewise emphasizes the nature of the ministerial vocation in his message series titled "The Unsearchable Riches of Christ," preached for his New Brunswick congregation in August 1737. In this message, Tennent teaches that the ministry vocation is a noble, honorable, pleasant, and profitable work. It is a noble work since it aims at the subject of highest importance. It is honorable work because it is carried out by divine appointment and blessing. And, overall, it is a pleasant work, "especially at such Times, when the blessed God enlarges his Servants' Hearts by his Love, and succeeds their Labours by his Power. O' then it's a sweet Recreation, to spend themselves to Faintness in labouring for Souls."[30] And even still, Tennent says, it is a profitable work, not in temporal reward but in "distinguishing Glory in the next World."[31]

Such emphasis upon the high calling of preachers could make us think that the revivalists were elevating the ministry to the priestly status of the ministers in the Roman church. However, this was certainly not the case. The revivalists plainly demonstrate their vocational boundaries shaped by their role as humble servants of Christ. Yet, as Edwards explains, "ministers of the gospel, as Christ's servants and officers under him, are appointed to promote the designs of that great work of Christ, the work of salvation."[32] Ministers are coworkers with Christ, sent as he was, "and as co-workers with him, to preach good tidings to the meek, to bind up the broken-hearted, to proclaim liberty to the captives, and the opening of the prison to them that are bound, and to comfort all that mourn."[33] Davies makes a

28. Edwards, *Sermons and Discourses, 1743–1758*, 97.
29. Edwards, *Sermons and Discourses, 1743–1758*, 344–45.
30. Tennent, *Unsearchable Riches of Christ*, 30.
31. Tennent, *Unsearchable Riches of Christ*, 30.
32. Edwards, *Sermons and Discourses, 1743–1758*, 341.
33. Edwards, *Sermons and Discourses, 1743–1758*, 90.

similar distinction saying, "When all ministers are upon a level, and their office is not attended with secular honours and riches, they had not such room, or temptation to ambition; and the highest character they can aspire to, is that of humble laborious servants of Christ and the souls of men."[34]

The ministry is an office to be magnified but not for the reasons offices are normally magnified. Davies challenges ministers:

> Let them 'magnify their office,' not by assuming airs of superiority, or by making ostentatious claims to powers that they have nothing to do with, but by rejoicing more in it, than in crowns and thrones—by supporting it with dignity, that is, acting up to their high character; and by so exercising it as to render it an extensive blessing to the world. This will be the best expedient to keep themselves and their office above contempt, and to gain the approbation of God and man.[35]

The revivalists agreed with the apostle Paul who wrote to Timothy, "If any man aspires to the office of overseer, it is a fine work he desires to do" (1 Tim 3:1).

While the vocation of preacher is a fine work, Davies emphasizes, "still it is a work."[36] The ministry is not an office to be flippantly held but is, as Edwards stresses, one in which the preacher must "spend and be spent" for his listeners.[37] Davies teaches, "It is not a post of honour, profit, or ease, . . . it is a work."[38]

The duties of the minister make it a work.[39] Davies explains, "It may properly be called a work, if we consider the duties of the office, which require the utmost assiduity, and some of which are peculiarly painful and laborious."[40] The minister must do all the work of a Christian—working out his own salvation, struggling with temptation, discharging his Christian duties to God, his hearers, and himself. But besides this, there is "a great, an arduous and laborious work *peculiar* to the office" of a minister "which

34. Davies, *Sermons*, 3:540.

35. Davies, *Sermons*, 3:558–59.

36. Davies, *Sermons*, 3:549.

37. Edwards, *Sermons and Discourses, 1743–1758*, 174.

38. Davies, *Sermons*, 3:551.

39. Davies delineates this work saying, "To the office of a gospel minister . . . it belongs to preach the word; to administer the sacraments; to concur in the ordination of persons duly qualified to this office; and to rule the church of God." Davies, *Sermons*, 3:540.

40. Davies, *Sermons*, 3:549.

not only is sufficient to exhaust all his time and abilities, but which requires daily supplies of strength from above to enable him to perform it."[41] He must study so that his messages might be delivered with power. He must visit the sick as well as frequent the homes of his parishioners for private discipleship and instruction. And he must do it all "with zeal, fidelity, prudence, and incessant application, as the main business of life"[42] while always giving "no offence to anything, that the ministry be not blamed; but in all things to approve himself as the minister of God: (2 Cor vi. 3,4,)—to preach Christianity out of the pulpit, by his example as well as in it, by his discourses; and to make his life a constant sermon."[43] The duties alone make the vocation of preaching a daily work—a calling that consumes one's life.[44]

Accompanying any great work are hardship and discouragement as well as victory and applause. The rise and fall of each can be overwhelming. Since preaching is a great work, the rise and fall of victory and defeat are par for the course. Edwards experienced such victory and pain in his dismissal from Northampton, a place where he saw both the pinnacle of revival and the gorge of church conflict. Davies and Tennent experienced

41. Davies, *Sermons*, 3:549.

42. Davies, *Sermons*, 3:550.

43. Davies, *Sermons*, 3:550.

44. Davies challenges, "You are now entering upon a life of painful labour, fatigue, and mortification. Now you have nothing to do but to work for your Lord and Master: to work, not merely for an hour or two once a week, but every day, in every week, and through your whole life. If you enter into your closet, it must be to pray. If you enter into your study, it must be to think what you shall say to recommend your Master, not yourself; and to save the souls that hear you. If you enter into the pulpit, it must be not to 'preach yourself, but Christ Jesus the Lord;' (2 Cor 4:5,) not to set yourself off as a fine speaker, a great scholar, or a profound reasoner, but to preach Christ crucified, . . . and to beseech men, in his stead, to be reconciled to God; to warn every man, and teach every man, that you may present every man perfect in Christ Jesus. (Col 1:28.) If you go into the world, and mingle in conversation, it must be to drop a word for Christ; and let mankind see, that you live, as well as talk, like a Christian. If you travel about from place to place, among necessitous vacancies, it must be to diffuse the vital savour of your Master's name, and not your own. If you settle, and undertake a particular charge, it must be to watch for souls, as one that must give an account; and industriously to plant and water that spot which is laid out for you in the Lord's vineyard." *Sermons*, 3:551–52. Davies adds, "This work will leave no blanks in your time, but is sufficient to employ it well. It will leave none of your powers idle, but requires the utmost exertion of them every one. It is the work of your Sundays, and of your weekdays—the work of your retirement, and your social hours—the work of soul and body—of head and heart—the work of life and death: a laborious, anxious, uninterrupted work. But, blessed be God! it is, after all, a good work." Davies, *Sermons*, 3:552.

victory and pain in their ministries as well, even if perhaps to a lesser degree than Edwards. Still, each man persevered through success or hardship and encouraged others to do the same. Davies says preachers should persist in their work "with fortitude and perseverance, in spite of all the discouragements of unsuccessfulness and the various forms of opposition that may arise from earth and hell—to abide steady and unshaken under the strong gales of popular applause, and the storms of persecution—to bless, when reviled; to forbear, when persecuted; to entreat, when defamed."[45] Tennent echoes,

> Notwithstanding all that Contempt that is pour'd upon, and Opposition made against the faithful Ministers of Christ, by ignorant and wicked Men; and notwithstanding the many Discouragements that do attend their Work, partly from the centorious Reflections of good Men, and partly from its own Weight and Difficulty, and their Weakness, Coldness, and sometimes Unsuccessfulness; or from the Temptations of the Enemy of Souls; . . . . Partly from the Straits they are sometimes exposed to, on the Account of their Support; among a poor, penurious, and ungrateful People. I say, notwithstanding all the aforesaid Particulars, the ministerial Work, is a great *Privilege*.[46]

To the revivalists, the preaching vocation is one of high calling and hard work that results in both encouragement and discouragement, yet, when faithfully administered, is always attended by God and accomplishes the will of God.

Such a tremendous and important work demands execution by a person of sufficient merit and strength. Preaching might seem to require the work of a more divine being, even an angel perhaps, "and yet," Davies explains, "this work must be done—done habitually, honestly, conscientiously, by us frail mortals, that sustain this office; or else we shall be condemned as slothful and wicked servants. This thought must forever sink our spirits, were it not that Christ is our strength and life."[47] God calls and equips men to carry out this vocation. Still, before a man ever stands to preach, the inner conviction of that man concerning the holy calling has to be considered. "Was he a hireling or a shepherd? Was he a professional

45. Davies, *Sermons*, 3:550.

46. Tennent, *Unsearchable Riches of Christ*, 29.

47. Davies, *Sermons*, 3:550.

middleman or a voice for God?"[48] The revivalists assert that the preacher is a shepherd; the preacher is a voice for God. Such an emphasis is clearly seen in Tennent's famous sermon "The Danger of an Unconverted Ministry." In this message, Tennent raises questions of both doctrine and style, but the underlying issue is character—the inclination of the minister's heart and the fitness to his calling. Some years previous, in the preface to his two sermons preached at New Brunswick in August 1737, Tennent speaks of the unsearchable riches of Christ and, as Paul did, of being the greatest of all sinners, not worthy to be called a servant of God much less a minister of Christ. But he continues, "Yet I do rejoice in the Office that God has called me to, notwithstanding all the Difficulties that do embarrass it; and so far as I know my own Heart, I wou'd not lay it down for all the World. *For woe is me, if I preach not the Gospel*."[49] God calls humble men who will spend and be spent for their congregations. The man who remains focused on his vocation can be used by God.

Preaching is a high calling, and imperative to good preaching is this calling upon a man. Still, a man must accept the requirements of his calling. Such requirements, as identified by Edwards, Tennent, and Davies, further indicate the role of the preacher in their homiletical theology. Such requirements emphasize the nature of one's preparation as a man of God and his relationship with his listeners.

Preachers Are to Be Converted, Pious, and Well-Studied

Conversion Essential

One of the charges levied against the revivalists by some of the established clergy centered on the question, "Who is truly qualified to preach?" Many of the Old Lights charged the New Lights with believing that the call of God did not consist in their being regularly ordained but rather in some invisible movement of the Holy Spirit. Further, the Old Lights disliked the New Light emphasis that unconverted ministers are ineffective in leading sinners to salvation.

48. Turnbull, *Jonathan Edwards*, 111.

49. Tennent, *Unsearchable Riches of Christ*, vi. Tennent signed the preface August 20, 1737, as "Your very unworthy pastor."

After being ejected by his synod in May 1741, Tennent responded by publishing his own account of the episode. In this work Tennent clarifies both the objections of the synod and provides his response. Tennent writes,

> We believe that there is a Necessity of previous Tryals and Ordination in order to the Ministry; and that such who are regularly set apart, being sound in Doctrine, and blameless in Life, however, their inward State may be, are true Ministers in the Sight of the Church, and that their Ministrations are valid. But in the meantime we think that none should undertake the ministerial Work but those that are truly gracious; those that are inclined of God thereto: For we know not how a graceless Man can be faithful in Ministry.[50]

As to the challenge of unconverted ministers being ineffective in leading souls to salvation, Tennent says, "God, as an absolute Sovereign, may use what Means he pleases to accomplish his Work by. We only assert this: that Success by unconverted Ministers Preaching is very improbable, and very seldom happens, so far as we can gather."[51]

Slightly over a year previous, in March 1740, Tennent had offered his most scathing attack on the unconverted clergy in his sermon "The Danger of an Unconverted Ministry." This message intensified the firestorm of revival criticism and led to Tennent's ejection from the synod. Though Tennent later recanted some of his harsher language and sentiments, he remained steadfast in his conviction that effective ministers should be converted themselves.[52]

An unconverted man may pursue the prestige of a ministerial position, but he will never be effective in fulfilling the purpose of a minister. Tennent charges,

> Men that do not follow Christ, may fish faithfully for a good name, and for worldly Pelth; but not for the Conversion of Sinners to God. Is it reasonable to suppose, that they will be earnestly concerned for others Salvation, when they slight their own? . . . God Almighty does not send Pharisees and natural Men into the Ministry: For how can those Men be faithful, that have no Faith? It's

50. Tennent, "Remarks Upon a Protestation," quoted in Heimert and Miller, *Great Awakening*, 169–70.

51. Tennent, "Remarks Upon a Protestation," quoted in Heimert and Miller, *Great Awakening*, 170.

52. Tennent grieved that this message was repeated and reprinted so often because it made him look like a firebrand, and he was really nothing of the sort.

> true Men may put them into the Ministry, thro' Unfaithfulness, or Mistake; or Credit and Money may draw them, and the Devil may drive them into it, knowing by long Experience, of what special Service they may be to his Kingdom in that Office: But GOD sends not such hypocritical Varlets.[53]

Unconverted ministers will never be effective because they are not sent by God, and they preach an inaccurate gospel. Tennent says these ministers preach a works-righteousness, always "Driving, Driving, to Duty, Duty . . . that it will recommend natural Men to the Favour of God."[54] Such a sermonic theme is expected from men who know nothing of the saving mercy of Christ. Because works righteousness is not acceptable to God, the minister will be ineffective. In his journal, Whitefield provides one of the classic summations of Tennent's teaching, writing, "He convinced me more and more that we can preach the Gospel of Christ no further than we have experienced the power of it in our own hearts. Being deeply convicted of sin, by God's Holy Spirit, at his first conversion, he has learned experimentally to dissect the heart of a natural man."[55]

Though Tennent was the most boisterous advocate for a converted ministry, Edwards and Davies also called for such a seemingly obvious, yet oft neglected, requirement. Edwards says the inner holy ardor of a minister's soul allows the minister to be a "burning light: a minister that is so, has his soul enkindled with the heavenly flame; his heart burns with love to Christ, and fervent desires of the advancement of his kingdom and glory; and also with ardent love to the souls of men, and desires for their salvation."[56] We can see here the natural progression salvation brings: love for Christ leads to desires to advance his kingdom that leads to a love for the souls of men and a desire for their salvation. A pastor's preaching will naturally reflect his passions.

Davies likewise encouraged ministers to be saved. Taking Num 27:16–18 as his own prayer, Davies bids his Hanover congregation farewell, hoping and praying that the Lord would bring them a pastor: "a man in whom is the Spirit, who may go out and come in before you; that the congregation of the Lord be not as sheep without a shepherd."[57] To all three men, conver-

53. Tennent, "Danger," 77.

54. Tennent, "Danger," 79.

55. Whitefield, *Journals*, 348.

56. Edwards, *Sermons and Discourses, 1743–1758*, 92.

57. Davies, *Sermons*, 3:645.

sion was an essential part of the role of the preacher and, thus, a vital part of their homiletical theology.

Piety Natural

If a preacher is genuinely converted, the revivalists believed he will endeavor to have a vibrant relationship with Christ. Such piety provides a minister a growing spiritual relationship, encouragement for his work, and effectiveness in his vocation.

Tennent notes in a preface to a collection of sermons, "I do without boasting, inform you, that I obtained these following Sermons of Jesus Christ the King of the Church, with many Prayers and Tears."[58] His pious relationship with Christ had made such a reception possible.

In his farewell message to Northampton, Edwards encourages his former congregation to seek in their next pastor a man with an established character of "serious religion and piety" not only because all churches need such a preacher but also because their church is in particular need of such a man:

> 'Tis of vast importance that those who are settled in this work should be men of true piety, at all times, and in all places; but more especially at some times, and in some towns and churches. . . . If you should happen to settle a minister, who knows nothing, truly of Christ, and the way of salvation by Him, nothing experimentally of the nature of vital religion; alas, how will you be exposed as sheep without a shepherd! . . . You will need one that shall stand as a champion in the cause of truth and the power of godliness.[59]

Edwards believed ministers should imitate Christ. In an ordination sermon titled "Christ the Example of Ministers," Edwards's theme is a minister's relationship with God. The minister is to follow Christ's example "in that universal and eminent holiness of life, which he set an example of in his human nature."[60] In another sermon, Edwards says, "Ministers, in order to their being burning and shining lights, should walk closely with God, and keep near to Christ; that they may ever be enlightened and enkindled

58. Tennent, *Unsearchable Riches of Christ*, vii.

59. Edwards, *Sermons and Discourses, 1743–1758*, 487–88.

60. Edwards, *Sermons and Discourses, 1743–1758*, 336.

by him. And they should be much in seeking God, and conversing with him by prayers."[61]

Davies also wholeheartedly sought a growing relationship with God. His personal piety attracted followers, including many former Anglicans who had turned away from their own spiritually dead clergy. Davies believed a deep relationship with God made the good, hard work of the preacher successful in accomplishing God's will while also encouraging the minister in troubling times. Davies challenged an ordination candidate saying, "It becomes us to be often on the knee at the throne of mercy, petitioning for help and success: and if we are, in any measure, blessed with either, we should arrogate nothing to ourselves, but ascribe all glory to him, who condescends to distribute gifts to men, and to crown these gifts with his Divine blessing."[62] Davies knew, however, that not every season of a minister's life is crowned with joy and blessing. Every minister faces seasons of discouragement. Whenever these discouragements come, the minister's pious faith will uphold him, thus his relationship with Christ is imperative.

> Therefore, in an humble dependence upon divine assistance, you resolve to continue in it, whatever discouragements arise from a sense of your own imperfections, or from the unsuccessfulness of your labours in the world. And at times you feel, that God is with you, as a mightily terrible one; and causes his pleasure to prosper in your hands; and renders your hardest labours your highest delights: and then, oh then, you would not exchange your pulpit for a throne nor envy ministers of state, if you may be but ministers of the glorious gospel.[63]

The minister should never trust in his own labors, only the Lord.[64]

When God is free to work through a minister, his power is set free to accomplish his will. Godliness in the minister results in power in the pulpit. Edwards believed that the preacher's heart must be "full of much of the holy ardor of a spirit of true piety." Godliness produces power because "true grace is no dull, inactive, ineffectual principle; it is a powerful thing; there is an exceeding energy in it; and the reason is, that God is in it." When God is in it, the "inward holy ardor" of the minister's soul "is exercised and manifested in his being zealous and fervent in his administrations." The

61. Edwards, *Sermons and Discourses, 1743–1758*, 100.

62. Davies, *Sermons*, 3:559.

63. Davies, *Sermons*, 3:548.

64. Davies, *Sermons*, 3:32.

minister is a burning light whose "spiritual heat and holy ardor" is "communicative, and for the benefit of others."[65]

While the minister should maintain piety on a daily basis, he is to pursue it to an increasing degree in times of awakening because God himself is working at an increased level. In the midst of his revival reflections, Edwards writes, "We need a double portion of the Spirit of God at such a time as this. . . . The state of the times extremely requires a fullness of the divine Spirit in ministers, and we ought to give ourselves no rest till we have obtained it."[66]

A converted minister, like any Christian, should grow in his relationship with God. Even though this relationship takes effort and discipline, the results of such piety are well worth it.

Study Expected

For all their emphasis upon piety, the revivalists realized that piety alone would not provide the minister all he needed in the pulpit. If, as Tennent believed, the sermon was a clergyman's most important duty, then study was both needed and expected.

For example, during the first Presbyterian ordination in Virginia, Davies gives instruction upon the office of an ordinary minister of the gospel, or pastor/teacher. Time employed in study is essential. The minister is "to employ his hours at home, not in idleness, or worldly pursuits, but in study and devotion, that his head and heart may be furnished for the discharge of his office."[67] This need is the only way for a minister to be instant in season and out of season, preaching the word with zeal and effect (2 Tim 4:2).

Likewise, Edwards notes that the pastor/teacher must be able and apt to teach. Because of this, he has to be "well-studied in divinity, well acquainted with the written Word of God, mighty in the Scriptures, and able to instruct and convince gainsayers."[68] Further, he must be "apt to teach, ready to instruct the ignorant, and them that are out of the way, and diligent in teaching, in public and private; and careful and faithful to declare the whole counsel of God, and not keep back any thing that may be profitable

65. Edwards, *Sermons and Discourses, 1743–1758*, 92.

66. Edwards, *Some Thoughts Concerning the Revival*, 507.

67. Davies, *Sermons*, 3:549.

68. Edwards, *Sermons and Discourses, 1743–1758*, 93.

to his hearers."[69] Diligence to study and preparation will make the minister most effective. Though some people may think that human learning is of little or no use to a preacher, Edwards disagrees, "An increase of knowledge, without doubt, increases a man's advantage either to do good or hurt, according as he is disposed."[70] A minister should be disposed to do good; therefore, good learning is helpful.

The revivalists expected preachers to study hard for messages. This study begins with their initial training. Though many eighteenth-century preachers did not have access to the more prestigious universities of England or the colonies, as shown in chapters 2 and 3, many of them attended log colleges or studied under other awakened preachers. They were trained to study the Scriptures, often in the original languages. As Old suggests, "They had studied and studied hard, but somehow one detected more than a patina of learning. One sensed the glow of holiness. The preachers of the Great Awakening clearly knew God."[71]

Blend of Light and Heat Needed

The emphasis upon both piety and study demonstrates that Edwards, Tennent, and Davies did not separate the heart from the head. Whereas some eighteenth-century preaching emphasized preaching to the head alone (light) and the extremists of the Awakening promoted preaching to the heart alone (heat), these major leaders of the Awakening preferred a careful balance of the two. Edwards, in his reflections on the true excellency of a minister, says that the uniting of light and heat in a minister "shows that each is genuine, and of a right kind, and that both are divine."[72] Edwards explains what happens when only one of these components is available:

> When there is light in a minister, consisting in human learning, great speculative knowledge and the wisdom of this world, without a spiritual warmth and ardor in his heart, and a holy zeal in his ministrations, his light is like the light of an *ignis fatuus*, and some kinds of putrifying carcasses that shine in the dark, though they are of a stinking savor. And if on the other hand a minister has warmth and zeal, without light, his heat has nothing excellent in it,

69. Edwards, *Sermons and Discourses, 1743–1758*, 93.

70. Edwards, "Distinguishing Marks," 282.

71. Old, *Moderatism, Pietism, and Awakening*, 156.

72. Edwards, *Sermons and Discourses, 1743–1758*, 95.

> but is rather to be abhorred; being like the heat of the bottomless pit; where, though the fire be great, yet there is no light.[73]

Such a balanced preaching ministry of unified light and heat will not only be amiable but also profitable. In *Some Thoughts Concerning the Revival*, Edwards writes, "Zeal and courage will do much in persons of but an ordinary capacity, but especially would they do great things if joined with great abilities."[74] When light and heat work in partnership, the preacher's "light will be like the beams of the sun, that do not only convey light, but give life; and converts will be likely to spring up under their ministry, . . . and the souls of the saints will be likely to grow, and appear beautiful."[75]

God attends the preaching of the minister who has an abiding relationship with him and has prepared well both his soul and sermon for the preaching moment. When the preacher is thoroughly prepared and the sermon has been carefully developed through study and prayer, as if received from Christ himself, the man of God is ready to preach. Such preaching will be effective; if not in that moment, certainly in time. But when such effects occur, Davies reminds ministers to give the glory to God, saying, "Good ministers love to be humble, to lie in their proper sphere, and would have God to have all the glory, as the great efficient; and when we ascribe the work of God to the instrument, we provoke him to withdraw his influence, that we may be convinced of the mistake."[76]

Preachers Are to Maintain a Good Relationship with Their Listeners

Maintain Rapport with the Congregation

The revivalists recognized that the preacher needs rapport with his congregation if he expects to be heard. In 1741, Edwards's father had been at odds with his parishioners for three years. Edwards's solution was to have two young revivalists come into his father's stalemated church with their fresh, enthusiastic approach. In his letter inviting Eleazar Wheelock to be one of these revivalists, Edwards indicates the need for rapport between pastor and parish. He writes, "The minds of people there will be more open to

73. Edwards, *Sermons and Discourses, 1743–1758*, 95.

74. Edwards, *Some Thoughts Concerning the Revival*, 509–10.

75. Edwards, *Sermons and Discourses, 1743–1758*, 96–97.

76. Davies, *Sermons*, 3:32.

your preaching than to my father's, against whom they have such a personal prejudice."[77] Edwards indicates that, for the local pastor, rapport with his people is foundational for effective ministry. Edwards's plan of bringing in supply preachers proved successful in aiding his father's situation.

Love the Congregation

In a message titled "The Church's Marriage to Her Sons, and to Her God," preached for the installment of Samuel Buel as pastor in East Hampton on Long Island, September 19, 1746, Edwards illustrates the love relationship between pastor and congregation as a marriage:

> A faithful minister, that is in a Christian manner united to a Christian people as their pastor, has his heart united to them in the most ardent and tender affection: and they, on the other hand, have their hearts united to him, esteeming him very highly in love for his works' sake, and receiving him with honor and reverence, and willingly subjecting themselves to him, and committing themselves to his care, as being, under Christ, their head and guide.[78]

The minister, as an undershepherd, is under obligation to love the church because Christ, "the great shepherd and bishop of souls" loved the church and has made her his bride.[79] The minister's heart is to be united to the people "not for filthy lucre or any worldly advantage, but with a pure benevolence to them, and desire of their spiritual welfare and prosperity and complacence in them as the children of God and followers of Christ Jesus." And yet, the heart of the congregation should be united to their minister as well, loving and honoring him with "a holy affection and esteem." However, Edwards corrects the motive for such love. He says the congregation is not to love merely because the minister admires them or tickles their ears or raises their curiosity or gratifies their fleshly principles with "florid eloquence" but because they receive him "as the messenger of the Lord of Hosts, coming to them on a divine and infinitely important errand, and with those holy qualifications that resemble the virtues of the

77. Edwards, *Letters and Personal Writings*, 90.

78. Edwards, *Sermons and Discourses, 1743–1758*, 173–74.

79. Edwards, *Sermons and Discourses, 1743–1758*, 173.

Lamb of God."[80] Such a relationship brings great joy to the minister and congregation alike.

Though Edwards was dismissed from his Northampton pastorate because of an irreconcilable doctrinal difference, Edwards did not spite the congregation and left them saying, "How often have we met together in the house of God in this relation? How often have I spoke to you, instructed, counseled, warned, directed, and fed you, and administered ordinances among you, as the people which were committed to my care, and whose precious souls I have the charge of!"[81] Even in parting, Edwards's love for Northampton was evident.

Of the three preachers herein considered, perhaps Davies enjoyed the greatest rapport with his congregation. Upon leaving his charge in Hanover for his new role as president of the College of New Jersey, Davies tells his congregation that he had endeavored to declare the whole counsel of God among them and held nothing back.[82] He had done this because he loved them. He acknowledges their tender love for him and tells them that their pastor will "always tenderly love you, wherever he goes, and whatever you think of him."[83] There's had been an "endeared friendship."[84] Certainly, this relationship is partly why Davies enjoyed such a fruitful ministry in Hanover.

When a pastor and congregation have a "prevalence of benevolence," distractions due to personality conflicts and personal preferences are minimized and the Spirit of God is free to accomplish the Christ-given task of making disciples.[85] Preachers who love their people will labor to bring them to Christ and help them grow in Christ. In "The Apostolic Valediction Considered and Applied," Davies's farewell sermon from Hanover, Davies maintains that a disposition of love ingratiates ministers with mankind, thereby promoting ministers' usefulness in several ways.[86] First, he writes,

80. Edwards, *Sermons and Discourses, 1743–1758*, 174.

81. Edwards, *Sermons and Discourses, 1743–1758*, 475.

82. Davies, *Sermons*, 3:647.

83. Davies, *Sermons*, 3:643.

84. Davies, *Sermons*, 3:643.

85. Davies, *Sermons*, 3:505. "It is comparatively easy to a minister, who ardently loves his people to make them sensible he does love them, and is their real friend, even when he is constrained to put on the appearance of severity." Likewise, a true friend will listen to his minister friend encourage or admonish him from the pulpit.

86. Davies, *Sermons*, 3:503.

> When a minister in his congregation appears in a circle of friends, whose affections meet in him as their common centre, then his labours are likely to be at once pleasing and profitable to them. When the heart is open to the speaker, his words will gain admission through the same door of entrance.[87]

Second, such a love enables and excites ministers to exercise the ministry in such a manner as tends to affect their hearers and "make deep impressions upon their hearts."[88] "When men see the confessed lover of souls in the pulpit, it is natural for them to say, 'Now it is proper I should be attentive, and regard what I hear; for I am convinced the speaker aims at my best interest.'"[89] Third, it will "make a minister of the gospel diligent and laborious in his office."[90] Love will keep the minister busy. Love will excite him to preach the word, to be instant in season and out of season. Love will turn his conversations in the right direction. And love will cause him to bow the knee, inspiring prayers "with a kind of almighty importunity."[91] Fourth, the ardent love of souls will enable ministers "to bear all the hardships and difficulties" they may "meet with in the discharge of it, with patience, and even with cheerfulness."[92] Love is "strong to suffer." The love of lesser things (fame, riches, honor) has conquered many a mountain, how much more can a high love of souls? Fifth, such a love would restrain ministers from everything "low, disgraceful, or offensive" in their ministrations, conversations, and designs.[93] Such "prevalence of benevolence" could only have a "happy effect" upon the exercise of the ministerial office.[94] What preacher would not desire such an effective and enjoyable ministry among his people?

The role of the preacher was foundational to the homiletical theology of Edwards, Tennent, and Davies. They believed that how the preacher portrayed himself and carried out his office would influence his effectiveness. The most effective preacher would be a converted and pious man who was fulfilling his vocation as a preacher. As such, he would endeavor to grow

87. Davies, *Sermons*, 3:503.
88. Davies, *Sermons*, 3:507–8.
89. Davies, *Sermons*, 3:508.
90. Davies, *Sermons*, 3:509.
91. Davies, *Sermons*, 3:509–10.
92. Davies, *Sermons*, 3:510.
93. Davies, *Sermons*, 3:512.
94. Davies, *Sermons*, 3:503.

faithfully in the Lord as well as study diligently so he might correctly impart the word of God to his beloved congregation.

THE ROLE OF SCRIPTURE

Whereas much Enlightenment preaching was moralistic and only slightly, if at all, related to Scripture, the preaching of Edwards, Tennent, and Davies, was grounded in Scripture. For them, Scripture was divine, infallible, authoritative, and sufficient and, thus, served as both the source of and criterion for preaching.

Scripture Is Divine, Infallible, Authoritative, and Sufficient

Edwards, Tennent, and Davies were the products of traditions that valued Scripture. The Puritan preachers from whom Edwards descended were men "who not only held a high view of the Word, but also held a high view of preaching that Word."[95] The Presbyterian fathers of Tennent and Davies were no less committed to Scripture.

The Puritans and Presbyterians alike were Protestants, and a foundational principle of the Protestant Reformation was the authority of Scripture. Therefore, it was almost natural for awakened Protestants like Edwards, Tennent, and Davies to elevate Scripture as they promoted revival. David Larsen says the Awakening was "a revival of the Reformation in a real sense."[96] This link between Protestantism and the Awakening can be readily seen in one of Davies's sermons. After asking the question, "What is an apostolic New Testament bishop?" Davies quotes William Chillingworth, a prominent Protestant from a previous generation. Davies says, "This inquiry will lead you to your Bibles: and I hope, you are all so far Protestants, as to join with the great Chillingworth in saying, 'The Bible! the Bible! is the religion of Protestants.'"[97]

95. Bickell, *Light and Heat*, v. Holland says, for the Puritans, "The Bible was the root of all authority. Whatever doctrine was developed for the day had its origin and justification in the Bible." Holland, *Preaching in American History*, 115.

96. Larsen, *Company of the Preachers*, 359.

97. Davies, *Sermons*, 3.534. William Chillingworth (1602–1644) was an English churchman who researched Catholicism and Protestantism, eventually deciding upon Protestantism. His work *The Religion of Protestants: A Safe Way to Salvation* (1637), emphasizes the sole authority of the Bible. Davies is paraphrasing an oft repeated statement

Such a return to Scripture not only affected the content of messages but also kept ministers in check. Though the minister might enjoy powers and privileges in society and be the only one allowed to speak for God in public assemblies, still, "because sermons had to be based on *Sola Scriptura*, even the minister's authority was limited."[98]

More than any other concepts related to Scripture, Edwards, Tennent, and Davies emphasized that Scripture was divine in origin, infallible in content, authoritative in force, and sufficient in guidance. These were their descriptions of the Scriptures.

Scripture Is Divine, Authoritative, and Infallible

To these men, Scripture was divine in origin. This belief was the foundational premise of their thoughts upon Scripture. The apostle Paul's words in 2 Tim 3:16 were close to their hearts: "All Scripture is inspired by God and profitable for teaching, for reproof, for correction, for training in righteousness." The conviction concerning Scripture's divinity will be evident in the comments below concerning the other aspects of Scripture.

Because Scriptures were given by divine inspiration, they are, as Tennent says, "infallibly true and of divine authority."[99] The infallibility and authority of Scripture go hand-in-hand, giving Scripture power. At times this power of infallible authority is demonstrated with sword-wielding boldness; at other times, it is demonstrated with quiet resolve. The preacher draws his confidence in preaching from both.

Edwards demonstrates this sword-wielding boldness when he says that Scripture "is the great and standing rule which God has given to his church, to guide them in all things relating to the great concerns of their souls; and 'tis an infallible and sufficient rule."[100] One feels in Edwards's words a bold, unyielding confidence. Scripture stands resolutely, sword drawn, as the "standing rule."

Still, at other times, the infallible authority of Scripture has a quiet power that is demonstrated in quiet resolve. Here the picture is much more of a knight standing confident with sword in scabbard rather than of a

---

of Chillingworth.

98. Stout, *New England Soul*, 19. Stout is speaking of New England Puritans in the 1600s.

99. Tennent, *Twenty-Three Sermons*, 64.

100. Edwards, "Distinguishing Marks," 227.

knight wielding sword in battle. Davies reflects upon this quiet strength in his sermon on the Christian religion:

> The measures [the biblical writers] took were a plain declaration of their religion; and they wrought miracles for its confirmation. . . . Here I cannot but take particular notice of that matchless simplicity that appears in the history of Christ and his apostles. The evangelists write in that artless, calm, and unguarded manner, which is natural to persons confident of the undeniable truth of what they assert; they do not write that scrupulous caution which would argue any fear that they might be confuted. They simply relate the naked facts, and leave them to stand upon their own evidence. They relate the most amazing, the most moving things, with the most cool serenity, without any passionate exclamations and warm reflections.[101]

As the apostles had a quiet confidence in the infallible truth and authority of the things they wrote, so the preacher should have such confidence when he proclaims the text. If the apostles saw no need to belabor their facts, though their facts may seem to be fantasy, why should the preacher? He should not. The preacher should stand with quiet resolve upon the infallible authority of Scripture.

Depending upon the situation, the preacher may choose to stand with the sword-wielding boldness of Scripture or with the quiet resolve of Scripture. Whatever the case, he should be confident in the infallibility and authority of the divine word of God. If he is, his preaching will unleash the power of God's word.

Scripture Is Sufficient in Guidance

Because Scripture is divine in origin, infallible in content, and authoritative in force, it is naturally sufficient in guidance as well. Davies best demonstrates this belief in his sermon "The Divine Authority and Sufficiency of the Christian Religion." Even though his message focuses on the Christian religion in general, Davies deals much with the subject of Scripture. One can see in this message Davies's high belief not only in the sufficiency of the Christian religion but also in the sufficiency of Scripture. Davies states that everything he wishes to prove is found in his text:

101. Davies, *Sermons*, 1:91.

> If I can prove that Christianity offers all the ends of a religion from God; if I can prove that it is attended with sufficient attestation; if I can prove that no sufficient objections can be offered against it; and that men have no reason at all to desire another; but that this proves ineffectual for their reformation and salvation, there is no ground to hope that any other would prove successful; I say, if I can prove these things, then the point in debate is carried, and we must all embrace the religion of Jesus as certainly true. These things are asserted or implied in my text, with respect to the Scriptures then extant, *Moses and the prophets.*[102]

All the proof is available in the Old Testament. However, Davies goes on to say that Christians have even more available. He says,

> We have not only Moses and the prophets, but we have also Christ, who is a messenger from the dead, and his apostles; and therefore, surely, 'if we do not hear them, neither will we be persuaded, though one rose from the dead.' The Gospel is the last effort of the grace of God with a guilty world; and if this has no effect upon us, our disease is incurable that refuses to be healed.[103]

Scripture is sufficient. Later in his message, Davies delineates the ways Scripture is sufficient. He says the Scriptures give "sufficient instructions what we should believe, or are a sufficient rule of faith."[104] Scripture gives "faint discoveries of natural reason," the "clearest and most majestic account of the nature and perfections of the Deity," an account of the present state of human nature, as degenerate," "a welcome account of a method of recovery from the ruins of our apostasy, through the mediation of the Son of God," and a view of "the invisible worlds."[105] Everything from life in this day to how to have life in the morrow is covered in Scripture. It is completely sufficient.

To men like Edwards, Tennent, and Davies, Scripture was divine in origin, infallible in content, authoritative in force, and sufficient in guidance. After declaring the divine origin of Scriptures in his message "The Divinity of the Scriptures," preached in New Brunswick in April of 1738, Tennent demonstrates that the word of God should be heard "believingly, as the very Word of God," "attentively, with due Reverence and Concern,"

102. Davies, *Sermons*, 1:73.

103. Davies, *Sermons*, 1:76–77.

104. Davies, *Sermons*, 1:77.

105. Davies, *Sermons*, 1:78–79.

"applicatively, searching ourselves by what is Spoken," and "obediently, acting in our after walk, according to the Word of God we hear."[106] If people choose to reject Scripture, it is their fault, not God's. Davies says, "If they are unbelievers now, it is not for want of evidence, but through willful blindness and obstinancy; and as they that will shut their eyes can see no more in meridian light than in the twilight, so they that reject a sufficiency of evidence would also resist a superfluity of it."[107]

Scripture Is the Source of Preaching

Because Scripture is divine in origin, infallible in content, authoritative in force, and sufficient in guidance, Edwards, Tennent, and Davies believed it must be the source of preaching. Edwards displays this belief in *Some Thoughts Concerning the Revival.* Those who were critical of the revival often used extra-biblical arguments and little Scripture. In response, Edwards says, "Those that I am speaking of, will indeed make some use of Scripture, so far as they think it serves their turn; but don't make use of it alone, as a rule sufficient by itself, but make as much, and a great deal more use of other things, diverse and wide from it, to judge of this work by."[108] Edwards believed Scripture was sufficient and, therefore, should be the source of preaching as well as for arguments concerning spiritual and ecclesial issues. Upon his departure from Northampton, Edwards encourages his congregation to seek in their next pastor a man who will use the Bible as his source for preaching even more than he had. He proclaims,

> May you have a minister, of greater knowledge of the Word of God, and better acquaintance with soul cases, and of greater skills in applying himself to souls, whose discourses may be more searching and convincing; that such of you as have held fast deceit under my preaching, may have your eyes opened by his; that you may be undeceived before that great day.[109]

Edwards believed the best minister will use Scripture in all the ways given by the apostle Paul in 2 Timothy. Such preaching would be effective,

106. Tennent, *Divinity*, 168. Whereas in other messages Tennent delineates a number of applications, for this part of his message he simply says, "The Application of this is easy, if you are but willing." Davies, *Sermons*, 1:169.

107. Davies, *Sermons*, 1:106.

108. Edwards, *Some Thoughts Concerning the Revival*, 296.

109. Edwards, *Sermons and Discourses, 1743–1758*, 478–79.

especially when performed by a man with renewed rapport with the people of Northampton.

Davies demonstrates a similar belief in his departing sermon from Hanover. Davies says he had endeavored to declare the whole counsel of God.[110] He states,

> Your consciences bear witness, "that you have had precept upon precept, and line upon line," during my ministry among you—That I have not shunned to declare to you all the counsel of God, Acts 20:27; and have kept back nothing that was likely to be profitable to you. Acts 20:20. I have warned you, in season and out of season—I have reproved, rebuked, and exhorted you, with all long-suffering and doctrine. 2 Tim 4:2. I have preached to you as a dying man to dying men.[111]

A man passionate about preparation for eternity will have Scripture, all of Scripture, as the source for his preaching.

Awakened preachers saw the need for sermons to be grounded in Scripture. Scripture was the source of authority because Scripture was from God.

Scripture Is the Criterion for Preaching

In his book *The Modern Preacher and the Ancient Text*, homiletician Sidney Greidanus notes, "The affirmation that the Bible serves as source for preaching and lends authority to preaching does not entail that the congregation must blindly accept whatever is said, for the other side of the coin is that the Bible also functions as the criterion of preaching."[112] Edwards, Tennent, and Davies believed their listeners should not judge preachers according to their splendid presentation or elocution but rather by their use of the Scripture. Listeners should "test the word that is spoken to see if it is indeed worthy of acceptance as the Word of God."[113] This topic will be further treated below in the discussion of the role of the listener in preaching.

For men like Edwards, Tennent, and Davies, Scripture was the primary tool laid upon the sermonic workbench. Because Scripture is divine, infallible, authoritative, and sufficient and serves as both the source of and

110. Davies, *Sermons*, 3:647.

111. Davies, *Sermons*, 3:654–55.

112. Greidanus, *Modern Preacher*, 14.

113. Greidanus, *Modern Preacher*, 14.

criterion for preaching, it is indispensable in preaching. Awakened preachers returned to many of the beliefs of their forefathers and, once again, elevated the authority and sufficiency of Scripture in preaching. The result was awakening. As Larsen states, "At the epicenter of any spiritual detonation is the recovery of the preaching of the Word of God."[114]

THE ROLE OF THE HOLY SPIRIT

By himself, a preacher has nothing to say. Any significance to his words is given by the Spirit. As Stott says, "To address a congregation without any assurance that we are bearers of a divine message would be the height of arrogance and folly."[115]

Whenever Edwards, Tennent, and Davies stood to preach, they knew they did so only by the grace of God. They also knew that if their preaching had any effect, it was because of the Holy Spirit's empowerment. Therefore, any glory that came from preaching was due the Spirit and not the preacher. These men trusted Paul's words to the Corinthians: "I planted, Apollos watered, but God was causing the growth. So then neither the one who plants nor the one who waters is anything, but God who causes the growth" (1 Cor 3:6–7). The preacher has his task to perform, but the Holy Spirit gives the effect. As Tennent says in a message upon God's divine mercy, "Sinners are always under God's control and within the reach of his arm."[116]

The Holy Spirit Empowers the Words of the Preacher

Though the preacher and his crafting of the message are vital to the sermonic process, it is the Spirit who gives power to the words. Davies calls for this power, saying,

> We have the gospel, we have preaching, we have all the means of salvation; but something is wanting to give them life to make them efficacious, and bear them home upon the hearts of sinners with that almighty energy which they have sometimes had. . . . And what is it? It is Thou, eternal Spirit.[117]

114. Larsen, *Company of Preachers*, 359.

115. Stott, *Between Two Worlds*, 96.

116. Tennent, "Divine Mercy," in Alexander, *Sermons and Essays*, 40.

117. Davies, *Sermons*, 2:428.

One could have all of the components of a powerful event and still have nothing. The components of text, sermon, preacher, and listeners need something to put them together and cause them to interact and react. That something is Someone, the Holy Spirit of God. A preacher's efficacy depends upon the Holy Spirit's "superintending influence."[118]

Religion flourishes or declines, "not so much according to external means, as according to the degree of divine influence."[119] One sermon may leave a listener "cold and hard-hearted, while another, no better in itself, sets him all on fire."[120] It is neither the preacher nor his methodology that brings the effect; it is the Holy Spirit.

In "The Success of the Ministry Owing to a Divine Influence," Davies makes his case for the urgency of the Spirit's influence in preaching. This message on 1 Cor 3:7 and preached at Hanover on November 19, 1757, is a good representation of this portion of the homiletical theology of Edwards, Tennent, and Davies.

Davies believed that an absence of effectiveness in preaching was linked to an absence of the Holy Spirit. People may enjoy the message and attend faithfully, but the deficiency of life transformation indicates a neglect of the Spirit. Davies proclaims,

> When we see people enjoy the frequent cultivations of the gospel, and the means of spiritual fruitfulness, and yet few new trees of righteousness planted, and those that have been planted seemingly withering and unfruitful, we cannot but conclude that something is wanting: without which all the means they enjoy will be of no service. We should naturally turn our thoughts to an inquiry, what was wanting, had we tilled our lands from year to year without a crop? . . . There is certainly something wanting, which is of greater consequence than anything we have. Here are the gospel, and its ordinances . . . ; here is a minister . . . ; here are the hearers that crowd our sanctuary. . . . And what, then, is wanting? Why God, that alone can give the increase, is not here by the influences of his grace: and in his absence, "neither he that planteth is anything, nor he that watereth:" they all are nothing together; and may labour till dooms-day, and never convert one soul.[121]

118. Davies, *Sermons*, 3:9.

119. Davies, *Sermons*, 3:25.

120. Davies, *Sermons*, 3:28.

121. Davies, *Sermons*, 3:12.

The success of the ministry of the gospel "entirely depends upon the concurring influences of divine grace; . . . without the divine agency to render the gospel successful, all the labours of its ministers will be in vain."[122] At the same time, however, if the Spirit is present, there will be effectiveness. In a later message, Davies says,

> If [God] be with you, he will cause his church among you to flourish, and adorn every individual in it with the beauties of holiness. If the God of love and peace be with you, he will cause love and peace to prevail among you, and render you a society of friends and brethren, walking unanimously to the same heavenly country, like affectionate pilgrims. If he be with you, his gospel will not be that languid, feeble, inefficacious thing that it has been for some time.[123]

The same lack of concern for the Spirit's presence will get the same results "till ministers and people are brought to the dust before God, to acknowledge their own weakness and entire dependence upon Him."[124] If a preacher wants to see results, he must "invite the blessed agent to accomplish his work, instead of provoking him to leave."[125]

Men like Edwards, Tennent, and Davies understood that ministers work both with and for God in their preaching. Just as in the natural world God "makes use of the instrumentality of the husbandman to till the ground, to sow the seed, and water it" and yet "it is he that commands the clouds to drop down fatness upon it," so also, "in the world of grace, God uses a variety of suitable means to form degenerate sinners into his image, and fit them for a happy eternity." Chief of these is the ministry of the gospel. "Ministers are sowers sent out into the wild field of the world, with the precious seed of the Word."[126] Ministers work with God for the common purpose of accomplishing God's grand scheme of redemption.[127]

Still, while ministers work with God for a common purpose, they should not think they are his equals. Ministers also work *for* God. They work for God, who is carrying out his grand scheme of salvation, and for

122. Davies, *Sermons*, 3:12.
123. Davies, *Sermons*, 3:651–52.
124. Davies, *Sermons*, 3:31.
125. Davies, *Sermons*, 3:33.
126. Davies, *Sermons*, 3:9–10.
127. Davies, *Sermons*, 3:554–55.

Jesus Christ, who originally gave the preacher his commission.[128] And because preachers work for God, each will one day have to give an account of his stewardship to the Master.[129]

To discharge their office with diligence, ministers need constant supplies of divine grace.[130] Humanity is spiritually dead (Eph 2:1) and blind (2 Cor 4:4) and in need of someone to open their eyes. However, as Davies explains, a conundrum exists: "Clay cannot open the eyes of the blind." A clay man cannot open the eyes of another clay man. It is only when one man is in God's "almighty hands" that blinded eyes can be made to see.[131] A "clay" minister needs the Holy Spirit to open his eyes and mouth so that he may speak life to his "clay" congregation.

People sometimes struggle in articulating the relationship of the Holy Spirit and preaching. As the theologian of the Awakening, Edwards considered this subject. In 1742, he published *Some Thoughts Concerning the Present Revival of Religion in New England* in five parts. In this treatise, Edwards seeks to defend the revival as a work of God, encourage others to promote the work, defend those promoters who had been injuriously blamed, offer suggestions for corrections to the Awakening, and provide suggestions for how people might promote the revival. It is in the fourth part of his treatise that Edwards deals with the Spirit's assistance in preaching. Edwards says that some had "greatly misunderstood" the Spirit's role and were seeking "after a miraculous assistance of inspiration, by immediate suggestion of words to them" by the Spirit.[132] Edwards teaches, however, that the more excellent way is to have the "gracious holy assistance of the Spirit of God." Edwards explains this assistance, saying,

> The gracious, and most excellent, kind assistance of the Spirit of God in praying and preaching, is not my immediate suggesting of words to their apprehension, which may be with a cold dead heart, but by warming the heart and filling it with a great sense of those things that are to be spoken of, and with holy affections, that sense and those affections may suggest words. Thus indeed the Spirit of God may be said, indirectly and mediately to suggest words to us, to indite our petitions for us, and to teach the preacher what to say; he fills the heart, and that fills the mouth; as we know that when

128. Davies, *Sermons*, 3:552–54.

129. Davies, *Sermons*, 1:651.

130. Davies, *Sermons*, 3:559.

131. Davies, *Sermons*, 3:14–15.

132. Edwards, *Some Thoughts Concerning the Revival*, 437.

> men are greatly affected in any matter, and their hearts are very full, it fills them with matter for speech, and makes 'em eloquent upon that subject; and much more have spiritual affections this tendency, for many reasons that might be given.[133]

This assistance requires at least two things. First, the preacher must have a pious relationship with God through which the Spirit is free to work. Second, the preacher must study. The man who attempts to preach without these is guilty of presumption. If a man can preach without these, he is the exception rather than the norm.[134]

Revivalists knew that even the most talented preacher needs the Holy Spirit to empower his words. In 1745, Edwards warned one of his Scottish correspondents that God could humble even the most naturally gifted minister. He writes,

> God has lately done great things before our eyes, whereby he has shown us something of his wonderful power and mercy; but has withal so disposed things, that events have tended remarkably to show us our weakness, infirmity, insufficiency, and great and universal need of God's help; we have been many ways rebuked for our self-confidence and looking to instruments, and trusting in an arm of flesh; and God is now showing us that we are nothing, and letting us see that we can do nothing.[135]

Davies sums up the proper attitude of a godly preacher saying, "Good ministers love to be humble . . . and would have God to have all the glory, as the great efficient; and when we ascribe the work of God to the instrument, we provoke him to withdraw his influence, that we may be convinced of the mistake."[136] Only the Holy Spirit can empower the words of the preacher.

The Holy Spirit Applies the Message to the Listener

Inherent to the Holy Spirit's work of empowering the preacher's words is his applying those words to the listener. In the preface to a sermon collection, Tennent says that God, because of his grace, "has accepted and blessed my sincere though weak Attempts, for the Conviction, Conversion,

133. Edwards, *Some Thoughts Concerning the Revival*, 437–38.

134. Edwards, *Some Thoughts Concerning the Revival*, 438.

135. Edwards, *Letters and Personal Writings*, 181.

136. Davies, *Sermons*, 3:32.

and Consolation of some of you, for which I bless the most high God."[137] Tennent knew that the Holy Spirit not only empowers the words of the preacher, but applies the message of those words for conviction, conversion, or consolation.[138]

Edwards agreed. In his sermon "God Makes Men Sensible of Their Misery Before He Reveals His Mercy and Love," preached in the fall of 1730, Edwards declares that God works through imprecatory preaching and other methods of inducing spiritual humiliation to lead people to conviction so that they might ultimately experience his love. In picturesque language, Edwards proclaims, "Before God opens prison doors, he makes 'em see that they are shut up, that they are closed prisoners, and that there is no way that they can get out."[139] Upon preparing to leave his Northampton charge, Edwards shares his hope that whomever the congregation secures as their next pastor will not be in the way of Christ's work among them through his Spirit. He proclaims,

> Whoever may hereafter stand related to you as your spiritual guide, my desire and prayer is, that the great Shepherd of the sheep would have a special respect to you, and be your guide . . . , and that he who is the infinite fountain of light, would "open your eyes, and turn you from darkness unto light, and from the power of Satan unto God; that you may receive forgiveness of sins, and inheritance among them that are sanctified, through faith that is in Christ."[140]

For years, Edwards had battled errant doctrine in Northampton with the Spirit's assistance. He left that pulpit hoping that a different Spirit-filled man could finally bring about change.

Edwards, Tennent, and Davies held great confidence in the Spirit's work. Such understanding encouraged them in troublesome times and allowed them to celebrate in victorious ones. They all believed, as Davies, that "God will not forget their honest, though feeble, and frequently unsuccessful labours in his own work."[141] He will empower a preacher's words, apply his words, and eventually, when he lifts the charge from the preacher's shoulders in heaven, he will reward his words.

137. Tennent, *Unsearchable Riches of Christ*, vii.

138. See Tennent, *Sermons on Important Subjects*, 184–208.

139. Edwards, *Sermons and Discourses, 1730–1733*, 156.

140. Edwards, *Sermons and Discourses, 1743–1758*, 481.

141. Davies, *Sermons*, 3:557.

THE ROLE OF THE LISTENER

Turnbull states that eighteenth-century listeners, especially those in the Calvinist traditions, "came to church to listen to the pastor as the mouthpiece of God."[142] Because the sermon was the agency of God in conversion and the destiny of the soul was the most important fact of life, Turnbull says, "attention was assured and offered, generally, to the preacher and his message."[143] The word *generally* in Turnbull's statement is important. As was shown in chapters 2 and 3, even in the churches that held a high regard for preaching, lethargy could exist and often did exist. Therefore, one can only say that preachers were "generally" given the attention of their congregation.

The revivalists, however, grasped the attention of their audiences. The revivalists were likely successful in doing so because they realized that listeners are more than just an audience assembled for a religious talk; they are participants in the great scheme of God.[144] In their messages, no matter their style of delivery or methodology, these preachers embarked on a sermonic journey and made sure their listeners went along for the ride. They knew that any congregation may be composed of both Christians and heathens, but they were all humans and sinners in need of a word from God. Therefore, men like Edwards, Tennent, and Davies called their people out of sleep and gave them active roles in the preaching event.

The revivalists challenged their listeners to participate in the event of preaching. In fact, in their messages, one senses that this task was delivered to the listeners with fervor. Near the end of one ordination message, Davies turns his attention to the laity in the audience and emphasizes their need to work with the minister in his office of preaching:

> You must, also, hence see, that it is your concern to concur with ministers of the gospel in promoting the benevolent and important ends of their office. Endeavor so to attend upon their ministrations, as that you yourselves may be saved by them. And endeavor

142. Turnbull, *Jonathan Edwards*, 60.

143. Turnbull, *Jonathan Edwards*, 60.

144. Ritschl says, "The sermon is not a full and proper sermon because the words which come out of the preacher's mouth are true and Biblical. The sermon is an event in and of the Church. There is an inseparable relation between the proclamation and the congregation. But the preaching has priority over the hearing, inasmuch as the call has priority over the response." Ritschl, *Theology of Proclamation*, 127.

> by your conversation and example, and all methods in your power, to make them useful to others.[145]

Without listeners hearing and heeding the message, even the best preaching will fail.

Listeners are important. Therefore, listeners, whether they be Christian or heathen, had a prominent role in the homiletical theology of Edwards, Tennent, and Davies. These men believed their listeners were to receive ministers as the mouthpiece of God and come to worship prepared to hear and heed the message so that they may be changed by God.

The View of the Listener: Sinner

Central to the role of the listener in the revivalists' homiletical theology was their view of the listener. Edwards, Tennent, and Davies viewed all humans as sinners. Whereas some in the eighteenth century proposed that man was getting increasingly better, awakened preachers saw the opposite. Man was as sinful as he had always been. Humans were still fallible, and the revivalists were unafraid to say so. Old states that such a view of humanity actually commended the awakeners to their age:

> It was this by which so many of their contemporaries came to realize that they were the realists of the day. So much of the eighteenth century was frivolous and artificial, and yet the artificiality fooled no one. It was an age of satire as well, yet few people were willing to speak of death and judgment, at least not as honestly as [the] evangelical preachers.[146]

Because listeners are lost and estranged from God, the preacher's task is to confront sinners, appraise their estrangement from God, and help them to see the need for repentance and salvation. Also, believers will be warmed by remembering the gospel.

The revivalists' dim view of human nature could often appear overly negative. One needs only to read Tennent's scathing rebuke of the unconverted clergy to feel this. However, Marsden humorously defends Edwards's dim view by reminding the reader that Edwards's "grandmother was an incorrigible profligate, his great-aunt committed infanticide, and

145. Davies, *Sermons* 3:560.

146. Old, *Moderatism, Pietism, and Awakening*, 158.

his great-uncle was an ax-murderer."[147] It would be hard to not have a dim view with such a lineage!

More often than not, the view of listener as sinner was communicated as Davies did in an evangelistic message to his beloved congregation in Hanover in 1757:

> When I consider I am speaking to an assembly of sinners, guilty, depraved, helpless creatures, and that, if ever you be saved, it will be only through Jesus Christ, in that way which the gospel reveals; when I consider that your everlasting life and happiness turn upon this hinge, namely, the reception you give to this Saviour, and this way of salvation; I say, when I consider these things, I can think of no subject I can more properly choose than to recommend the Lord Jesus to your acceptance, and to explain and inculcate the method of salvation through his mediation; or, in other words, to preach the pure gospel to you; for the gospel, in the most proper sense, is nothing else but a revelation of a way of salvation for sinners.[148]

Davies's dim view of humanity is evident; however, this view does not cause him to be vindictive and hateful toward his congregation. Instead, because he loves the people, he challenges them to accept Christ.

Davies's emphasis upon the expectation of ministers to love souls has already been noted. In the same message in which he admonished ministers to do this, he did the same to listeners. "The love of souls is the duty of hearers as well as ministers."[149] The first implication of such teaching is the hearers should love their ministers as "the friends, the lovers of your souls."[150] The second is that they must love their own souls. If ministers "are so strongly obliged to love the souls of others, surely you must be obliged to love your own."[151]

Though to some Tennent and Edwards might not always appear loving in their words, it is evident that they held a similar view. For example, in his message "Zeal, an Essential Virtue of a Christian" preached in April 1740, Edwards spoke of love as the principal affection needed in zeal. He says, "Zeal is an inward heat or fervency of spirit, and love is the flame

147. Marsden, *Jonathan Edwards*, 22.

148. Davies, *Sermons*, 1:109.

149. Davies, *Sermons*, 3:514.

150. Davies, *Sermons*, 3:514.

151. Davies, *Sermons*, 3:516.

whence that heat comes. This is the fire that fills the soul with that holy fervor that is called zeal."[152] For Edwards, a love for God came first. This love fans a Christian's zeal to serve God in all ways, including the evangelism of lost souls.

Listeners Must Receive Ministers as the Mouthpiece of God

Edwards, Tennent, and Davies were the products of Christian traditions that valued the ministerial office. This valuing caused them to reflect upon the role of the preacher in preaching as well as how the preacher should be received by the congregation. Above all, listeners are to receive the minister as a called authority and support the minister so he might effectively carry out his calling. Still, they were to depend upon the Holy Spirit, not their human minister alone.

Receive the Minister as a Called Authority

Congregations should recognize their minister as God-called and, therefore, authoritative in his message. This recognition is especially needed in the local church, but the principle actually applies wherever a minister may speak. Edwards explains that wherever a minister "is providentially called to preach the Word of God, or minister in holy things he ought to be received as a minister of Christ, and the messenger of the Lord of Hosts to them."[153]

Davies helped his congregation fulfill their role of receiving their minister by placing them in a unique relationship to him. In one message he asks his congregation to consider themselves "as hearers not of a preacher formed out of the clay like yourselves, but of the Lord Jesus Christ. Suppose him here in person treating with you about your reconciliation to God, and what regard you would pay to a proposal made by him in person." Whatever regard they would show Christ, is the same as they should show Davies as he spoke in Christ's "name and stead."[154]

152. Edwards, *Sermons and Discourses, 1739–1742*, 141.

153. Edwards, *Sermons and Discourses, 1743–1758*, 172.

154. Davies, *Sermons*, 1:141.

Support the Minister

In an age when many ministers were tax-supported, a discussion on the role of the congregation's support of the minister may seem redundant. However, the support Edwards, Tennent, and Davies expected from their people went beyond finances. While adequate financial provisions were expected, support was also to be given in numerous other ways. Edwards summarizes these in "Christ, the Example of Gospel Ministers":

> It is your duty and interest well to support your minister, so it concerns you to pray earnestly for him, and each one to do what in him lies in all respects to encourage and help him, and strengthen his hands, by attending diligently to his ministry, receiving the truth in love, treating him with the honor due to a messenger of Christ, carefully avoiding all contention with him, and one with another. And take heed in particular, that you do not forsake him to follow those, who under pretense of extraordinary purity are doubtless doing the devil's work, in separating themselves, and endeavoring to draw off others from the ministers and churches in the land in general.[155]

Listeners are to support their minister by praying for him, encouraging and helping him, attending and receiving his messages, treating him with honor and respect, and avoiding contention with him and others.

Of all these methods of support, however, prayer was the most important and foundational. Both Davies and Edwards addressed this subject at ordination assemblies. In one of these sermons, after directing most of his comments to the candidate, Davies addresses the listeners, pleading with them to "see how much ministers need the assistance of your prayers."[156] In an ordination message, Edwards beseeches the laity to "earnestly pray" for their minister "that he may be filled with divine light, and with the power of the Holy Ghost, to make him so."[157] Such praying will be "for the greatest benefit to yourselves; for if your minister burns and shines, it will be for your light and life."[158] Much of a minister's effectiveness depends upon his congregation's prayer life.

155. Edwards, *Sermons and Discourses, 1743–1758*, 347–48.

156. Davies, *Sermons*, 3:559.

157. Edwards, *Sermons and Discourses, 1743–1758*, 101. This message was preached on August 30, 1744.

158. Edwards, *Sermons and Discourses, 1743–1758*, 101.

Depend upon the Holy Spirit

Though many of the revivalist ministers were naturally gifted in preaching, they also encouraged their congregations to depend upon the Holy Spirit over-and-above their ministers. Talented and anointed ministers were important, but they could also easily distract the people from the Spirit of God.

In a message to his church in Hanover, Davies agrees that "faithful and accomplished ministers are singular blessings to the places where they labour, because it is by their instrumentality that the Lord is wont to work." But Davies further instructs his congregation, saying, "But still let us remember, that even a Paul or an Apollos is nothing, unless the Lord give the increase. One text of Scripture, one sentence, will do more execution, when enforced by divine energy, than all the labours of the ablest ministers upon earth without it."[159] Depending upon the Spirit allows God to be free to act. However, Davies says, depending upon the instruments provokes God to leave. In another sermon, Davies exposes the result of such an ill-guided choice:

> You may still have your favourite minister; you may still have sermons, and all the ordinances of the gospel: but alas! "hearing you shall hear, and not understand; and seeing you shall see, and not perceive:" and the very means that ripen others for heaven, will only cause you to rot and putrefy, till you drop, as it were by your own weight into hell. . . . for the absence of the Spirit is the great reason why sinners attend upon the ministry of the gospel without any real advantage.[160]

A congregation may have everything needed for great effect—a great preacher, sermons, the ordinances, and a full congregation—but without the Spirit, little will happen.

While he would have agreed with Davies's conclusions, Edwards gives an additional reason for depending on the Spirit over a minister. In his famous *Some Thoughts Concerning the Revival*, Edwards flatly demonstrates the erratic nature of humans and the designations and labels they give men, especially preachers. In Edwards's day, preachers were either "alive" or "dead." Edwards challenges his readers to be careful of calling one preacher dead and another alive simply because today's "alive" may be tomorrow's "dead." All it will take to demote the most alive minister today is for another

159. Davies, *Sermons*, 3:31.

160. Davies, *Sermons*, 3:635–36.

minister to come along tomorrow who excels in some way.[161] Human labels are fickle; God's Spirit is constant.

Listeners Must Come to Worship Prepared to Hear and Heed

Tennent insisted that listeners must "attend with diligence upon the preached Word; for it is by the foolishness of preaching that God saves those that believe."[162] Because listeners play an important role in preaching and are saved through preaching, the revivalists believed listeners need to prepare for worship so that they may hear and heed what God says to them. This preparation includes both piety and study. Such preparation allows listeners to respond to the instruction and call of God. Unlike the Jews who hardened their hearts against the prophets and against Christ and his apostles, and continued unreformed and impenitent, modern listeners should hear and heed the call. Responding is the listeners' job. It is sinful for listeners to remain indifferent.

Edwards spoke to this indifference in his most biting sermon. First written in 1730 or early 1731, Edwards's sermon titled "Stupid as Stones" is the most piercing condemnation of the people of Northampton that Edwards delivered until his "Farewell Sermon" of 1750. In this message, Edwards is disappointed with his congregation not because of corrupt doctrine or disagreement but because of indifference. This message surfaces Edwards's livid frustration for the listener who has no enthusiasm for the preacher's message.[163] Such a problem caused Edwards to remind his congregation that their indifference did not frustrate God's word or plan, it simply caused it to be accomplished in a manner other than the preacher originally planned. Taking his text from Ezek 3:27, Edwards says that God forewarned Ezekiel "that the going and preaching the Word of God to [the Jews in Judea] would be like going amongst briars and thorns and scorpions. They would show themselves so perverse, so proud and spiteful."[164] Edwards states the doctrine of his sermonic text: "When God sends his messengers to preach his word, his word shall not be in vain; or, God shall

161. Edwards, *Some Thoughts Concerning the Revival*, 478.

162. Tennent, "Divine Mercy," 46–47.

163. Valeri, editor's introduction to Edwards, *Sermons and Discourses, 1730–1733*, 173.

164. Edwards, *Sermons and Discourses, 1730–1733*, 175.

not be frustrated when men hear or whether they forbear."[165] Edwards's point is that God "will obtain his end, let men treat his word how they will."[166] God's word will not return void.

Edwards believed listeners refuse to hear the message for various reasons. Some of them have yet to respond to Christ in salvation and refuse to do so. Others do not want to give up "their vices and ways of known sin."[167] Many come "only in conformity to custom."[168] They hear the words but without reflection and application to their life. Still others are "intent upon something else" whether it be other persons in attendance, business affairs, the "lusts in their imaginations," a conversation with their neighbor, or a good day's sleep in the pew.[169] Nevertheless, though they do not hear, God's word does not return void. God is glorified even in their indifference because such indifference condemns them in their sin. Edwards's application is for both ministers and listeners. First, "ministers should not neglect faithfully to preach the Word of God, however, regardless men are of their message."[170] While disinterested men are discouraging, the ministers do not always know God's purposes. Second, ungodly listeners should consider that by so opposing God, they do not hinder his word but actually fight against their own souls.[171] Instead, they should aim to hear and obey the word so they may be profited for their spiritual good.[172]

Piety and Study Are Important for Listeners as Well as Ministers

The revivalists knew that an unprepared listener would be an indifferent listener. However, listeners were much more likely to hear and heed a message if they were mentally and spiritually prepared for that message. Therefore, piety and study and the blending of mind with heart are just as important for listeners as they are for ministers.

This blending of both mind and heart was a unique emphasis of the revivalists. The established churches tended to emphasize the head, whereas

165. Edwards, *Sermons and Discourses, 1730–1733*, 176.
166. Edwards, *Sermons and Discourses, 1730–1733*, 176.
167. Edwards, *Sermons and Discourses, 1730–1733*, 178.
168. Edwards, *Sermons and Discourses, 1730–1733*, 179.
169. Edwards, *Sermons and Discourses, 1730–1733*, 179.
170. Edwards, *Sermons and Discourses, 1730–1733*, 182.
171. Edwards, *Sermons and Discourses, 1730–1733*, 183.
172. Edwards, *Sermons and Discourses, 1730–1733*, 183.

"pietism tended to separate the religion of the head from the religion of the heart. The emphasis of Jonathan Edwards, Samuel Davies, and Gilbert Tennent was to give equal importance to piety and learning."[173] Such balance prepares listeners to hear the word just as it prepares ministers to preach the word.

The revivalists expected listeners to study the Scriptures for themselves. They should not leave such matters to ministers alone. Edwards says, "Those doctrines of divinity which relate to the essence, attributes, and subsistencies of God, concern all; as it is of infinite importance to common people as well as to ministers, to know what kind of being God is."[174]

Christians should also "improve in personal religion" so that a decline in religion may be avoided. As he left his charge in Hanover, Davies challenged the church to continue growing spiritually even though they might be pastorless for a time:

> Far be it from me, my brethren, to think that now, when you are deprived of your minister, you may lawfully make a stand in your Christian progress, or allow yourselves to slide down the slippery, descending road of apostacy. You are still obliged to grow in grace, and in the knowledge of our Lord and Saviour Jesus Christ.[175]

Obviously, the preacher is not the only source of grace. "The throne of grace is still accessible," Davies says, for "your closets are still open for you; and you may enjoy the sweet privilege of secret devotion." Interestingly, Davies reminds his congregation, which began as a religious reading society, to turn to the Bible and the "unusual variety of excellent books" that were within their reach because these could make them wise unto salvation even when they did not have the opportunity of "attending upon the public ministry." The Hanover group could even "receive advantage" from an occasional visit to the public ministry in the established church, and Davies challenges his people to "always retain those catholic principles" he had endeavored to inculcate upon them and to seek spiritual good "wherever it may be obtained."[176]

173. Old, "Gilbert Tennent," 133.

174. Edwards, *Sermons and Discourses, 1739–1742*, 92.

175. Davies, *Sermons*, 3:645.

176. Davies, *Sermons*, 3:645.

Respond to the Instruction and Call from God

Sermons are not empty words. They are the words of God communicated through a God-called, authoritative servant to a congregation. Therefore, listeners should hear and heed both the instructions and call of God.

In one of his most lovingly composed letters, Edwards communicates this role of the listener to an eighteen-year-old convert of Suffield, Massachusetts, who was without a pastor. Edwards instructs, "When you hear sermons, hear 'em for yourself: though what is spoken in them may be more especially directed to the unconverted, or to those that in other respects are in different circumstances from yourself. Yet let the chief intent in your mind be to consider with yourself, in what respects is this that I hear spoken applicable to me and what improvement ought I to make of this for my own soul's good?"[177] He also encourages her to pray for the ministers of Christ.[178]

Davies challenges his listeners to be "pliable, self-diffident, and submissive; not obstinate, head-strong, and self-willed."[179] Hearers have every reason to listen because they are dying men who will soon face the Supreme Judge.[180] Yet, Davies knew that in any congregation there are those who hear and heed and those who do not or who cannot hear or heed due to impenitence. Taking Matt 13:14 as his text for a sermon titled "The Guilt and Doom of Impenitent Hearers" for the Hanover congregation on November 12, 1758, Davies says,

> It is a threatening from God, not that he would recall the commission of his ministers, or remove them, but that he would give them a commission in wrath, and continue their ministry, as a judgment upon their hearers. . . . A threatening that they shall hear, that is, that their life and rational powers, the ministry of the word of God, and all things necessary for hearing, shall be continued to them; but by all their hearing they shall not understand; they shall not receive instructions that will be of any real service to them: they shall not understand any thing to a saving purpose. Their knowledge may be increased and their heads filled with bright notions and speculations; but all their improvements will be of no solid or

177. Edwards, *Letters and Personal Writings*, 92.
178. Edwards, *Letters and Personal Writings*, 95.
179. Davies, *Sermons*, 3:647.
180. Davies, *Sermons*, 3:647.

> lasting advantage to them; so that their hearing is equivalent to not hearing, and their understanding to entire ignorance.[181]

There are great differences among the people who attend a sermon, "though they mingle in the same assembly, hear the same preacher, and seem to stand upon the same footing."[182] Each individual listener's preparation to hear and heed is vital.

It is vital because if a listener is not prepared, he or she may miss God. As has been previously noted, many people who were in church during this age were not converted. Some were, as Davies says, "in the right only by chance."[183] Davies warns listeners to hear and heed so they might obtain definite faith instead of chanced faith:

> If you believe the Christian religion to be divine, because you hardly care whether it be true or false, being utterly unconcerned about religion in any shape, and therefore never examining the matter; if you believe it true, because you have been educated in it; because your parents or ministers have told you so; or because it is the religion of your country; if these are the only grounds of your faith, it is not such faith as constitutes you true Christians; for upon the very same grounds you would have Mahometans in Turkey, disciples of Confucius in China, or worshippers of the Devil among the Indians, if it had been your unhappy lotto be born in those countries; for a Mahometan, or a Chinese, or an Indian, can assign these grounds for his faith, Surely, I need not tell you, that the grounds of a mistaken belief in an imposture, are not a sufficient foundation for a saving faith in divine revelation. I am afraid there are many such implicit believers among us, who are in the right only by chance.[184]

Listeners who are in the right only by chance need to respond to a rational, well-grounded faith, "instead of that which is only blind and accidental."[185]

Tennent admits that some people did not hear the message simply because they did not like the message. In the preface to his published sermon "The Preciousness of Christ to Believers," preached in New Brunswick,

181. Davies, *Sermons*, 3:617–18.

182. Davies, *Sermons*, 3:618.

183. Davies, *Sermons*, 1:73.

184. Davies, *Sermons*, 1:72–73.

185. Davies, *Sermons*, 1:73.

August 1738, he says, "As for ignorant, prophane, and pharisaical Persons, I expect that some of them will be offended: Well, let them Grumble and Snarl it does by shew their Rottenness and Hypocrisy."[186] Certainly, Tennent had the dimmer view of his listeners and readers! In his scathing rebuke of the unconverted ministers, Tennent declares that congregations do not always mind a poor minister; often, they are content with a good (albeit spiritually dead) minister. A dead minister requires no response:

> Isn't this the Case of Multitudes? If they can get one, that has the Name of a Minister, with a Band, and a black Coat or Gown to carry on a Sabbath-days among them, although never so coldly, and insuccessfully; if he is free from gross Crimes in Practice, and takes good Care to keep at a due Distance from their Consciences, and is never troubled about his Insuccessfulness; O! think the poor Fools, that is a fine Man indeed; our Minister is a prudent charitable Man, he is not always harping upon Terror, and sounding Damnation in our Ears, like some rash-headed Preachers, who by their uncharitable Methods, are ready to put poor People out of their Wits, or to run them into Despair; O! how terrible a Thing is that Dispair! Ay, our Minister, honest Man, gives us good Caution against it.[187]

Tennent's sarcasm is obvious, but his point is direct. Listeners would rather not have to hear and heed, but it is their responsibility under God to do so.

In addressing some of the Awakening's excesses, Edwards admitted that outcries and responses were sometimes extreme, yet he rejoiced in it "much more than merely in an appearance of solemn attention."[188] Excessive response was better than no response at all! No response at all was sinful. As Davies says, "Every instance of willful sinning against knowledge is the most dangerous and provoking manner of sinning."[189]

God is able to work most effectively when listeners are fulfilling their role in preaching. A congregation that receives its minister as the mouthpiece of God and comes to worship prepared to hear and to heed is more likely to be blessed by God than one that remains indifferent to the things of God. At times, the congregations of Edwards, Tennent, and Davies were

186. Tennent, *Preciousness of Christ*, 245.

187. Tennent, "Danger," 86–87.

188. Edwards, *Some Thoughts Concerning the Revival*, 399.

189. Davies, *Sermons*, 3:633.

indifferent. During those days, these courageous preachers woke their congregations and called them to response.

The response must not be to the preacher. The response must be to God. In his analysis of the Awakening, Edwards says that many who went to hear a preacher "have not been able to resist the power and the spirit with which he spake; have sat trembling under the Word, and gone away from it weeping."[190] Many went to hear a preacher, but, instead, they heard from God.

If awakening is to continue and thrive, Edwards declares it will take every living soul. Reflecting upon the revival he writes, "Not only magistrates and ministers, but every living soul, is now obliged to arise, and acknowledge God in this work and put to his hand to promote it, as they would not expose themselves to God's curse."[191] But this is true not only for awakening but preaching in general as well. When the Holy Spirit, the Scriptures, the preachers, and the listeners are all fulfilling their roles in preaching, God can work to bring about positive effects.

THE ULTIMATE AIM OF PREACHING

Because listeners are either lost sinners in need of salvation or saved sinners in need of edification, the revivalists believed the ultimate aim in preaching is "to wash and cleanse the souls of men."[192] Like the Puritans before them, the revivalists held that the word of God had priority in the divine-human relationship. Therefore, "preaching surpassed other activities in worship, in which human beings addressed God through prayer and singing."[193]

The Preacher's Task the Same as Christ's: Preach the Gospel

The work of ministers is in many respects like the work of Christ, especially in terms of his saving and prophetic offices. Yet, as Edwards explains, there is one important difference: "that ministers are to speak and act wholly

190. William Cooper's preface to Edwards, "Distinguishing Marks," 220.

191. Edwards, *Some Thoughts Concerning the Revival*, 379.

192. Edwards, *Sermons and Discourses, 1743–1758*, 335. Edwards based this on Eph 5:26 where Paul says Christ gave himself for the church "so that He might sanctify her, having cleansed her by the washing of water with the word."

193. Valeri, "Preface to the Period" in Edwards, *Sermons and Discourses, 1730–1733*, 15.

under Christ, as taught of him, as holding forth his word."[194] Even the most celebrated minister is still an undershepherd of the Chief Shepherd.

Since Christ has brought the gospel, preachers are to proclaim the gospel. Christian preaching should stand out among other preaching or speeches of the day. Anything that does not proclaim Christ is less than Christian preaching.

The awakeners challenged the idea of "natural religion." This type of religion seeks God in creation. Natural religion found special favor among the deists and other proponents of the Enlightenment because it allowed one to believe in God (or a god) without having a relationship with God (god). While the revivalists acknowledged that God has revealed himself in creation, they also agreed with the apostle Paul who said nature has done little more than to make men without excuse (Rom 1:20). Natural religion is good for one thing: making people aware of God. The additional preaching of the gospel is essential. Men and women need a relationship with God. In his message "The Unsearchable Riches of Christ," Tennent insists, "If Ministers do not preach Christ, and direct Sinners to Him, they do not preach the Gospel, but the *Religion of Nature*."[195] Without the gospel, men and women cannot have a relationship with God.

The preaching of the gospel by faithful ministers is, as Edwards says, the "principal means that God uses" to present the gospel to people and "to exhibit Christ and His love and benefits to His elect people" as well as "for the bringing up the church, as it were, from her childhood, till she is fit for her marriage with the Lord of glory."[196] Both evangelism and edification were important, but evangelism was the primary goal.[197]

In a sermon titled "The Preaching of Christ Crucified, the Means of Salvation," preached upon 1 Cor 1:22–24, Davies says the preaching of Christ crucified is "the ground, the substance, and marrow of the gospel; and it is this, above all other things, that its ministers ought to preach and inculcate. It should have the same place in their sermons which it has in that gospel which it is their business to preach; that is, it should be the foundation, the substance, the centre, the drift of all."[198] Davies declares,

194. Edwards, *Sermons and Discourses, 1743–1758*, 341.

195. Tennent, *Unsearchable Riches of Christ*, 29.

196. Edwards, *Sermons and Discourses, 1743–1758*, 185.

197. Preachers could and should preach other topics and Scriptures. However, the ultimate and chief aim was the conversion of sinners.

198. Davies, *Sermons*, 1:621.

> The sufferings of Christ, which had a dreadful consummation, in his crucifixion, their necessity, design, and consequences, and the way of salvation thereby opened for a guilty world, these are the principal materials of our preaching; to instruct mankind in these is the great object of our ministry, and the unwearied labour of our lives. We might easily choose subjects more pleasing and popular, more fit to display our learning and abilities, and set off the strong reasoner, or the fine orator; but our commission, as ministers of a crucified Jesus, binds us to the subject; and the necessity of the world peculiarly requires it.[199]

Here Davies holds his homiletical theology above any crowd-pleasing methodology.[200]

In a message titled "The Wisdom of God in Redemption," Tennent stresses the need for preaching the gospel:

> Pray, is not the Business of Pastors after God's Heart, to feed the People with Knowledge and Understanding? And is it not the Design of their Office to turn Sinners from Darkness to Light? But what need is there of this Institution at all, what need of any Labours to instruct Mankind, if Men had sufficient Light without it in themselves? Is not Preaching at any Time or Place, on this Plan, an Absurdity, a meer Farce? And why did the Apostles take so much Pains in traveling and preaching? Why did they run such Risques, and endure such Hardships? Was it to do a superfluous Business, to teach People what they knew already, or might know without their Assistance? If so, was this prudent in them (seeing they carried on no Business of Merchandize or Traffick in their Travels to enrich themselves) or a good Argument that they had the full Exercise of their Reason? Pray did they suffer Stripes,

199. Davies, *Sermons*, 1:621.

200. Pilcher says, "The preparation of souls for imminent death was in fact the core of Davies's theology. To better prepare his listeners for the ultimate event, Davies demanded a unity of Christian life—a unity of inward belief and outward action. He concentrated on behavior here on earth and called for Christians to emulate Christ by living a life of virtue and holiness, a life of positive righteousness rather than negative goodness. Such a theology had certain positiveness that fitted the time and place." Davies preached both to sinners and lukewarm church members. Pilcher, *Samuel Davies*, 66. Sprague says Davies knew "his time for active service was short, and that the demand for evangelical labour in the region around him was most urgent," therefore, he "addressed himself to his work with a strength of purpose and a simple dependence on Divine aid, that gave a mighty power to his ministrations." Sprague, "Memoir of President Davies," quoted in Davies, *Sermons*, 1:14.

> Imprisonment, or Death, like wife Men, or Fools, for doing what was needless, judge ye.[201]

Preaching is too arduous a task to spend one's time at it for no spiritual benefit.

Spirit-transformed listeners are the true source of joy for ministers. Tennent tells one congregation, "You cannot give the faithful Ministers of Christ so much Pleasure any other Way, as by turning to God, for this they study, pray, groan and weep; your Conversion would make their Hearts glad, in all their Labours and Sorrows; nor can you grieve their Spirits so much any other Way, as by your Obstinancy in Sin."[202] For sinners to wash and cleanse their souls is the ultimate aim of preaching. A methodology may assist the accomplishment of this aim, but it must always remain a servant of it.

As pastors assigned to the weekly task of preaching, Edwards, Tennent, and Davies worked faithfully at their sermonic workbenches with an eye to fine-tuning their messages and lectures for each week. As they did, they also hammered out their homiletical theology.

Each man was a keen thinker who both formed and practiced his homiletical theology with skill and insight. In the end, scholarly and stiff Edwards, fiery and outspoken Tennent, and scholarly and eloquent Davies arrived at similar homiletical theologies even though their methodologies may have been quite different.

For these men, the roles of the preacher, Scripture, Holy Spirit, and listeners in preaching stand out as the fundamentals of their homiletical theology. Because these men were admired and followed by other preachers, they spoke extensively concerning the role of the preacher. As Edwards says, they believed that "the roof of the church's mouth is the officers in the church that preach the Gospel; their word is to Christ's beloved like the best wine, that goes down sweetly; extraordinarily refreshing and enlivening the saints, causing them to speak, though before they were mute and asleep."[203] Because they are so important to the preaching task, preachers must work hard at their vocation. They must be converted, pious, and well-studied so that they might be both educationally and spiritually empowered to be effectively used by God. They must have a good relationship with their listeners so the message they share will be not only heard but heeded as well.

201. Tennent, *Sermons on Important Subjects*, 89.

202. Tennent, *Sermons on Important Subjects*, 291.

203. Edwards, *Some Thoughts Concerning the Revival*, 403.

Any preacher who stands to preach should do so on the authority of Scripture. The revivalists firmly held that Scripture is divine, infallible, authoritative, and sufficient. Therefore, it should be both the source and criterion of preaching. While a preacher should be widely read and offer engaging material to his listeners, the true power in the words came from the Scriptures. The sermon should be grounded in Scripture, built upon Scripture, and judged by Scripture.

When a godly minister stands to preach with a strong, biblical message, the Holy Spirit can most effectively perform his role in the preaching event. Edwards, Tennent, and Davies knew that the Holy Spirit gives power to the words of the preacher. It is he who sets those words to flight, so they may land in the listeners' ears and ultimately their hearts. He is the one who applies the message to each listener, bringing about life transformation.

Still, no matter how well-prepared and godly the preacher is or how grounded in Scripture the message is, or how involved the Holy Spirit is, the message is most effective when the listeners also perform their role in preaching. God can work in spite of listeners, but he generally chooses to work with them. Even though men and women are sinners, God still desires a transforming relationship with them. But these listeners have certain responsibilities when they come to hear the word of God preached. They must receive their ministers as the mouthpiece of God, realizing that ministers are given their authority by God. Because of this important level of authority, listeners should support their ministers and depend upon the Holy Spirit as they listen to them. However, even before the worship service begins, the listeners have the task of preparing themselves to hear and heed the word—to till the soil of their hearts so the seeds might be planted, sprout, and grow in them.

These leaders of awakening considered their ultimate aim in preaching to be the cleansing of the souls of humanity. Humans are sinners: lost sinners need salvation and saved sinners need edification. Essentially, the preacher's task is the same as Christ's—to preach the gospel.

In one of his hymns, Davies celebrates the joyful results of preaching within a church. Gospel preaching began with Christ and continues to pastors and people today. As with many sacred hymns, theology is evident within the words. In this case, it is specifically a homiletical theology:

> With grateful hearts come let us sing,
> The gifts of our ascended King;

Though long since gone from earth below,
Through every age his bounties flow.

The Saviour, when to heav'n he rose
In splendid triumph o'er his foes
His gifts on rebel men bestowed,
And wide his royal bounties flow'd.

Hence sprang th' apostles' honoured name,
More glorious than the hero's fame
Evangelists and prophets hence
Derive the blessings they dispense.

In humbler forms, to bless our eyes,
Pastors from hence and teachers rise;
Who, though with feebler rays they shine,
Still gild a long-extended line.

From Christ their various gifts derive,
And fed by Christ their graces live;
While, guarded by his mighty hand,
'Midst all the rage of hell they stand.

Thus teachers, teachers shall succeed
When we lie silent with the dead!
And unborn churches, by their care,
Shall rise and flourish large and fair.

Pastors and people join and sing,
This constant, inexhausted spring,
Whence through all ages richly flow
The streams that cheer the church below.[204]

204. Davies, *Sermons*, 3:560–61.

CHAPTER V

Contributions to The Awakening's Effectiveness

WHEN PREACHING MATTERED: EXTRAORDINARY RESULTS

THE FIRES OF REVIVAL eventually reduced to coals and finally to ashes. By 1776, the Awakening was over in all parts of the American colonies. It had largely ended in the Middle and New England Colonies by the mid to late 1740s and in the Southern Colonies by 1776.[1] Still, while the Awakening was over, its effects remained. God makes beauty of ashes. Though many Christians returned to church life as usual and were content to gather the revival's ashes and display them on their ecclesiastical mantles, some dusted the ashes away and looked for growth. New life grew from the ashes in both the churches and society of all three colonial regions.

The effectiveness of the First Great Awakening is difficult to verify historically. Bumsted and Van de Wetering accurately state, "Both pro- and anti-revival assessments of the Awakening's popularity were obviously influenced by what the observers wanted to believe."[2] Therefore, the enumerated results of the revival vary from historian to historian, often depending upon personal conclusions about whether or not the local revivals were

1. By 1794 the people in the South had grown so impious that at least one revivalist had even given up trying to hold weekday meetings. Jarratt, *Life of the Reverend.*

2. Bumsted and Van de Wetering, *What Must I Do*, 128.

part of a general awakening. Maxson notes that opponents of the revival, such as Edwards's nemesis Charles Chauncy, represented it "as a tempest of ungoverned passions that swept over the colonies, leaving wreckage everywhere in the alienations and divisions in families, neighborhoods, and churches, the undermining of cherished institutions, and a relapse into indifference, debauchery, and irreligion."[3] However, Maxson says, an impartial study that is free from the partisan and denominational biases of the period "leads to a very different conclusion."[4] That conclusion is, despite the negative ramifications of split churches, emotional excesses, and the like, the Awakening did produce many positive effects. The most frequently listed and properly evidenced positive results include increased converts and personal devotion, church growth and expansion, missionary zeal, a renewed ministry, as well as several social contributions. These effects cannot be ignored, even by the most careful revival critic.

Increased Converts and Personal Devotion

Stout says, "The Great Awakening was the most momentous occasion in the spiritual life of colonial America."[5] The increased number of converts and personal devotion reported by many ministers and laymen is indicative of the Awakening's impact on the spiritual life of the colonies.

Increased Converts

While it is impossible to determine an exact number of conversions in the American colonies during the First Great Awakening, estimates range from several thousand to as many as five hundred thousand.[6] Such estimates are only "limited by a historian's attitude toward revivalism and by the total population of the American colonies."[7] Detailed records were not kept or have not survived for most areas and even Prince's *Christian History* seldom contains figures. Relevant records are particularly lacking in the Middle

3. Maxson, *Great Awakening*, 139.

4. Maxson, *Great Awakening*, 139.

5. Stout, "Transforming Effects," 127.

6. Most authors indicate that the later number is especially hard to maintain given a total colonial population of around one million in 1740. See Noll et al., *Eerdman's Handbook*, 114.

7. Bumsted and Van de Wetering, *What Must I Do*, 129.

Colonies and the South. In New England, where records are best, estimates range from twenty-five thousand to fifty thousand converts during a time when the population of New England was roughly 350,000.[8] In *The Great Awakening: Documents on the Revival of Religion, 1740–1745*, Richard L. Bushman sums up the number of conversions in the following way:

> People from all ranks of society, of all ages, and from every section underwent the new birth. In New England, virtually every congregation was touched. It was not uncommon for ten to twenty percent of a town, having experienced grace, to join the church in a single year. In the middle colonies, the Presbyterians were most affected, although Whitefield, himself an Anglican, preached to people of all denominations. The Awakening did not penetrate far into the South until after 1744, but then Presbyterian evangelists made rapid inroads into Anglican strongholds in Virginia as well as among their own congregations in the backcountry. It is safe to say that most of the colonists in the 1740s, if not converted themselves, knew someone who was, or at least heard revival preaching.[9]

For further discussion concerning the numbers of converts and the growth brought to the colonial churches, please see the section below titled "Church Growth and Expansion."

Personal Devotion

Even more frequently mentioned than conversions were signs of repentance and concern.[10] Increased personal devotion was a result of the Awakening. For example, William Cooper of Boston's Brattle Street Church remarked

8. Lescelius, "Great Awakening," 33. Joseph Tracy proposes fifty thousand converts. He states, "We must remember that the practice of admitting to the communion all persons neither heretical nor scandalous, was general in the Presbyterian church and prevailed extensively among the Congregational churches. In consequence, a large portion of the communicants in both were unconverted persons. Multitudes of these were converted. Of course, there was no census of the unconverted members of the several churches, or of the conversions among them; nor would any of them be counted as additions to the churches. In some cases, the revival seems to have been almost wholly within the church, and to have resulted in the conversion of nearly all the members. A large addition ought to be made, on this score, to the estimated number of conversions." Tracy, *Great Awakening*, 391.

9. Bushman, *Great Awakening*, xii.

10. Gaustad, *Great Awakening*, 104.

that in one week during the revival more people came to him in repentance and concern than did in the preceding twenty-four years of his ministry.[11] Many of these persons had been churchgoers or even Christians for years, but the revival awakened their devotion to Christ. A deeper loyalty to the externals of religion developed. Church attendance increased, and pastors added lectures and sermons to their weekly church schedules. When enough meetings were not available to meet the demand, religious exercises were held in homes. Some young people, as those in Northampton, formed piety groups. The Massachusetts General Court even enforced a stricter observance of the Lord's Day, evidencing the revival's influence on society as a whole. Many people experienced renewed personal devotion as a result of the revival.

The revival in Northampton reached its peak in 1740 and 1741 after Whitefield's visit. In a letter dated December 14, 1740, Edwards reported the early effects upon personal devotion. Edwards writes that the state of religion "has been gradually reviving and prevailing more and more, ever since you was here. Religion is become abundantly more the subject of conversation; other things that seemed to impede it, are for the present laid aside."[12] Edwards also indicates that many children and youth had experienced salvation, including some of his own children.

The Awakening brought a fresh emphasis upon the Christian experience, especially experiential piety. Ministers encouraged their people to devote their daily lives to loving God and serving their neighbors. Increased prayer was encouraged.[13] In addition, the desire developed to see the church membership rolls purified of all but the truly regenerate. The Half-Way Covenant was repudiated by many Congregational and Presbyterian leaders and their churches.[14]

11. Prince, *Account of the Revival*, 18.

12. Edwards to the Reverend George Whitefield, in *Letters and Personal Writings*, 87.

13. Edwards wrote *An Humble Attempt to Promote Explicit Agreement* to encourage prayer.

14. The Half-Way Covenant was a compromise adopted by Congregational churches in colonial New England to deal with declining full church membership. Originally, only those who could testify to a personal conversion were admitted as full members and could have their children baptized. By the 1660s, many second-generation colonists couldn't make such a public profession of faith, which meant their children were ineligible for baptism. To address this, churches allowed these unconverted but baptized adults to be "half-way" members: they could have their children baptized and participate in some aspects of church life but were excluded from full privileges like communion and church voting until they experienced conversion.

Church Growth and Expansion

The First Great Awakening brought an immense amount of vitality to churches. Many churches reported phenomenal growth and new denominations exploded onto the colonial scene. Though Gaustad is correct in concluding that the Awakening was not a mass movement of people desiring church membership,[15] there was a general upsurge in those seeking membership during the revival.[16] Good records remain for both Connecticut and southeastern Massachusetts. Bumsted and Van de Wetering provide a helpful analysis of these numbers from which the following discussion is largely taken.

In Connecticut, an average of eight people joined each of the colony's congregations each year from 1730 through 1740. During the height of the revival between 1741 and 1742, the average reached thirty-three a year.[17] A similar phenomenon occurred in southeastern Massachusetts. During the height of revival there between 1742 and 1743, the average reached twenty-five. Table 3 demonstrates the average number of annual admissions to churches in these two regions of New England.

15. Gaustad, *Great Awakening*, 103. Noll also states, "It is possible that the Awakening, while not increasing the rate of conversion when calculated over the long run, did keep the rate at its former level when it otherwise might have fallen." Noll et al., *Eerdman's Handbook*, 115.

16. There was a low proportion of church membership in colonial America—never more than one-third of New England's adults, and as few as 5 percent of southern adults. By contrast, 54 percent of Americans claim to be church members and approximately 40 percent attend church regularly. Jones, *Assessing the Nation's Religious Composition*.

Interestingly, in the colonial period, church attendance was always higher than church membership. Noll explains the reason: "In New England the scrupulousness with which residents looked upon conversion (not to speak of the fear which some souls felt at testifying before a full congregation) made joining the church a major step indeed. In the south the absence of bishops prevented proper confirmations, and in the middle colonies a more rapidly shifting population kept formal membership low, But in every region a large number of people attended church who were not actually members." Noll et al., *Eerdman's Handbook*, 75.

17. Noll, *History of Christianity*, 97.

Table 3: Average Number of Annual Admissions to Particular Churches in Two Regions of New England, per Church, 1733–1747[18]

Year	Southeastern Massachusetts	Connecticut
1733	6.3	8.5
1734	5.7	7.5
1735	4.4	19.5
1736	14.1	12.5
1737	7.0	8.7
1738	5.6	11.2
1739	4.8	8.5
1740	4.9	7.3
1741	8.0	43.4
1742	37.4	22.7
1743	12.3	5.2
1744	4.9	4.5
1745	3.5	3.8
1746	2.3	3.3
1747	2.0	3.5

Taking an average of the churches in the two regions for the period 1741–1744, the height of the New England revival, gives the following mean annual admissions per church:

1741	25.7
1742	30.0
1743	8.8
1744	4.7

The four year total is 69.2. When this is multiplied by the approximately four hundred churches in New England during the period, one yields a total for admissions to church membership during the revival years of around twenty-seven thousand. This is a substantial figure and is in keeping with many of the reports from the period.[19]

18. Bumsted and Van de Wetering, *What Must I Do*, 130. Figures for southeastern Massachusetts are based on a table in Bumsted, *Pilgrim's Progress*, 290–91. Figures for Connecticut are based on a table in Vos, "Great Awakening in Connecticut," 171–72.

19. Certainly, as Bumsted and Van de Wetering emphasize, "People were *always* being converted, *always* joining churches." Thus the emphasis should not be upon gross additions but net additions. The authors figure the net gains to be approximately twenty persons per New England church. The total net gain is just over eight thousand for New

Not only did church membership and attendance increase, but the number of churches increased as well. Gaustad claims that separation by New Lights was the chief cause of new churches in New England.[20] The members of these schismatic churches challenged the propriety of public taxation for ministerial support, violated the traditional rules of ordination, protested against admitting the unconverted to communion, objected to cold, formal, "dead" preaching, and practiced spontaneous, zealous personal religion.[21] These new churches had profound effects on New England. They destroyed the New England parish system and weakened the structure of the establishment. However, not all of the new churches were the result of splits. Around 150 were founded upon the natural increase of towns and parishes.[22]

The churches of various denominations in the Middle Colonies saw expansion and organization as a result of the Awakening. Though definite numbers are not available, it is apparent that the Presbyterians grew in number and influence, with the Second Presbyterian Church of Philadelphia becoming the center of New Light influence under the pastoral leadership of Gilbert Tennent.[23] Also, the operations of the Moravians attracted universal attention. Mission work helped plant additional churches in the Middle Colonies and other parts of the colonies, especially the South.

The Southern Colonies experienced increased churches but of a different persuasion than before the Awakening. Before the revival, the liturgy and law of the South were Anglican; after the Awakening, the power and prominence of Anglicanism waned. In its place were Presbyterians, Baptists, and

England to which must be added perhaps several thousand who joined churches outside the establishment or had no churches to join. The authors point out, however, that "the Great Awakening did not greatly increase the number of church members in New England over the long run. It appears, instead, to have drawn on a fairly constant pool of individuals who would eventually have joined churches anyway. Colonial Americans accepted religion as a central feature of their lives, and the revival appeals to a population willing—even anxious—to join churches. Not totals, but timing, is the important factor." Bumsted and Van de Wetering, *What Must I Do*, 132.

20. Gaustad, *Great Awakening*, 114.

21. Gaustad, *Great Awakening*, 115.

22. Gaustad, *Great Awakening*, 114–15.

23. New Light Presbyterian churches in the New York Synod increased from twenty-two to seventy-two congregations from 1745 to 1758. The Old Side decreased from twenty-five to twenty-two. It was not migration or immigration that caused this growth, but, as Maxson says, "The Great Awakening itself supplies the only sufficient answer." Maxson, *Great Awakening*, 116.

Methodists, denominations that continue to hold dominance in the South to the present day. As was previously noted in the second chapter, the southern revival began with the Virginia Presbyterians, continued to the North Carolina Baptists, and concluded with the Methodists. The total number of southern congregations, both Protestant and Roman Catholic, soared from 343 in 1750 to 1,118 in 1776. Anglicanism increased in number of churches during these years (188 to 304) yet greatly declined in prominence (54.8 percent of the total churches to 27.3 percent of the total). By the time of the Revolution, Anglicans led Presbyterians by only 3.3 percent and Baptists by 4.7 percent, and in every southern colony the new evangelicals outnumbered Anglican communicants.[24] From 1750 to 1776, Baptists saw the greatest increase in congregations and prominence, rising from 7.9 percent of all congregations to 22 percent.[25] Quakers saw the next greatest increase, growing from no congregations to 111 congregations, or 10 percent of the total. Methodist societies increased from obscurity to 3.4 percent of the total.[26]

The newer denominations experienced rapid expansion as a result of the First Great Awakening. The peak of the Presbyterian revival was in 1756. Though the fever pitch waned between 1750 and 1776, the Presbyterians established more than two hundred churches in the South.[27] Baptists in the South experienced revival first in 1755 with the establishment of the Sandy Creek Church in North Carolina, which experienced explosive numerical growth in its first three years, increasing from six to six hundred members. The Baptist revival saw several ebbs and flows but became a rushing movement in the 1770s. As a result of the Awakening, Baptists "emerged from relative obscurity to become the largest denomination in America."[28] The Methodist revival began as a movement to revive the Anglican Church. However, as Anglicanism refused to change, Methodism eventually took on

24. Heyrman, *Southern Cross*, 13.

25. Heyrman, *Southern Cross*, 261. Heyrman supplies a table of estimated church membership, 1750–76, which includes the following denominations: Anglican, Baptist, Methodist, Presbyterian, Quaker, German Reformed, Lutheran, Roman Catholic, Dunker, Moravian, Dutch Reformed, Mennonite, and French Reformed.

26. It should be noted that even with all the gains in numbers, the new evangelical churches only included at most 10 percent of the adult white southern population in 1776 and only a negligible percentage of African Americans. Heyrman notes that the large Presbyterian representation could have been due to Scots-Irish migration into the region rather than an influx of native-born southerners into the churches. Heyrman, *Southern Cross*, 13.

27. Heyrman, *Southern Cross*, 13.

28. Hinson, "Baptist Experience in America," 195.

its own identity. The Methodist segment of the Southern Awakening began in the summer of 1775 and ran through 1776. Methodist circuits expanded rapidly. For example, key leader and itinerant George Shadford added six hundred to his circuit in 1775 and eighteen hundred in 1776.

Other denominations throughout the colonies benefited as well. Cragg says, "The Lutherans, under Mühlenberg, consolidated their forces. . . . The Reformed Churches, both Dutch and German, had been languishing in apathy; the Awakening galvanized them into life and probably saved them from extinction."[29] Pilcher says, "The strength of any colonial religious body was eventually determined by the degree of its acceptance of the Great Awakening."[30] Table 4 illustrates the number of churches in the eight major colonial denominations and their growth from 1660 to 1780.

Table 4: Number of Churches—Eight Major Colonial Denominations[31]

Total Number of Churches:
1660: 154
1700: 373
1740: 1,176
1780: 2,731

	1660	1700	1740	1780
Anglican	41	111	246	406
Baptist	4	33	96	457
Congregational	75	146	423	749
Dutch Reformed	13	26	78	127
German Reformed	0	0	51	201
Lutheran	4	7	95	240
Presbyterian	5	28	160	495
Roman Catholic	12	22	27	56

While every denomination, with the exception of the Roman Catholics, grew by nearly 900 percent, Baptists and Presbyterians show by far the greatest percentage increase. Baptists saw an 11,325 percent increase and Presbyterians a 9,800 percent increase.

29. Cragg, *Church*, 180.

30. Pilcher, *Samuel Davies*, 64.

31. Adapted from Noll et al., *Eerdman's Handbook*, 97.

Noll also provides a table regarding the population and number of churches in 1750. This chart is helpful because it gives a snapshot of the church-to-population ratio near or just after the conclusion of the Awakening in all three colonial regions. Table 5 presents Noll's findings.

Table 5: Population and Number of Churches, 1750[32]

	Churches	Population	Ratio Churches:Population
New England	576	350,000	1:606
Middle Colonies	590	275,000	1:467
South	296	310,000	1:1046

Missionary Zeal

Table 5 illustrates that a need for missions existed in the colonies in the mid to late eighteenth century. The white population was growing and geographically expanding, making the need for new churches apparent. There were also large numbers of Blacks and Indians[33] living in or near the settled regions. Awakened individuals realized that these groups needed the good news of Christ as well.

The missionary zeal of churches grew as a result of the Awakening. People came to serve not only themselves but one another and wanted to improve society.[34] More importantly, people were not only concerned for their own souls but for the souls of others as well. The leaders of the Awakening sought to reach all peoples—slave and free, rich and poor, educated and uneducated. In this way, the revivals served as a "leveling force" in American colonial society.[35] Ministers took the gospel beyond their own

32. Adapted from Noll et al., *Eerdman's Handbook*, 76. This table covers the eight major denominations included in Table 4. The population figures refer to Caucasians only.

33. These are the names frequently given these groups in the primary and chief secondary sources. However, from here on, this book will use the currently accepted terms for these groups. "Blacks" will be referred to as "African Americans" and "Indians" as "Native Americans."

34. Stearns, *Great Awakening*, 54.

35. Sweet, *Revivalism in America*, 41.

colony.[36] Benevolent institutions sprang up to serve the needs of many.[37] Social barriers began to break down, which allowed the gospel to reach the under classes, such as Native and African Americans.

The Puritans had purposed to evangelize the Native Americans since the establishment of the Massachusetts Bay Colony in 1630.

Seal of the Massachusetts Bay Colony[38]

The Massachusetts seal echoed the Macedonian call of Paul (Acts 16:9), picturing a Native American with arms outstretched saying, "Come over and help us." However, more conflict than mission often occurred. Actual mission endeavors did not take place until ministers John Eliot (1604–1690) and Thomas Mayhew Jr. (1621–1657) put missionary programs into practice in the mid-seventeenth century. Eliot printed the first Bible in a Native American language (Natick dialect), which was also the first Bible printed in North America.[39] With the First Great Awakening a century later, the mission to the Native Americans gained new momentum. "The revival gave an impulse to the work at nearly all the [missionary] stations."[40] John Sargeant (1710–1749) was a missionary to the Housatonic

36. Maxson indicates that the revivalists in the Middle Colony were influential in carrying the revival to the South, especially to Virginia. Middle colony influence upon the Hanover Revival was noted in the second chapter of this dissertation. Maxson, *Great Awakening*, 99–103.

37. Armstrong, 11.

38. Secretary of Massachusetts, "History."

39. Library of Congress, "Eliot Indian Bible."

40. Tracy, *Great Awakening*, 398.

tribe in Stockbridge, Massachusetts, who experienced success, including baptizing 182 of the tribe.[41] David Brainerd (1718–1747) was one of the outstanding missionaries to the Native Americans in New York and Eastern Pennsylvania.[42] Eleazor Wheelock (1711–1779) and Samson Occom (n.d.) worked among the tribes in New Hampshire and founded there the forerunner of Dartmouth College. Edwards also served as a missionary to the Native Americans between his Northampton pastorate and his presidency of the College of New Jersey.

The most successful and lasting mission work was among the African Americans. Maxson calls the evangelization of the slaves and freedmen "the greatest missionary triumph of the eighteenth and nineteenth centuries."[43] Davies especially did admirable work among this people group.[44] Davies's congregation was in the center of plantation country, and his parishioners included many slaves who sat in the meetinghouse. He and other southern ministers sought the evangelization and education of the slaves. Though some planters later objected saying that baptism into the Christian church made their slaves prouder and inspired them with thoughts of freedom, many awakened ministers and their churches were able to evangelize the slaves without this fear from the Old Dominion.[45] Davies was one of the first leaders, if not the first, to be actively concerned in the education of African Americans.[46] Though he owned slaves and did not preach against the institution of slavery, "he expressed whatever doubts he had about the institution simply by refraining from praising it."[47] Some people claimed that slavery in the colonies was a more fortunate state for the Africans than freedom in Africa because it afforded them the opportunity to be evangelized. Davies never affirmed such a view; rather, he deplored certain aspects of the system of slavery.[48] Eventually, the evangelism among the African Americans had

41. McDow and Reid, *Firefall*, 225.

42. Brainerd's work and publications made a great impact upon the life of other missionaries, such as William Carey, noted founder of the modern missions movement. Lescelius, "Great Awakening," 34.

43. Maxson, *Great Awakening*, 92.

44. See Pilcher, *Samuel Davies*, 107–18.

45. Bumsted and Van de Wetering, *What Must I Do*, 137.

46. Pilcher, *Samuel Davies*, 108.

47. Pilcher, *Samuel Davies*, 111.

48. Pilcher, *Samuel Davies*, 111. "While the Awakening may have provided spiritual solace and improved treatment for Negroes and Indians, it did not produce any voices demanding the fundamental alterations in their relationship to white society. Urgings

a positive effect on that demographic, especially in the South. Evangelical churches founded by African American pastors began to spring up in Southern cities after the American Revolution. They appealed both to freedmen and highly skilled slaves. While "their status was more a product of the new philosophies let loose by the Revolution and by changing economic conditions in the South than a direct result of the Great Awakening . . . the black evangelists had absorbed both the techniques and the doctrinal assumptions of the revival."[49] The prominence of the African American church today is a testimony to the evangelization that resulted from the Awakening.

Some churches divided as a result of the newfound missionary zeal. Gaustad notes, "When a church or minister refused to become evangelistic, a schism would often result, this leading to the formation of a new and fervent group or to an alliance with some already existing ecclesiastical body whose missionary concern was obvious."[50]

Renewed Ministry

McDow and Reid list "role models for church leadership" as one of the results of the Awakening.[51] The leaders of the Awakening do serve as excellent role models for gospel ministers. The reason this is true is because they benefited from and promoted a renewed ministry. Ministers experienced renewal through both their educational opportunities and renewed theologies.

Educational Impetus

The Awakening roused an impulse toward education. The Congregationalists, Presbyterians, and Anglicans required formal education prior to, or as part of, the ordination process for their ministers. Unfortunately, as noted previously, it was difficult for young men to receive ministerial training in

for abolition of the slave trade, emancipation of the Negro, and a better deal for Indians continued to be faintly heard from moralists and those (like the Quakers) who remained completely outside the revival. . . . A generation after 1740, Samuel Hopkins of Newport would find some moral arguments in pietism against Negro slavery. But it is difficult to connect these events directly with the Great Awakening." Bumsted and Van de Wetering, *What Must I Do*, 150.

49. Bumsted and Van de Wetering, *What Must I Do*, 138.

50. Gaustad, *Great Awakening*, 105.

51. McDow and Reid, *Firefall*, 226.

the colonies prior to the Awakening. This led to the importation of many ineffective but, nevertheless, academically "qualified" ministers from Europe. Thankfully, men like William Tennent realized the need for accessible theological education. Tennent's Log College is widely recognized as the forerunner of modern seminaries. Cragg states, "Though the Great Awakening encouraged the preaching of uneducated men and often appealed to the emotions rather than to the reason, it coincided with a notable expansion of educational enthusiasm."[52] Likewise, the Awakening led more young men to pursue the ministry for the right reasons. This naturally led to more converted ministers and improved churches. Colleges soon multiplied in number to provide for the training of these men, especially those from the dissenting denominations. In 1740, Harvard, William and Mary, and Yale were the only colonial colleges. By the revival's end, several more were founded, most by Christian groups, including the College of New Jersey at Princeton by Presbyterians in 1746, Rhode Island College (later Brown University) by Baptists in 1764, Queen's College (later Rutgers) by Dutch Reformed in 1766, and Dartmouth by Congregationalists in 1769.[53] Pennsylvania and Columbia were also founded as a result of the Awakening.[54] Maxson notes, "The debt of education in the United States to the great Awakening is merely suggested, not adequately expressed, by the enumeration of the colleges which were the direct fruits of the revival."[55] By the time of the American Revolution, New England had more clergy per population than anywhere else, and these five generations of clergy delivered at least five million sermons, the average colonial churchgoer listening to seven thousand sermons in a lifetime.[56]

Theological Renewal

The pre-Awakening colonists existed amidst numerous theological ideas—Calvinism, Arminianism, Arianism, Unitarianism, Universalism. The more extreme of these ideas experienced increasing popularity due to the

52. Cragg, *Church*, 180. By "uneducated men," Cragg is referring to the many lay preachers who itinerated during the Awakening.

53. Noll et al., *Eerdman's Handbook*, 116. Dartmouth was an outgrowth of Eleazor Wheelock's Indian School that had been founded in 1754.

54. Sweet, *Revivalism in America*, 147–48.

55. Maxson, *Great Awakening*, 99.

56. Stout, *New England Soul*, 3–6, 13–15.

Enlightenment. The central issues of evangelical Christianity were severely tested. The Awakening, in response, championed these issues. Gaustad lists the debated issues as follows: "general or particular Atonement, a human or divine Christ, reason or revelation, reform or regeneration, free or earned grace."[57] Christians divided numerous times over these issues as evidenced by the numerous denominations that grew as a result of the revival. Though one might lament such division within the church, the divisions were largely among evangelical Christians who were busily seeking to do their best to interpret God's word and to do his will. There was sometimes "fervent evangelism without intellectual discipline,"[58] but there is no need to lament over such.[59] Before the revival, heresy was growing, but, as Tracy notes, "The revival set bounds for the progress of heresy."[60]

For all the many theological issues debated during the Awakening, the First Great Awakening gave renewed emphasis to two important issues in theology: justification by faith and a regenerate church.

The revivalists "championed the Reformation—and more importantly the New Testament—emphasis on justification by faith"[61] and many other doctrines related to it. During the fall of 1745, twenty friends of the revival met to affirm a "Testimony" concerning the revival. This document attributes much of the revival's success to the regular preaching of Scripture and numerous key doctrines, including:

> The all seeing eye, purity, justice, truth, power, majesty, and sovereignty of God; the spirituality, holiness, extent and strictness of the law; our original sin, guilt, depravity and corruption by the fall; including a miserable ignorance of God and enmity against him, our predominant and constant bent to sin and creatures above him; our impotence and aversion to return to him; our innumerable and heinous actual offences, and thereby our horrid, aggravated guilt, pollution and odiousness in his eyes; his dreadful and efficacious wrath and curse upon us; the necessity that his law should be fulfilled, his justice satisfied, the honor of his holiness, authority, and truth maintained in his conduct towards us; our utter impotence to help ourselves, and out continual hazard of being

57. Gaustad, *Great Awakening*, 126.

58. Gaustad, *Great Awakening*, 129.

59. If any lament is made, it should be over the extreme evangelists who developed doctrinal novelties and practices that contributed to the rapid decline of the Awakening.

60. Tracy, *Great Awakening*, 399.

61. McDow and Reid, *Firefall*, 225.

> sent into endless misery; the astonishing displays of the absolute wisdom and grace of God in contriving and providing for our redemption; the divinity, mediation, perfect holiness, obedience, sacrifice, merits, satisfaction, purchase and grace of Christ; the nature and necessity of regeneration to the holy image of God by the supernatural operation of the divine Spirit; with the various parts of his office in enlightening our minds, awakening our consciences, wounding, breaking, humbling, subduing and changing our hearts, infusing his saving graces, exciting and helping us in the exercise of them, and in all obedience, witnessing with our spirits that we are the children of God, and raising his consultations and joys in us; the difference between his saving graces and merely moral virtues without sanctification, whereby multitudes are deceived to their eternal ruin; in special, the nature and necessity of receiving Christ, so as to be actually united to him and have entire and everlasting interest in him, to be forthwith justified by his imputed righteousness, adopted into the number of the children of God, entitled to all their privileges assured in the covenant of grace, have Christ as our mediatorial and vital Head of all good, with his constant dwelling and acting by his Spirit in us; and then, in continual acts of faith, deriving from his fresh supplies of spiritual liveliness and comfort, as also light and strength for every duty and to carry on our satisfaction; the nature of gospel obedience and holiness, and their necessity, not as the matter of our justification, but as the fruit and evidence of justifying faith, and to glorify God and enjoy him the principal end of both our creation and redemption: and lastly, the sovereignty of the grace of God in this whole transaction, from its original, in the decree of election, to its consummation in glory.[62]

The revival championed these and other doctrines of evangelical Christianity to a greater or lesser degree depending upon the Christian denomination involved.

The revivalists also placed increased emphasis on a truly regenerate church membership. This was a natural consequence since most of the colonial revivalists were Reformed in orientation. A "cold and formal Arminianism" had prevailed in the days preceding the revival.[63] Maxson explains that the national churches of England, Scotland, and Holland, which existed in the colonies as well, "received candidates into full church-membership

62. Quoted in Tracy, *Great Awakening*, 400–401. Tracy gives no other bibliographic information.

63. Tracy, *Great Awakening*, 399.

if they possessed a competent degree of religious knowledge and lived a moral life. It was hoped that such were converted."[64] The revivalists did not place much hope in the supposed Christians who filled the churches. They assumed that a large percentage of the church membership was not regenerate, "addressed them as such, and exhorted them to seek clear evidence of conversion."[65] Therefore, numerous church members were converted in addition to those outside of the church who professed faith in Christ. As noted in Tennent's legendary "Danger of an Unconverted Ministry," the revivalists also believed a number of the ministers were unconverted. The Awakening "fully and finally killed the doctrine that an unconverted ministry might be tolerated."[66] The new ministerial schools ensured salvation of their students, and congregations became insistent that their ministers give evidence of genuine faith.

Social Contributions

The church was not the only part of the colonies affected by the Awakening. The social fabric renewed as well. The moral climate changed, and the colonies unified.

Bumsted and Van de Wetering state, "If a high level of immorality was one of the classic complaints of the clergy before the revival, the revival's effect upon moral conduct would inevitably become a test of its efficacy."[67] For years, preachers, especially those of Puritan persuasion, had been calling for improved morality. Unfortunately, as was shown in chapter 2, their preaching largely fell on deaf ears. However, as people were genuinely converted during the Awakening, their morality naturally improved. Others, while perhaps not converted, presumably saw the change in their friends or at least sensed that their life was not being lived the best, and put down their vices for a time. Bumsted and Van de Wetering conclude,

> During the height of local revivals, a "public reformation" of the visible behavior of colonial Americans *did* occur. For a short time at least, fewer people visited taverns and more attended religious services. At least publicly, the population exhibited patterns of

64. Maxson, *Great Awakening*, 144.
65. Maxson, *Great Awakening*, 144.
66. Tracy, *Great Awakening*, 394.
67. Bumsted and Van de Wetering, *What Must I Do*, 143.

> behavior that were approved by the standards of traditional Christian morality.[68]

Though many people returned to their carnal ways in the wake of the revival, the moral climate of the colonies did change as revival swept through the land.

There was another important social effect of the Awakening—the unification of the colonies. Witham states, "Although the term *America* had been around, now it was increasingly used to talk about a single religious people."[69] Some scholars propose that the Awakening even helped prepare the colonies for the Revolutionary War. The revival built in people a desire for religious liberty.[70] Before the Awakening, indifference to religion was widespread and tolerance was no problem. Afterward, however, religion was vitally important to the awakened colonists and problems arose. A growing impatience with the alliance of church and state surfaced. As the idea of religious liberty grew, so did the idea of liberty at large. The revival's emphasis upon the salvation of the individual soul helped give credence to the idea of individual freedom. The religious rhetoric of the day gave America the biblical themes of liberty and order.[71] Mark Shaw says that it was really the "Spirit of '40" and not the "Spirit of '76" that birthed America. Shaw proposes that while America had its organization birth in 1776, the organic birth began in 1740. What America experienced in 1740 was "an inner American revolution, a spiritual declaration of independence that made the political reshuffling thirty-six years later an inevitability."[72] Noll states that the Awakening was the first truly national event. The diverse colonies became one nation as bonds were made and ties with the various

68. Bumsted and Van de Wetering, *What Must I Do*, 147; emphasis added.

69. Witham, *City Upon a Hill*, 46.

70. The dissenting congregations in all three colonial regions fought for religious freedom. As previously noted, Davies was active in achieving religious freedom for Presbyterians in Anglican Virginia. In addition to religious freedom, religious democratization grew in influence. The power of the church came to rest in the pew instead of the pulpit. As a result of both growing religious freedom and religious democratization, "after the Awakening, it was possible, even fashionable to leave the established church to join a separate society, a Baptist or Anglican church, or perhaps to hold religious services in a private home. Church minorities were now more outspoken than ever before." Gaustad, *Great Awakening*, 113.

71. Witham, *City Upon a Hill*, 2.

72. Shaw, "Spirit of 1740," 7.

mother countries loosened. Terms such as *liberty*, *virtue*, and *tyranny*, though already powerful, were given more energy in the revivals.[73]

The First Great Awakening had impressive positive effects upon the American colonies. Converts increased in number and church members grew in their personal devotion. Churches grew, increased in number, and reached new areas. Missionary zeal advanced the church beyond its own walls and race, giving rise to missions to the Native and African Americans. Renewed churches produced a renewed ministry that, in turn, produced more renewed churches. In addition, colonial society felt the sweep of revival.

THE CONTRIBUTIONS OF THE REVIVALISTS' HOMILETICAL THEOLOGY

Revival: Caused By . . . or Contributed To . . .?

What caused the revival? This question is often posed by scholars of early American religious history. Numerous possible causes have been given, ranging from the super religious, which views the revival as primarily a unique movement of the Holy Spirit, to the simply secular, which views the revival as the result of the demographic immigration and migration of religious people. However, in studying the Awakening, these two extremes should be avoided. Secular and religious scholars alike should consider both the non-spiritual and spiritual factors that potentially could have caused the Awakening. Yet, as Noll admits, "The final evaluation . . . will depend less upon the evidence of history than upon the convictions of historians."[74] In the end, it is impossible to define the factor or factors that *caused* the revival.

Regardless of what caused the First Great Awakening or what a scholar believes caused it, the revival was a successful, verifiable, historical event. With this in mind, instead of looking for causes of the Awakening, one might look for the factors that *contributed* to the Awakening's success. With this slight focal shift, many of the factors that are commonly listed as causes for the Awakening may instead be noted as contributors to its success. For example, certainly, the natural demographic growth and geographic expansion of America contributed to the revival. As more people immigrated to the colonies, more could be converted or join churches, and, as people migrated

73. See Noll, *History of Christianity*, 110–12.

74. Noll et al., *Eerdman's Handbook*, 114.

into new areas, new churches could be established. Also, certainly, diseases, economic difficulties, and natural phenomenon heightened people's sensitivities. People in the colonies, especially those in the rural outreaches, experienced daily hardships that needed real spiritual answers. The New England earthquake on October 29, 1727, and its nine days of aftershocks caused people to pay attention, especially since their ministers had been warning them for some time of impending judgment. Numerous scholars have made observations concerning environmental factors and "all of these observations lead toward the conclusion that environmental factors prepared the colonial population to embrace a spiritual message, which, even if it could not deal directly with such problems, brought inner peace and an escape from guilt."[75] Certainly, one might even speak of a special outpouring of the Holy Spirit contributing to the Awakening. Revival is a work of the Holy Spirit, and only during movements of the Spirit of God are so many people converted and so many communities transformed. One can conclude that all of these potential *causes* are certain *contributors* to the revival's effectiveness.

Homiletical Theology: One Contributor Among Many

What contributions did the homiletical theology of Edwards, Tennent, and Davies have upon the effectiveness of the Awakening within the American colonies? Certainly, this homiletical theology did not cause the revival or make the Awakening successful in a vacuum. It was simply one of the many factors, albeit an important one, which helped the fires of revival burn with force and breadth.

As one considers the Awakening's historical and homiletical contexts as well as the Awakening's results alongside the homiletical theology of Edwards, Tennent, and Davies, he may propose several possible contributions this theology of preaching had upon the Awakening's success. These contributions are organized around the five components of the homiletical theology discussed in chapter 4.

Contributions of the Preacher

As stated in chapter 4, Edwards, Tennent, and Davies believed the office of the preacher to be a high calling from God to men whom he specifically

75. Noll et al., *Eerdman's Handbook*, 114.

equips for the homiletical task. Therefore, preachers should be savingly converted and practice piety in their personal and public lives. Likewise, because preachers participate in the work of redemption, they are to be well-studied in the Scriptures. Still, ministers are not noisy gongs or clanging cymbals, but are to speak the redemptive word of God to listeners with whom they have a relationship and with whom God desires a relationship.

Such a view of the preacher's role in preaching increased the effectiveness of preachers, thereby helping the Awakening to be effective. Revivalists who held to these principles became more devoted to the Lord and their calling, held a deeper commitment to scriptural authority, and desired to pastor truly regenerate churches. Likewise, the high expectations for the study and preparation of preachers prompted the development of accessible education.

Vocational Preachers Devoted Themselves to Their Work

The revivalists believed preachers who are fulfilling a vocation will be more effective than those who are merely filling an occupation. The positive results of the First Great Awakening reveal this to be true. It was churches with this kind of pastor, regardless of his denomination, which attracted the greatest number of listeners and realized the majority of converts.

The revivalists were consumed by their calling. They put forth the prayer and study required for effective preaching. As the revivalists labored at their sermonic workbenches and the fruit of that labor was shared from the pulpit, transformation took place in the lives of the listeners. The transformation was likely possible because similar change had already taken place in the preachers. Congregations enjoy good sermonic presentations but they can also sense the preacher's sincerity of heart. As people noted the sincerity of heart and faith in the revivalists, they responded to the Spirit's prompting in their lives. Davies once commented on the need for devotion to calling:

> It is an easy thing to make a noise in the world, to flourish and harangue, to dazzle the crowd, and set them all agape, but deeply to imbibe the spirit of Christianity, to maintain a secret walk with God, to be holy as he is holy, this is the labor, this the work.[76]

This "more important work" was especially accomplished by Davies. Pilcher notes, "Davies' striking combination of [fine pulpit] qualities, plus

76. Davies, *Sermons*, 1:60.

his dignity and solemnity, readiness to answer the needs of a frontier people, and exemplary personal life, led increasingly large numbers of Anglicans to turn away from the cold, rationalistic sermons and uninspired lives of their Church of England clergy."[77] Such "turning away" from dead churches happened a great deal during the Awakening,[78] but, as has been shown, so did "turning to" faith in Christ of those previously unchurched.

Because awakened ministers were devoted to their work, they also invested themselves in discipling their people after conversion. As has been previously shown, the ministers often met with small groups or individuals to provide additional instruction in the faith. These were practices adopted from Richard Baxter and the German Pietists.[79]

The awakened ministers stood out from the rest of the clergy because of their devotion to their vocation. There is little doubt this devotion helped them to be mightily used by God in their ministries.[80]

Devoted Ministers Inevitably Had a Commitment to Scriptural Authority

The revivalists delved into the Scriptures on a daily basis. Because of their interest in piety, they spent time in devotional reading and prayer. Because of their commitment to study in preparation for preaching, they also invested themselves in exegetical study. These men worked with the original

77. Pilcher, *Samuel Davies*, 54–55.

78. Though Gilbert Tennent had earlier encouraged people to leave their churches for those led by awakened preachers, he later lamented this practice because of the division it was causing within the church. In a letter to Reverend Dickinson on February 12, 1742, Tennent writes in a postscript, "The late Method of setting up *separate Meetings*, upon the *suppos'd unregenerancy* of Pastors of Places, is *enthusiastical, proud*, and *schismatical.* All that Fear GOD, ought to oppose it as a most dangerous Engine to bring the Churches into the most damnable Errors and Confusions: The Practice is built upon a twofold false Hypothesis, viz. Infallibility of Knowledge; and that unconverted Ministers will be used as Instruments of no good to the Church." Quoted in Lovejoy, *Religious Enthusiasm*, 108. Tennent goes on to state that such exposing of supposed unconverted ministers serves only to provoke them and declares the revivalists as arrogant.

79. Crawford, *Seasons of Grace*, 66.

80. This is not to say that devotion to vocation will always lead to the kind of results seen during the First Great Awakening. As has already been demonstrated, the Awakening was a confluence of many contributing factors. Devoted ministers were only one of these factors. Devotion to calling does not always lead to positive results. The ministry of Jeremiah is a perfect example of one who perfectly executed his calling but saw little positive results.

languages, read books of theology, and conversed or corresponded with other ministers about theological and ecclesiastical issues.

It is difficult to prove whether the revivalist's commitment to scriptural authority came before or developed out of their pious and diligent study. On the one hand, these men were the product of traditions that valued Scripture and held to a high degree of scriptural authority. On the other hand, many of the ministers in the days before the Awakening and those who disapproved of the Awakening were part of these same traditions. Still, the revivalists' devotion to scriptural authority stands out as more instrumental to their ministries.

It would seem, then, that the revivalists possessed, at least, a heightened or more sincere commitment to scriptural authority than their brothers in the same traditions. This is a fair conclusion because, as has been shown, many of the colonial ministers in the days preceding the revival were not pious, some were even unconverted, and a great number were merely filling a position instead of fulfilling a calling. Their sermons were moralistic essays that had little or no relationship to the word of God. The revivalists were different. They were converted, pious, spiritually growing believers who were committed to the truth of the Bible. Therefore, Scripture had to be the source and criterion for preaching. More will be said about the specific contributions of this scriptural authority under "Contributions of the Scripture" below.

High Expectations for Preachers Resulted in Accessible Education

Perhaps the most enduring results of the Awakening were the educational institutions that were founded in the revival's wake. These schools resulted from a need for accessible education, but such education was needed because the expectations of preachers were so high. The ministers coming from Europe to the colonies were educationally qualified but theologically impotent. The ministers from Harvard were not much better, since the school produced the majority of the Arminian, Old Light ministers. Yale had been founded in 1701 as a more pietistic and orthodox alternative to Harvard, but it was inaccessible to the majority of the colonies.[81] In the days preceding the Awakening, this situation was frustrating; nevertheless, it was largely accepted. The Awakening, however, made this situation absolutely unacceptable.

81. Stout, *New England Soul*, 220.

As revival spread, awakened congregations and clergymen alike became insistent that better education and more properly trained ministers were needed. Ministers needed to be trained in piety as well as the Scriptures if they were to become effective expositors of the Bible. These were fundamentals of the revivalists' homiletical theology. The expectations for complete theological study were raised beyond what was currently being taught in the institutions. As early as the 1720s, Stoddard, a Harvard graduate, began calling for more than merely "good education," insisting that education alone was insufficient to make an able minister.[82] As previously shown, the Log College, the other schools like it, and the permanent institutions they birthed became the solution to the problem of accessible and complete theological education. These schools encouraged the salvation of their students, helped these students develop a vibrant relationship with Christ, and gave them the tools necessary to study conscientiously for sermons. An educational momentum was generated. As the new schools produced ministers who held to their high standards, these ministers, in turn, instilled similar values in their converts and ministry protégés, sending even more ministers to the schools. While accessible education may have eventually come about without the Awakening, the fact remains that the Awakening caused an educational impetus in the colonies.

Regenerate Preachers Sought to Grow Regenerate Churches

As genuinely converted ministers entered or continued in their pastorates, they desired for their congregations to become truly regenerate and labored to this end. Their labor was born out of a genuine love for the sinners who sat before them each week. Though the Enlightenment promoted the idea that humanity was becoming increasingly good, the Awakening realized humanity was as sinful as ever. Preachers and congregants alike were sinners—either sinners saved by grace or sinners bound for destruction. Therefore, each revivalist, like many of their Puritan predecessors, ministered as a dying man to dying men. They had a fervency and interest in the lives of their people, both in leading them to salvation and answering the hard questions of life that they faced every day. This love for their congregation motivated the revivalists to preach Christianity with words from the pulpit as well as with their lives out of the pulpit. Their devoted lives were a constant sermon in an effort to see life transformation occur in

82. Stoddard, *Defects of Preachers Reproved.*

the congregation as a whole.[83] Conversions were important, but life transformation was paramount. Just as men were warned not to confide in "the fading flowers of floating, fleeing passions," so, too, was a preacher's work finally measured by the enduring fruits of his sermons.[84]

Contributions of the Scripture

The preaching of Edwards, Tennent, and Davies, and men like them, stood out amid the Enlightenment preaching of their day largely because of its foundation in Scripture. As stated previously, for these men, Scripture was divine, infallible, authoritative, and sufficient; therefore, they believed it should serve as both the source of and the criterion for preaching.

This view of the role of Scripture in preaching contributed to the effectiveness of the Awakening by lending greater biblical authority to sermons. The increase in receptivity can be linked to greater biblical authority. God has promised that his word will not return void (Isa 55:11). However, if his word is not proclaimed, he has promised nothing, nothing at all. The moralistic preaching before the Awakening contained little biblical content; therefore, it had little biblical authority and few positive results. Awakened preaching was different.

Commitment to Scriptural Authority Led to Greater Biblical Authority in Sermons

The revivalists believed Scripture should be the source for preaching. These men said Scripture texts are "beams of the light of the Sun of righteousness; they are the light by which ministers must be enlightened, and the light they are to hold forth to their hearers; and they are the fire whence their hearts and the hearts of their hearers must be enkindled."[85] Edwards encouraged preachers to be "well studied in divinity, well acquainted with the written word of God, [and] mighty in the Scriptures."[86]

The revivalists held to these fundamentals because they accurately believed that true and ultimate authority resides in God. The Bible, God's

83. Davies, *Sermons*, 3:550.

84. Tennent, "Solemn Warning," quoted in Heimert, *Religion and the American Mind*, 233.

85. Edwards, *Sermons and Discourses, 1743–1758*, 100.

86. Edwards, *Sermons and Discourses, 1743–1758*, 93.

word given to men under the inspiration of the Holy Spirit, is God's authentic message. Because the Bible is God's authentic message, it bears his authority. Therefore, it has "the right to command belief and action."[87] Homiletician H. C. Brown Jr., in his book *A Quest for Reformation in Preaching*, states that there is a fundamental relationship between biblical authority and preaching. He writes,

> Since the only authentic document for authoritative content about God in personal revelation is the Bible, the task of the preacher is to use the Bible correctly in sermon preparation and delivery. *To the degree that the minister trusts the Bible to be accurate and authentic*, to the degree that he listens to the Holy Spirit while engaged in interpreting the Bible, to the degree that God's self-revelation is "built" into the sermon, and to the degree that the minister preaches his "biblical sermon" under the leadership of the Holy Spirit, *the message is authentic and authoritative*.[88]

In the italicized statements above, Brown demonstrates how a commitment to scriptural authority should lead to greater biblical authority in sermons. Greater confidence in Scripture will guide a preacher in developing and delivering a more biblically authentic and authoritative message. Because the revivalists' were committed to scriptural authority, they worked greater biblical authority into their sermons.

Working greater biblical authority into sermons meant two things. First, it simply meant they used more Scripture. For example, Larsen notes that Edwards "referred often to Scripture. In one set of fifteen sermons, he used 374 biblical quotations, an average of twenty-five per sermon."[89] Second, it meant they grounded their sermons in Scripture. They do not often read a text and then preach a message unrelated to the text.

Sermons enjoyed greater biblical authority as a result of the Awakening. This had positive results, as the next contribution of the role of Scripture indicates.

Greater Biblical Authority Contributed to Increased Receptivity

In an age when the authority of the church was compromised by ineffective ministers preaching biblically weak messages, greater biblical

87. Erickson, *Christian Theology*, 268.

88. Brown, *Quest*, 35; emphasis added.

89. Larsen, *Company of Preachers*, 376.

authority provided an environment for increased receptivity. Edwards, in his "Thoughts Concerning the Revival," indicates that greater biblical authority will lead to greater receptivity. He writes,

> [Ministers whom God is using to promote awakening] ought indeed to be thorough in preaching the Word of God, without mincing the matter at all in handling the sword of the Spirit [Eph 6:17], as the ministers of the Lord of hosts, they ought not to be mild and gentle . . . but should be sons of thunder. The Word of God, which is in itself "sharper than any two-edged sword," ought not to be sheathed by its ministers, but so used that its sharp edges may have their full effect, even to the "dividing asunder soul and spirit, joints and marrow" [Heb 4:12] (providing they do it without judging particular persons, leaving it to conscience and the Spirit of God to make the particular application).[90]

Only when the sword is unsheathed can it be used for its intended purpose.

It may be surprising that greater biblical authority would aid the preacher in the Age of Reason. After all, did not most people reject much of the Bible as superstition? Yes, but Brown explains that true authority is accepted by "sensible men," the very men the Enlightenment sought to produce. Sensible men have no problem with true authority—they have a problem with corrupted or abused authority:

> Only in the presence of true authority can there be true freedom. The absence of authority in the state produces tyranny while the absence of authority in education produces ignorance through a lack of learning. The absence of authority in personal conduct produces disgusting and revolting license. The absence of true authority in religion produces unbridled subjectivism on the one hand and authoritarianism, unlawful uses of authority, on the other. Authority obviously commends itself to sensible men.[91]

Perhaps this is why the notion of biblical authority took root among some "sensible men" during the Age of Reason, causing them to be increasingly receptive to biblical sermons. Even though the promoters of the Enlightenment rejected much of Scripture and denigrated God to a mere Creator, some "sensible men" may have realized the need for authority. The absence of true authority in religion had allowed the authoritarianism often practiced by the state churches, whether Catholic or Protestant, to grow.

90. Edwards, *Some Thoughts Concerning the Revival*, 423.

91. Brown, *Quest*, 31.

Likewise, it allowed the subjective, moralistic preaching to prevail. An emphasis upon biblical authority generated "true authority," as Brown calls it, resulting in "true freedom." This true freedom likely allowed ministers to boldly proclaim the word of God, the Holy Spirit to apply that word, and listeners to respond to the word. The result was increased receptivity as evidenced by the numerous converts and those persons demonstrating signs of repentance and concern during the Awakening.

Contributions of the Holy Spirit

The revivalists knew that no matter the skills of the preacher, by himself, a preacher has nothing to say. Any significance to his words is given them by the Spirit. The preacher has his task to perform, but the Holy Spirit gives the effect. Therefore, any glory that comes from preaching is due the Spirit and not the preacher. As stated in the previous chapter, the revivalists held that God's Holy Spirit will empower a preacher's words, apply his words, and eventually, when the Father lifts the charge from the preacher's shoulders in heaven, he will reward those words.

This portion of the awakened homiletical theology contributed to the effectiveness of the revival by promoting submission to the Spirit's work, thereby increasing homiletical humility on the part of the preacher. This confidence in the Spirit's power and submission to it by the preacher allowed greater freedom for the Spirit to apply the living word to living people.

Submission to the Work of the Holy Spirit Increased Homiletical Humility

Because the Holy Spirit gives the effect in preaching, awakened preachers spiritually submitted to the Spirit. They viewed themselves more as servants than as ambassadors.

This homiletical humility was demonstrated in the ministries of the three revivalists herein studied. Specifically, Edwards, Tennent, and Davies were not self-promoters. Though they published sermons and articles and defended the Awakening, they did not do so merely for personal advance. All three men invested themselves in their local pastorate for the majority of their ministry. When a chance for advancement in position presented itself, it was often only accepted with great resistance, as characterized by Davies's refusals to assume the presidency of the College of New Jersey. Because the men were focused on their charge, they invested themselves in that locale, pouring out their hearts each week to people with whom they had deep relationships.

Submission to the Holy Spirit apparently built holy unction within these men. Lee Eclov defines unction as "the anointing of the Holy Spirit on a sermon so that something holy and powerful is added to the message that no preacher can generate, no matter how great his skills."[92] The awakened ministers had godliness that allowed them to step into the pulpit with hearts that had been tested and cleansed by God. But they also exhibited the unction of Isaiah after the angel touched the fiery coal to his lips (Isa 6). Heimert notes, "Though the particular gifts of individual preachers did not go unnoticed, what was commonly noted was that which was shared." What was noticeably shared was an apparent attendance of Almighty power upon their eloquence.[93]

The Holy Spirit Was Given Freedom to Apply the Living Word to Living People

A generation before the revival, Solomon Stoddard had said, "The Spirit of the Lord must be poured out upon the People, else Religion will not revive. But when the Spirit is upon Ministers, it is a very hopeful sign."[94] It seems to be true that when the Holy Spirit is able to build within preachers homiletical humility and holy unction, he is more free to apply the proclaimed word to the listeners. He is given freedom to provide his internal witness. As theologian Millard Erickson says, the Holy Spirit "creates certainty of the divine nature of Scripture by providing evidences that reason can evaluate. He also gives understanding of the text through the exegete's work of interpretation."[95] An appropriate setting for this work took place in the preaching of the revivalists. These men linked strong biblical authority, competent hermeneutical study, eloquent homiletical craftsmanship, a love for the congregation, and a powerful dependence upon the Holy Spirit into a homiletical theology that could allow maximum effect. It is doubtful that such linkage alone caused the results, but it certainly created the circumstances through which the Spirit could bring revival.

92. Eclov, "How Does Unction Function?" in Robinson and Larson, *Art and Craft*, 81.

93. Heimert, *Religion and the American Mind*, 232.

94. Stoddard, "Benefits of the Gospel," quoted in Crawford, *Seasons of Grace*, 52.

95. Erickson, *Christian Theology*, 283.

Contributions of the Listener

The revivalists knew that listeners are important. Therefore, listeners, whether they are Christian or heathen, have a prominent role in preaching. Edwards, Tennent, and Davies believed listeners should receive ministers as the mouthpiece of God and come to worship prepared to hear and heed the message.

This foundational realization that listeners were recipients of the word of God and not mere spectators or rhetorical critics helped the Awakening achieve positive results by leading preachers to focus on a different goal in preaching as well as affording them increased authority as they earned this authority from their listeners. The result was expectant listeners who became transformed listeners.

A Change in View of the Listener Led to a Different Focus in Preaching

The Enlightenment proposed that man was getting increasingly better; awakened preachers saw the opposite. To them, men were sinners as they always had been. This view of humanity as sinners led to a different focus in preaching. The ultimate aim of preaching shifted from helping good people live good lives to "washing and cleansing the souls of men" whether they be saved or heathen.[96] Christian souls needed washing and cleansing just as much as the heathen. Perhaps the cleansing was to a lesser degree, but it was still needed. The shift in ultimate aim was discussed in the previous chapter. The contributions of this shift to the Awakening's success will be discussed below.

While it is difficult to determine which came first, the shift in ultimate aim or the change in view of the listener, it is probable that the change in view of the listener came first. Otherwise, if humanity was still inherently good, why would one need to shift focus from moral preaching to evangelical preaching? To make this shift in aim, one must take a more biblical view of humanity as those who have fallen short of the glory of God (Rom 3:23). Having made this change in view, the focus in preaching could be altered as well.

Some preachers began to preach more gospel or more Christ. This was discussed in the previous chapter. Some preachers also began to preach "terrors." The preaching of terrors was a sermonic form that attempted

96. Edwards, *Sermons and Discourses, 1743–1758*, 333.

to scare people away from hell. It became a fiercely debated topic during the Awakening. Edwards, however, provided well-balanced reasoning for preaching terrors in his *The Distinguishing Marks* when he said, "Some talk of it as an unreasonable thing to think to fright persons to heaven; but I think it is a reasonable thing to endeavor to fright persons away from hell, that stand upon the brink of it, and are just ready to fall into it, and are senseless of their danger."[97] If one's focus was the salvation of mankind, how could he not call to those in danger? As Crawford explains, the revivalists believed "men must be frightened out of hell with the law and lured into heaven with the Gospel. Second, they believed that the conversion of a man from a sinner into a saint involved a transformation of the affections, from love of sin to love of God."[98]

Once preachers began to view their listeners in a different light, they changed their ultimate aim in preaching. They shifted from keeping ease in Zion to calling people away from the terrors of hell. These men were preaching to change the heart. Like Paul before Felix and his wife, Drusilla, in Acts 24:24–25, these men stood with one aim. They did not proclaim sugarcoated sermonettes, they proclaimed the gospel—"righteousness, self-control, and the judgment to come" (Acts 24:25). For some, as with Felix, this was too much, too straightforward. But for the thousands who were awakened, it was what the Spirit used to transform their lives.

Preachers Were Given Increased Authority Because They Earned It

As previously noted, in the days preceding the Awakening, the prestige of the American pulpit had declined notably. This decline became disturbing to ministers well before the end of the seventeenth century. By the beginning of the 1700s, ministers were attempting to bolster their authority at every turn. For example, in New England, ministers objectified their office. In doing so, "they stressed the sacerdotal nature of the office, modified the link between the ministry and the gathered church, replaced lay with clerical ordination, formed ministerial associations, and emphasized their preaching function as the necessary means of grace."[99] These measures were especially promoted in ordination sermons. Between 1709 and 1740, dates that cover the height of the Awakening in New England, ministers there

97. Edwards, "Distinguishing Marks," 248.

98. Crawford, *Seasons of Grace*, 86.

99. Crawford, *Seasons of Grace*, 70–71.

published eighty ordination sermons.[100] These sermons challenged new ministers to exhibit the character and do the hard work that the office and calling of ministry required. As these genuinely converted and thoroughly equipped ministers entered their charges, they exhibited the qualities for which their ministerial fathers had called and the traits for which their listeners longed.

Modern-day homiletician Crawford Loritts writes, "Great preachers are good communicators, but good communicators are not necessarily great preachers. And the difference is authority."[101] Early on in the Awakening, Tennent said that ministers who were not sent of God and clothed with the Spirit lacked that divine authority "with which the faithful Ambassadors of Christ are clothed."[102] Therefore, since they have no work of the Spirit upon their life, they were "neither inclined to, nor fitted for, Discoursing, frequently, clearly, and pathetically, upon such important Subjects."[103] The result was a "common Mess" left to the people to be applied as they saw fit. These ministers "often Strengthen the Hands of the Wicked, by promising him Life. They comfort People, before they convince them; sow before they plow; and are busy in raising a Fabrick, before they lay a Foundation."[104] Tennent knew authority was needed and called for it. Though he later regretted some of the severity of his words, he still felt ministers needed the authority that is granted by God and recognized by a congregation.

The apparent result of the ministerial practices in New England and similar practices in the other regions was that ministers sought the spiritual authority for which Tennent had called and earned the authority usually given the office. Therefore, listeners had more reason to bestow increased authority upon their ministers. While this authority did not reach the heights that some of their forefathers had enjoyed, it did reach high enough to encourage listeners to listen. When they listened, they heard God's word, encountered God's Spirit, and were transformed.

100. Crawford, *Seasons of Grace*, 71.

101. Loritts, "Preaching That Raises our Sights," quoted in Robinson and Larson, *Art and Craft*, 36.

102. Tennent, "Danger," 78.

103. Tennent, "Danger," 78.

104. Tennent, "Danger," 78.

Expectant Listeners Resulted in Transformed Listeners

As shown in chapter 4, the revivalists instructed their listeners to receive their ministers as the mouthpiece of God and to come to worship prepared to hear and heed the message that the minister had been given by God. This instruction, when grasped by listeners, helped them to come with an expectant attitude and heart to worship.

As previously stated, congregations in the eighteenth century came to worship with some expectancy even before the revival. Since the meetinghouse and its pulpit were the center of community life, they came to it expecting to hear news, reports, and even a message of some sort by the preacher. However, they did not come so much expecting to hear from God.

As the Awakening took flame, expectancy changed. People packed meetinghouses to hear those who frequented the pulpit. Though many came expecting to see and hear well-known celebrity preachers, such as Whitefield, many also came on a weekly basis expecting to hear from God as the local pastor proclaimed the word of God. When people came with greater expectancy, they set one more circumstance in place for the possibility of greater transformation.

Contributions of the Ultimate Aim in Preaching

Because listeners are either lost sinners in need of salvation or saved sinners in need of edification, the revivalists believed the ultimate aim in preaching is "to wash and cleanse the souls of men."[105] Like the Puritans before them, the revivalists held that the word of God had priority in the divine-human relationship. Therefore, preaching is the preeminent act of worship.

Such a belief in the ultimate aim of preaching supplied awakened churches with a vibrant proclamation of the gospel. This proclamation of the gospel led to energetic, engaged church members as opposed to lethargic, apathetic church members.

The Urgency of the Gospel Inspired Effective Delivery

Effective delivery is not synonymous with eloquent delivery. Prior to the Awakening, sermon delivery was often eloquent but also completely ineffective. Various godly men in the era before the Awakening attempted a move

105. Edwards, "Christ the Example of Gospel Ministers," 593–94.

away from mere eloquence toward effectiveness.[106] In both England and America in the 1720s and 1730s, "preaching Christ" became a rallying cry for those ministers who were seeking changes in their churches. "Preaching Christ" was the revivalists' alternative to "the 'legalistic' and rationalist preaching that ignored grace and the Scriptures in favor of 'mere morality' and reason, preaching, they said, that taught philosophy rather than the Gospel."[107] Men such as Isaac Watts urged preachers to consider the usefulness of the sermon rather than the eloquence of it, and to preach Christ not philosophy, for it is the gospel alone that is the power of God to salvation.[108]

The revivalists adopted delivery styles that were not uniform but were effective. The delivery styles of Edwards, Tennent, and Davies have already been explained. These have been shown to be quite diverse, yet all three styles were effective in their own contexts. The revivalists did not follow one particular methodology that was patterned after Whitefield or any other prominent preacher. Rather, they and others like them, including Whitefield, functioned within what may be described as a realm of delivery methodology. This methodological realm is termed *impassioned overflow* in a discussion below under the heading "Homiletical Theology's Effect upon Homiletical Methodology." This "overflow" came out of the preacher's own experience of the gospel and his personal relationship with Christ. It was "impassioned" because this experiential relationship was personal, vital, and growing.

Since many of the revivalists believed the preaching of the gospel was the means of conversion, that God dispensed his grace through preaching, it was important for sermon delivery to effectively communicate the gospel message in an engaging and clear manner. Therefore, "preaching Christ," or Christocentric preaching, became more prominent. For example, Scottish minister Ebenezer Erskine (1680–1754) placed the emphasis in delivery upon the display of Christ's glory instead of the display of the preacher's eloquence. He wrote,

> It is the Spirit of the Lord, accompanying the preaching of the word, and displaying the glory of Christ therein. . . . It is not the flourish of words, it is not the force of human rhetoric, or flaunting

106. Crawford specifically mentions Cotton Mather and Solomon Stoddard as the leaders of two streams that finally converged to help produce a successful awakening. See Crawford, *Seasons of Grace*, 65–66.

107. Crawford, *Seasons of Grace*, 54.

108. See Watts, *Humble Attempt*, 24–34, 98.

> harangues of morality . . . no, it is a faithful display of the glory of Christ, a simple proposal of the gospel, an opening of the mysteries of the kingdom.[109]

But the mere mention of Christ did not mean a minister was preaching Christ. In fact, Tennent considered the frequent mentioning of the "Name of Christ" to be no better than the liturgical chants of Roman Catholicism—a substitution of "chimes and affected Tuning of the Words" for the substance of the gospel.[110] Nevertheless, "preaching Christ" through the methodological realm of "impassioned overflow" became prominent, and, as previously noted, sermon delivery became more engaging.

The Proclamation of the Gospel Led to Energetic, Engaged Church Members

If enlightened, moralistic preaching produced lethargic, apathetic church members, it is reasonable that the proclamation of the gospel could produce energetic, engaged church members. Homiletician Jeffrey Arthurs says God uses the ministry of his word to create and strengthen his body. "Through the foolishness of preaching God unleashes the power of His Word to form and grow his beloved church."[111] This seems to have been the case as a result of the "impassioned overflow" preaching of the gospel that occurred during the Awakening. Maxson notes that through the revival, "The seat of religion passed back from the head to the heart, and religion became again a force."[112]

In one of his ordination sermons, Edwards explains that religion will flourish when excellent gospel ministers go forth who hold in proper balance both light and heat, or head and heart:

> If a minister has light without heat, and entertains his auditory with learned discourses, without a savor of the power of godliness, or any appearance of fervency of spirit, and zeal for God and the good of souls, he may gratify itching ears, and fill the heads of his people with empty notions; but it will not be very likely to reach

109. Erskine, *Works*, 2:91.

110. Heimert, *Religion and the American Mind*, 231. See also Tennent, *Unsearchable Riches of Christ*, 26.

111. Arthurs, "Preaching Life into the Church," quoted in Robinson and Larson, *Art and Craft*, 57.

112. Maxson, *Great Awakening*, 140.

> their hearts, or save their souls. And if, on the other hand, he be driven on with a fierce and intemperate zeal, and vehement heat, without light, he will be likely to kindle the like unhallowed flame in his people, and to fire their corrupt passions and affections; but will make them never the better, nor lead them a step towards heaven, but drive them apace the other way. But if he approves himself in his ministry, as both a burning and a shining light, *this will be the way to promote true Christianity amongst his people*, and to make them both wise, good, *and cause religion to flourish among them in the purity and beauty of it.*[113]

This is what happened as a result of the preaching that occurred during the Awakening. Ministers who went forth proclaiming the gospel with both light and heat saw their church members become energetic and engaged. The increased number of services and persons seeking discipleship that have already been noted serve as testimony of this fact.

In sum, the homiletical theology of Edwards, Tennent, and Davies contributed to the effectiveness of the First Great Awakening in many ways. While this homiletical theology neither caused the Awakening nor made it effective on its own, it did contribute to the positive effects of the Awakening. Their particular views as to the role of the preacher, the role of the Scripture, the role of the Holy Spirit, the role of the listener, and their understanding of the ultimate aim of preaching resulted in specific changes among ministers and in churches that created the atmosphere for the Awakening to catch fire as well as helped fan the fire as it burned through various colonial towns and regions. There is no doubt that since preaching was the major vehicle for the spread of Awakening, the homiletical theology of its primary preachers contributed to its effectiveness.

HOMILETICAL THEOLOGY'S EFFECT UPON METHODOLOGY

As stated in chapter 1, successful preaching is not the result of homiletical methodology alone, but homiletical theology as well. While this book has focused on the later, still, a brief discussion should be included regarding how the revivalists' homiletical theology affected their methodology.

113. Edwards, *Sermons and Discourses, 1743–1758*, 96; emphasis added.

The Preaching Tradition Before the Awakening

Prior to the Awakening, Protestant clerics, in general, followed the Puritan tradition of preaching, known as the Puritan "plain style." Sermons in this style were to be written down only after sufficient prayer and were to be presented from memory or closely read from a manuscript. Close reasoning with logical development were expected in the sermon's development. Though a spiritual requirement of prayer and meditation existed, such spiritual discipline was only practiced by the most committed preachers. However, nearly everyone followed the methodology.

William Perkins (1558–1602), the sixteenth-century Puritan clergyman, established the "plain style" in *The Arte of Prophesying*. This work laid out a four-part plan for a true sermon:

1. To read the text distinctly out of the canonical Scripture.
2. To give the sense and understanding of it being read by the Scripture itself.
3. To collect a few and profitable points of doctrine out of the natural sense.
4. To apply (if he have the gift) the doctrine rightly collected to the manners of men in a simple and plain speech.[114]

The plain style sermon was famous for its many divisions and subdivisions. Each message sought to draw three elements from a text: doctrine, argument, and application. The teaching of doctrine was often the sermon's major objective. The Bible was the source of authority and every doctrine "had its origin and justification in the Bible."[115] Anything less would have smacked of popery. Illustrations were used, but they were simple and concrete, never allegorical. The pattern was argumentative and inductive. Listeners were not as expected to respond to the message as they were expected to critique how the message was presented. Holland states, "With critical acumen the members of the congregation judged the homiletical effectiveness of the sermon by its technique and spiritual truth."[116] This was the age of "pulpit oratory." Puritan congregants listened but they listened with an ear to criticism of the preacher rather than personal change of themselves.

114. Perkins, "Arte," 349.

115. Holland, *Preaching in American History*, 115.

116. Holland, *Preaching in American History*, 115.

This tradition emphasized the techniques of pulpit oratory whereby homiletical methodology often took precedence over homiletical theology. Early on in Puritanism, *how* something was said was as important as *what* was said. However, as time went along, *how* something was said slowly became more important than *what* was said. Sermon content was judged simply upon the basis of whether it was spiritually true or not. Life transformation through emphasis upon either evangelism or edification as the preaching objective became lost or at least diluted.

Anglicanism held to a different methodology. John Tillotson (1630–1694), the late-seventeenth-century Archbishop of Canterbury, had made popular a moralistic homiletical methodology. Tillotson practiced clarity of voice and moderation in doctrine. His rational sermons were well-organized essays that touched on morals and manners, but to a lesser degree on doctrine.[117] For Tillotson, "Every sentence counted. He avoided dramatic or poetic flourish. . . . This kind of sermon knew its audience, which often was smug and content. By logic and persuasion it offered moral wisdom and doctrinal order, not a concluding plea to sinners."[118] Moralistic themes were prominent; biblical content was not. The style quickly shaped Anglicanism, especially in the colonies where Tillotson's published homilies enjoyed a massive audience.

The devastating results of both the Puritan plain style and rational, moralistic preaching were summarized in chapters 2 and 3. Certainly there were exceptions, but generally both methodologies pursued weak ultimate aims for preaching and often resulted in boredom and/or indifference on the part of the congregations. This reception resulted in weakened spirituality throughout the colonies.

Awakened Preaching

The homiletical theology of Edwards, Tennent, and Davies presented a new aim for the preacher as well as a different task for the listener. While homiletical prowess could not hurt a preacher's task, it was no longer the preacher's ultimate aim—the salvation of sinners was. Likewise, while listeners should critically evaluate a message, the Awakeners believed a sermon should not be evaluated merely for its homiletical proficiency but rather for what effect the Spirit was able to work in one's life through it.

117. Witham, *City Upon a Hill*, 42.

118. Witham, *City Upon a Hill*, 42.

Such new and different emphases for both preachers and listeners resulted in some changes in the homiletical methodologies used by the revivalists.

Holland says, "The Great Awakening completely disrupted the Puritan style of preaching."[119] This is somewhat overstated. Certainly, the more flamboyant, extemporaneous preaching of Whitefield and those he influenced attracted the interest of sleepy congregants. Whitefield's influence caused many preachers to mimic or adopt his methodologies. However, nothing was "completely disrupted." As was shown in the third chapter, Edwards, whose style was closest to the Puritans, slightly altered his methodology after coming in contact with Whitefield, primarily in freeing himself from his notes; however, his methodology was still quite Puritan and never showed much resemblance to that of the more flamboyant Whitefield. Even Tennent, who early on was characterized as a rougher-hewn Whitefield, later fell into a more careful and less haranguing presentation. Davies seems to have always had his own methodology, which was one of fiery eloquence, blending both eloquent delivery and studied content.

Nevertheless, though Holland's point is overstated, changes did take place in methodology. From the time of the revival onward, it was no longer possible for a minister to be successful in the pulpit solely by his homiletical prowess. If a minister had homiletical prowess, fine, but he should also be spiritually alive—and that life should be evident in his presentation of the sermon. Holland correctly states,

> Whether a sermon was homiletically a work of art was no longer the criterion. A sermon now was judged by its effect. Style was secondary to conversion; organization gave way to immediacy. No longer did a sermon direct itself in close reasoning through the inductive process to a theoretical theological issue; rather, the sermon called for the sinner to admit his dependence on God and repent. The minister was judged by whether or not he could bring about this experience.[120]

Edwards and Davies in all of their messages, and Tennent in his later messages, serve as fine examples of preachers who balanced exhibiting a committed Christian life with skillful homiletic design, thorough exegesis, and structured arguments. One might say the revivalists' shift in methodology was from fashioned oratory to impassioned overflow.

119. Holland, *Preaching in American History*, 115.

120. Holland, *Preaching in American History*, 115.

Shift: Fashioned Oratory to Impassioned Overflow

Prior to the revival, clerics were primarily interested in engaging minds. Revivalists focused on changing hearts. This shift in focus necessitated a shift in methodology—from fashioned oratory to impassioned overflow. The eighteenth century reveals a movement away from a style of oratory that was ethical and rational in its content, disciplined and precise in its language, and unimpassioned in its presentation, toward a style that was evangelical in focus and emotive in use of language.[121] Edwards, Tennent, and Davies preached with a comfortable blend of both—preaching with soberness and passion.

As has been demonstrated, the revivalists maintained a balance between preaching to the mind and preaching to the heart. Motivated by a genuine concern for people, Edwards, Tennent, and Davies attempted to engage the mind with the doctrines of the faith while striking the heart with grateful affections. Because preaching had been so directed to the mind in the past, the revivalists' main innovation came in their ability to address the heart through the emotions. The revivalists effectively used their emotions as well as the emotions of their listeners to strengthen their preaching. However, the best revivalists did not exploit emotions but rather sought a genuine overflow of the heart.

Because the congregation's reaction was so important, the revivalists placed a renewed emphasis upon delivery. It was in delivery that the Holy Spirit was most actively at work among the listeners. Stout says, "As rhetorician, Edwards emphasized above all else the moment of delivery in preaching. Careful preparation and study were important but the Holy Spirit was most active through the sermon and the minister had to prepare himself for maximum concentration in that time."[122] Stout takes an unnecessarily dim view of Awakening preaching; still, he is correct in his conclusion that the revivalists aimed at the inspiration of the congregation in the moment whereas the rationalist essays were geared to the understanding and appreciation of informed audiences.[123]

Sermon delivery for Edwards, Tennent, and Davies consisted more of impassioned overflow than it did skilled oratory. Eloquence no longer focused on beautiful words but on a beautiful heart spilling forth with

121. Downey, *Eighteenth Century Pulpit*, 228.

122. Stout, *New England Soul*, 228.

123. Stout, *New England Soul*, 221.

meaningful words. The revivalists reclaimed for preaching "much of its former verve, power, and authority, though not, alas, its literary grace."[124] No amount of skilled methodology in presentation could replace or cover the fact that there was no relationship with Christ in the heart. Tennent made these sentiments clear in his famous "Danger of an Unconverted Ministry." He insisted that though a "natural" preacher may speak with polished wit and rhetoric and gild his message with "zeal, fidelity, peace, good order, and unity," because natural men do not have a true love of Christ and for the souls of their fellow-creatures, "their Discourses are cold and sapless, and as it were freeze between their Lips."[125] Crawford clarifies, "A fundamental agreement distinguished the evangelical persuasion: Religion is a matter of the heart. Unless the passions are moved, all the convincing arguments for the understanding are useless. The saving operations of the Spirit are an affective, not an intellectual experience."[126]

While revivalists made use of the passions and emotions, the best revivalists, as are here studied, held these in proper check. Edwards, in fact, shunned preaching that was geared "simply to play on the emotions by sensational means, dramatics, and shouting—techniques that became popular during the awakenings."[127] Edwards encouraged ministers to clearly and distinctly explain the doctrines of religion, "and unravel the difficulties that attend them and to confirm them with strength of reason and argumentations, and also to observe some easy and clear method and order in their discourses, for the help of the understanding and memory."[128]

What the revivalists wanted was "naturalness" in preaching, for they looked on this as "somehow synonymous with sincerity and benevolence."[129] In his sermon "The Love of Souls," Davies characterizes naturalness in preaching as that language which is motivated by genuine love for the congregation:

> Love has a language of its own—a language which mankind can hardly understand; and which flattery and affectation can but seldom mimic with success. Love . . . has its own look, its own voice, its own air and manner in every thing, strongly expressive

124. Downey, *Eighteenth Century Pulpit*, 227.

125. Tennent, "Danger," 78.

126. Crawford, *Seasons of Grace*, 86.

127. Marsden, "Edwards, Jonathan," 115.

128. Edwards, *Some Thoughts Concerning the Revival*, 386.

129. Heimert, *Religion and the American Mind*, 229.

> of itself. . . . The most studied and well-managed artifices of flattery and dissimulation have something in them so stiff, so affected, so forced, so unnatural, that the cheat may often be detected, or, at least, suspected.[130]

Likewise, Tennent acknowledged the power of human eloquence to touch men's hearts, but acknowledged that this alone was no evidence that the word was being preached in spiritual power. Tennent observed that when a preacher "delivers divine Mysteries with Sublimity of Sentiment, beautiful diction, and graceful Action, with what gentle Violence of such Discourses insinuate themselves into the Affections; but these natural Commotions are as transient as ineffectual."[131] The godly minister would endeavor to be natural in sermon delivery.

Since naturalness was desired, standards as to methodology were never clearly established. Heimert notes that "even extemporaneity was resisted as a standard, largely because it was understood that pulpit talent, like any other, had to be given leave to find its own personal and even idiosyncratic mode of expression."[132] This is a probable reason that the three revivalists herein considered practiced their own unique methodologies although they were within the realm of "impassioned overflow."

No longer did the preacher speak as one highly exalted from a lofty pulpit. He spoke as a dying man to dying men out of the impassioned overflow of his heart. For example, because Davies was sickly much of his life, he believed his time for active service was short and that his ministry was urgent, therefore, he "addressed himself to his work with a strength of purpose and a simple dependence on Divine aid, that gave a mighty power to his ministrations."[133] Like Davies, the other revivalists were no longer interested in merely engaging minds; they wanted to change hearts. Pilcher notes that the preparation of souls for imminent death was the core of Davies's theology.[134] He preached not only to sinners but also to lukewarm church members.[135] The focus was heart transformation.

130. Davies, *Sermons*, 3:505.

131. Tennent, "Solemn Warning," quoted in Heimert, *Religion and the American Mind*, 223.

132. Heimert, *Religion and the American Mind*, 232.

133. Sprague, "Memoir of President Davies," quoted in Davies, *Sermons*, 1:14.

134. Pilcher, *Samuel Davies*, 66.

135. Pilcher, *Samuel Davies*, 66.

Methodologies of Edwards, Tennent, and Davies

One of the biographers of Edwards and the biographers of both Tennent and Davies include brief discussions about the homiletical methodology of their subjects. It is evident in these discussions that the homiletical theologies of these men greatly influenced their methodologies.

Turnbull speaks of how Edwards often constructed a sermon. He says the usual methodology of Edwards was threefold:

> He *first* appealed to the emotions by self-interest. He believed that the passions were the prime movers in life, and therefore he was not afraid to appeal to those basic instincts of self-interest and fear. . . . The *second* feature . . . was to awaken the conscience for a verdict. He sought to bring out the nature of each choice and show its bearing upon the ultimate object of worthy living. . . . The *third* element . . . was to announce a threefold argument.[136]

His final threefold argument included (1) the unconverted are in a condition of infinite sinfulness and deserve infinite punishment, (2) this punishment is utterly beyond imagination, and (3) the only hope of escape is by accepting the gift of salvation from God.[137]

Tennent's homiletical theology linked directly with his homiletical methodology. Coalter says Tennent believed in a dual task of preaching. First, preaching should communicate what Tennent called a "historical faith," and second, preaching should aid the Holy Spirit in providing an "experimental knowledge" of the divine grace. These tasks led to vibrant piety in the church.[138] In his messages, Tennent wanted to accomplish these two tasks.

Pilcher insists that, for Davies, the need to reach the human heart was always first, and this could not be accomplished by reason alone. Pilcher says Davies believed "sinners must be made to see the magnificence, the awesomeness—the sublimity—of God and the Christian concept."[139] Davies hoped to bring about conviction that would be "followed by a sincere change of heart and a complete spiritual cleansing. The change would ultimately be evidenced in right living."[140]

136. Turnbull, *Jonathan Edwards*, 98.
137. Turnbull, *Jonathan Edwards*, 98.
138. Coalter, *Gilbert Tennent*, 42.
139. Pilcher, *Samuel Davies*, 48.
140. Pilcher, *Samuel Davies*, 72.

The conclusions of these scholars confirm that *what* Edwards, Tennent, and Davies believed about preaching directed *how* they preached. Because their ultimate aim in preaching was to see lives transformed, they designed their messages to reach this end.

F. L. Chapell, in *The Great Awakening of 1740*, states,

> The chief value of a revival of religion is seen in its permanent results, that live on long after the first excitement has passed away. God has promised that his spirit 'shall come down like rain upon the mown grass.' Now the value of the rain is not merely in the freshness which it sheds abroad while it is falling, but in the springing growth and maturity of the vegetation that results therefrom.[141]

Though the First Great Awakening had ended in all parts of the American colonies by 1776 and many would-be Americans returned to their sinful ways, the Awakening did produce many positive permanent results. These included increased converts and personal devotion, church growth and expansion, missionary zeal, a renewed ministry, as well as several social contributions. When taken together the results are one of the reasons the Awakening is termed *great*.

The homiletical theology of men like Edwards, Tennent, and Davies was one of the factors that contributed to the effectiveness of the revival. This chapter has proposed thirteen potential contributions the revivalists' homiletical theology made. These contributions were divided under the five segments of the homiletical theology. Ultimately, it seems, the well-balanced homiletical theology of the revivalists helped develop stronger preachers who delivered more effective sermons and grew healthier churches under the Holy Spirit's empowerment.

141. Chapell, *Great Awakening of 1740*, 126–27.

CHAPTER VI

Where Do We Go from Here?

The September 17, 2001, edition of *Time Magazine* contained an article titled "How Much Does the Preaching Matter?" The author's conclusion was that preaching matters to the degree that it can connect with "those who are hungry for a fresh experience of faith."[1] In the First Great Awakening, people were hungry for a fresh experience of faith, and they received it through the preaching of the revivalists. Preaching mattered.

For years before the First Great Awakening, ministers called for and prayed for revival. Their reasons for doing so were varied. Noll proposes, "New England ministers may have sought revival to shore up their status, mid-colony preachers may have thought revival would expand the outreach and deepen the spiritual life of their denominations, and southern Anglicans may have hoped that a deeper piety could be assimilated within a stable establishment." When the Awakening finally caught fire, however, it was a surprise.[2] It was a surprise because true revival is always a result of the Spirit's work, not the outcome of calculated means or methods. Though means and methods may create the atmosphere for revival, they do not cause revival. When revival came, it did not always look like everyone thought it should. At least some members of almost every denomination reacted adversely to the First Great Awakening; still, the majority of several groups embraced the revival and grew as a result.

As the revival spread, competent thinkers and practitioners like Edwards, Tennent, and Davies wrestled with the tough issues of the

1. Gibb, "How Much," 63.

2. Noll, *History of Christianity*, 90.

Awakening. This book has focused on their conclusions about preaching. The Awakening and its preachers gave renewed impetus to preaching by offering a new view of preaching. The task of preaching became so popular that by the time of the American Revolution, and the end of the Awakening, "Congregational clergy alone delivered more than two thousand sermons a week."[3] Edwards, Tennent, and Davies, and other revivalists like them, held to a homiletical theology that contributed in a number of ways to the effectiveness of the First Great Awakening within the American colonies.

This chapter will offer a summary of conclusions and some applications for contemporary preachers, as well as areas for ancillary study.

SUMMARY OF CONCLUSIONS

This book has argued that Edwards, Tennent, and Davies possessed a theology of preaching that contributed to the effectiveness of the First Great Awakening within the American colonies. It was a historically verifiable event with many positive permanent results, many of which were affected, at least in part, by the homiletical theology of the revivalists.

This book opens a new area of discussion for Awakening and homiletical scholarship by asking the question, "What role does one's homiletical theology play in the results of one's preaching and ministry?" Most preachers desire to be effective in their vocation. Unfortunately, the discussions about effectiveness have lingered long on the topic of homiletical *methodology* but have largely ignored the topic of homiletical *theology*. Preachers are often encouraged to "preach *like* . . ." instead of being challenged to "preach *because* . . ." or to "preach *for* . . . ." Too often, the emphasis is upon employing an effective methodology (preaching *like* . . .) instead of thinking through the deeper issues of a homiletical theology. The emphasis is usually on *how* one preaches instead of *who* may preach, *why* they preach, *what* they preach, and *to whom* they preach. Homiletical methodology is important, but it is not more important than homiletical theology. Therefore, this work has placed emphasis upon homiletical theology.

I encourage you, whether you are a preacher or a member of a congregation who sits under preaching each week, to reconsider the importance of homiletical theology. If effective preaching is vital to the ministry of the church and the church is vital to the commission of Christ then effective preaching is vital to the commission of Christ. Throughout history, effective

3. Witham, *City Upon a Hill*, 57.

preaching has always accompanied effective churches. As Peter Forsyth said, "With its preaching Christianity stands or falls."[4] If preaching is so vital, then consideration must be given to homiletical theology. Creativity is fine, varied methodologies are fine, but the most clever methodology will fail if the theological foundation is weak. The methodology may be effective in bringing people in but it will not likely be effective in seeing lives transformed by God.

Instead of being continually caught in a methodological preaching cycle like Fant describes, someone somewhere should break out of this cycle, focus on the deeper issues, and unearth enduring, effective preaching. The First Great Awakening provides one period of time during which this kind of preaching existed. Edwards, Tennent, and Davies were three of the greatest preachers of this period who worked primarily in the American colonies as pastors as well as supporters of the revival. Within the words of these men is found a homiletical theology that contributed to their effectiveness as well as the overall positive results of the First Great Awakening in the American colonies.

The historical context of the Awakening provided the development and influence of both reason and revival—two important features of the eighteenth century. The Enlightenment resulted in moral laxity, religious indifference, and philosophic revolt.[5] Though many cultural and philosophic changes took place, this dissertation has primarily focused on the changes brought about in religion. Enlightened men placed human reason over religion. A deity still existed, but biblical Christianity was quite unbelievable and was viewed as the product of a less reasonable age. Because humanity was so "enlightened," the view of humanity became increasingly positive. Original sin and human depravity were abandoned and in their place free will and the essential goodness of humanity was promoted.

The spiritual result of the moral and religious climate was darkened spirituality. Public worship was often ill attended and those who did attend were largely unconcerned. A melancholy ministry developed that only increased the spiritual depravity of the colonies as they offered weak preaching and an appealing ecclesiology that resulted in an unregenerate church.

The background for the Awakening was the decadent civilization of the "enlightened" eighteenth century. Such circumstances could have led to one of two ends: atheistic despair or spiritual revival. As I have confirmed,

4. Forsyth, 1.

5. Maxson, *Great Awakening*, 140.

a spiritual, general revival took place throughout the colonies in the mid-1700s. Beginning first in the Middle Colonies and then moving to New England and finally to the South, this Great Awakening burned through the colonies, fanned by the preaching of settled pastors like Edwards, Tennent, and Davies, as well as lay and ordained itinerants.

Within the historical context, the revivalists found their homiletical context in which they developed their theology of preaching. Preaching was the power that propelled the Awakening. Whereas sermons and preachers were nothing new, engaging sermons and convicted preachers were. Prior to the Awakening sermons were dry, lengthy, and produced few results. Awakened preaching, however, was fresh and new, and the ministers of revival preached with a new fervency and unction. People responded in mass. Consequently, revivalists increasingly used preaching to spread awakening. Edwards, Tennent, and Davies arose as the three key leaders of the First Great Awakening in their colonial regions. Their preaching, though somewhat varied in methodology, produced similar results. One commonality between the men was their homiletical theology.

In chapter 4, I described this homiletical theology with emphasis given to the roles of the preacher, Scripture, Holy Spirit, and listener. The ultimate aim of preaching was also discussed. The revivalists believed an effective preacher should be a growing, pious Christian who is consumed by his calling. His devotion to his work will be characterized by competent exegetical study with an aim to correctly imparting the word of God to his beloved congregation.

These men also believed Scripture is central to preaching. Scripture is divine, infallible, authoritative, and sufficient and, therefore, should serve as both the source of and criterion for preaching. But even the best preacher with a carefully studied and developed biblical message is not enough. The Holy Spirit also plays an important role in preaching. Any significance given to the words is given them by the Spirit. It is the Spirit who empowers the words of the preacher and applies the message to the listeners.

The revivalists understood listeners to be active participants in the sermon, not mere passive observers of a sermon. Listeners are to come to worship prepared to hear and heed the message delivered by the preacher, the mouthpiece of God. All listeners must heed the message because all listeners are sinners, whether converted or unconverted. Because all listeners are either lost sinners in need of salvation or saved sinners in need of edification, the revivalists believed the ultimate aim of preaching is to wash and cleanse the souls of men. The preacher's task is the same as Christ's—to preach the gospel. These are the basic tenets of the theology of preaching held by Edwards, Tennent, and Davies.

The revivalists' homiletical theology made numerous potential contributions to the Awakening's success. The most frequently listed and properly evidenced positive results of the First Great Awakening in the American colonies include increased converts and personal devotion, church growth and expansion, missionary zeal, a renewed ministry, as well as several social contributions. The revivalists' homiletical theology contributed to each of these in at least some small way.

The view of the role of the preacher contributed to the Awakening in several ways. It encouraged vocational preachers to be devoted to their work. These devoted ministers, who were pouring over the Scriptures each day, inevitably developed a deep commitment to scriptural authority that endued their sermons with greater biblical authority. Further, the high expectations for preachers resulted in the establishment of accessible and complete education, which included development of the minister's piety as well as competency in the Scriptures and theology. Much emphasis was placed upon regenerate preachers. These preachers endeavored to grow regenerate churches.

The commitment to scriptural authority led to greater biblical authority in sermons. This greater biblical authority contributed to increased receptivity. Numerous converts and increased piety were often the result.

As regenerate, pious ministers studied and imparted the Scriptures, they were increasingly submitted to the Holy Spirit's work through them. Therefore, the Spirit was given freedom to apply the living word to living people.

The realization that these living people, the listeners, were sinners in need of salvation or edification led to a different focus in preaching. As regenerate preachers proclaimed sermons with biblical authority, they earned increased authority themselves. Listeners came to services expecting to hear from God, which afforded them the opportunity to be transformed by God.

In all, the new aim in preaching led to energetic, engaged church members.

These members kept their minister accountable, reached out to their peers, and wanted to fulfill Christ's great commission. Ultimately, it seems, the well-balanced homiletical theology of the revivalists helped develop stronger preachers who delivered more effective sermons and grew healthier churches under the Holy Spirit's empowerment.

Though homiletical methodologies changed, they primarily did so as the result of the homiletical theology at their foundation. Davies confirms the emphasis upon one's relationship with God and his theology of preaching instead of external methodologies in one of his sermons:

> Sometimes a minister, who is a universal scholar, a masterly reasoner, and an accomplished orator, and withal, sincerely engaged for the conversion of sinners, labours in vain, and all his excellent discourses seem to have no effect; while another of much inferior accomplishments, is the successful instrument of turning many to righteousness. This cannot be accounted for without ascribing the distinction to the peculiar concurrence of divine grace; for if it depended upon the instruments, it would be quite the reverse. Sometimes a clear, convictive, and withal, solemn and warm discourse has no effect; while, at another time, the same doctrines, delivered in a weak, incoherent manner, have strange efficacy and reach the heart. Sometimes the reading of a sermon has been the means of awakening and careless sinners, when, at others times, the most solemn and argumentative preaching has been in vain. Sometimes we have seen a number of sinners thoroughly awakened, and brought to seek the Lord in earnest; while another number, under the very same sermon, and who seemed as open to conviction as the former, or perhaps more so, have remained secure and thoughtless, as usual. And whence could this difference arise but from special grace? We have seen persons struck to the heart with those doctrines which they have heard an hundred times without any effect. And indeed there is something in the manner of persons being affected with the word, which shows that the impression is not made by the word itself, or by any other power than divine.[6]

Methodologies vary but a strong understanding of what is being done in preaching and who is involved in the preaching event is most important.

APPLICATIONS FOR CONTEMPORARY PREACHERS

A homiletical historical study such as this is incomplete without offering some applications for contemporary preachers. What does all this

6. Davies, *Sermons*, 3:27.

information offer us for today? Though preachers today are ministering nearly three hundred years removed from the First Great Awakening, this study provides two primary applications for contemporary preachers. First, preachers must realize that homiletical methodology alone is not the answer to their struggle for an effective ministry. Second, preachers should develop their own personal homiletical theology. A third supplementary application may also be offered: ministers should find role models for church leadership among the leaders of the First Great Awakening.

Effective Ministry Takes More than Methodology

Preachers who desire to have effective pulpit ministries should realize that preaching itself is not broken and methodology alone is not the answer to their struggle for an effective ministry. The preaching ministry has always been a vital part of God's commission for the church. The First Great Awakening is one historical example that preaching at its best usually accompanied church life at its best. It has been shown that this effectiveness was not the result of homiletical methodologies alone.

Instead of chasing after the latest methodology, contemporary preachers should pause long enough to ask why the methodology works or even whether or not it really works. For example, is the methodology merely attracting a crowd or is it helping lives be transformed? This is a vital question. A large crowd does not necessarily evidence a movement of God any more than a small crowd evidences a lack of spiritual movement. The evidence of a movement of God comes from transformed lives—both converted sinners and edified saints. When a new methodological approach is presented, a preacher should study it to determine its root as well as its fruit. If the methodology fits his homiletical theology, he may employ it as one of many methods available to him.

Develop a Personal Homiletical Theology

Obviously, if contemporary preachers are to judge methodologies by their homiletical theology, then these preachers need to develop a biblically grounded theology of preaching. Preachers should spend time pondering what they feel the roles of the preacher, the Scripture, the Holy Spirit, and the listener are in preaching. They should also determine what they feel the ultimate aim of preaching should be. While there is certainly room for a variety of opinions within a homiletical theology, it seems that some minimal requirements do exist. These may be summarized as follows.

First, the preacher must be a regenerate and devoted Christian who is invested in his calling. This is basic to the New Testament. McDow and Reid state, "The contrasting preaching styles of these men give contemporary preachers the freedom to be themselves. Leadership is influence, and these men influenced others not by the appointment of external authority, but by character, conviction, and consistent message."[7]

Second, Scripture, as the word of God, must be the source of authority in the sermon. Authority must not rest in the preacher's office, the church's doctrines, or the culture's beliefs. All of these sources of authority must submit to the supreme authority of God's word as provided in the canon of Scripture.

Third, the Holy Spirit's role in preaching must not be neglected. He is an active participant in the preaching event. Both the hearts of the minister and the listeners should be prepared to hear from the Holy Spirit.

Fourth, listeners should be equipped to both hear and heed the message. Over time, listeners need to be instructed in how to develop an ongoing walk with the Lord so they may hear and heed the message. John Stott says, "The spiritual poverty of many churches throughout the world today is due more than anything else to either an unwillingness or an inability to listen to the Word of God. If individuals live by the Word of God, so do congregations. And a congregation cannot mature without a faithful and sensitive biblical ministry and without listening to the Word themselves."[8]

Fifth, the ultimate aim in preaching should include both evangelism and edification. Nearly every preaching event consists of both converted and unconverted listeners. Preaching should take into consideration both groups of listeners. While every sermon may not be able to address both groups, the course of one's preaching should.

Many Protestant ministers see their task and function quite differently than Edwards, Tennent, and Davies. As Bickell says, "Their time is dictated by the vision they have of the pulpit. Many 'share' rather than 'preach,' pray rather than pronounce blessings, and perform under a clouded vision of their ministry because they have no clear conviction about the nature of

7. McDow and Reid, *Firefall*, 226.

8. Stott, "Definition of Biblical Preaching," quoted in Robinson and Larson, *Art and Craft*, 28.

preaching."[9] Once a preacher has developed a well-balanced biblical theology of preaching, he can begin to both fulfill his vocation and evaluate his work by it. The results may not be as astounding as those of the First Great Awakening, but God will be free to work through the minister as he so chooses.

Find Role Models of Church Leadership

Contemporary preachers should read widely among effective historical preachers to find role models for church leadership. The ordination sermons especially provide much that is challenging and motivating to a minister even though he is nearly three hundred years removed from the original ordination candidate. When one reads these ordination sermons along with the biographies of these men of God, he finds effective role models for church leadership. The instructions the preachers gave to new ordinands are clearly evidenced in their own lives of ministry.

Contemporary pastors should be greatly challenged and humbled by these men. John Piper, a respected pastor and life-long student of Edwards, challenges twenty-first-century preachers by saying that preachers today are in no danger of mechanical imitation of men such as Edwards:

> We have fallen so far from their conception of preaching that we couldn't imitate it if we tried. I say "fallen" because, whether a manuscript should be read or whether a sermon should be two hours long, and its sentences complex and stories few, the fact is that the glory of these preachers was their earnestness—an earnestness that might be called gravity.[10]

Piper is correct. The success of these preachers was only partially based on their God-given gifts and abilities. Their primary success came from their earnestness and passion for the One whose word they proclaimed and for the proclamation of that word. Above all else, this is why people listened and why their lives were changed. Contemporary preachers should ask if their ministries have such "gravity."

The First Great Awakening first resonated in my soul twenty years ago during a course on church history. This interest was further developed during a doctoral seminar on spiritual awakenings. Since that time, I have

9. Bickell, *Light and Heat*, 1.

10. Piper, *Supremacy of God in Preaching*, 51.

fallen in love with homiletics and come to desire to become more effective at my own task of preaching.

It has been a joy to seek out the foundational principles that helped men such as Edwards, Tennent, and Davies contribute to the effectiveness of the First Great Awakening. These men did not have all of the answers. They were not perfect in their ministries. Their altars were not always filled. But they were used by God during a major move of his Spirit whereas other men were not. Their churches were touched whereas others were not. Why were they used by God? It seems that at least one reason was their homiletical theology caused them to be men whom God could use. Their commitment to God, their devotion to their vocation, their confidence in the authority of Scripture, their reliance upon the Spirit of God, their love for their congregation, and their understanding of what needed to happen in preaching allowed God to use them to bring further revival.

Some have looked with disdain upon the First Great Awakening as a mere period of religious excitement even invented by the preachers who became famous as a result. But these persons have missed the mark. Maxson correctly states that the Awakening "was more than wave on wave of excitement; it was a transforming process in the nation's life."[11] The numerous positive effects are undeniable. Truly, the American colonies were transformed by the power of Almighty God.

Today, America is in need of another "transforming process." May the Lord bring awakening to America again, and may he do so through its preachers.

11. Maxson, *Great Awakening*, 139.

Bibliography

Adam, Peter. *Speaking God's Words: A Practical Theology of Preaching*. Vancouver: Regent College Publishing, 1996.

Ahlstrom, Sydney E. *A Religious History of the American People*. New Haven: Yale University Press, 1972.

Aldridge, Alfred Owen. *Jonathan Edwards*. New York: Washington Square, 1964.

Alexander, Archibald. *Biographical Sketches of the Founder and Principal Alumni of the Log College*. Philadelphia: Presbyterian Board, 1851.

———, comp. *Sermons and Essays by the Tennents and Their Contemporaries*. Philadelphia: Presbyterian Board, 1855.

Allen, Tom. "Younger Pastors Ask: Is Preaching Out of Touch?" Pastors.com, 2004. https://web.archive.org/web/20060131040527/http://www.pastors.com/article.asp?ArtID=6183.

Alley, Robert Sutherland. "The Reverend Mr. Samuel Davies: A Study in Religion and Politics, 1747–1759." PhD diss., Princeton University, 1962.

Amory, Hugh, and David D. Hall, eds. *The Colonial Book in the Atlantic World*. Vol. 1 of *A History of the Book in America*. New York: Cambridge University Press, 1999.

Anchor, Robert. *The Enlightenment Tradition*. New York: Harper and Row, 1967.

Angoff, Charles, ed. *Jonathan Edwards: His Life and Influence*. London: Associated University, 1975.

Armstrong, John H. "Editor's Introduction." *Reformation and Revival* 4 (1995) 9–14.

Ashton, Thomas Southcliffe. *The Industrial Revolution (1760–1830)*. Oxford: Oxford University Press, 1968.

Atkins, Gaius Glenn, and Frederick L. Fagley. *History of American Congregationalism*. Boston: Pilgrim, 1942.

Balmer, Randall, and John R. Fitzmier. *The Presbyterians*. Westport: Greenwood, 1993.

The Barna Group. "Church Attendance." https://web.archive.org/web/20080209164058/http://www.barna.org/FlexPage.aspx?Page=Topic&TopicID=10.

Barth, Karl. *Homiletics*. Translated by Geoffrey W. Bromiley and Daniel Day. Louisville: Westminster John Knox, 1991.

———. *The Preaching of the Gospel*. Translated by B. E. Hooke. Philadelphia: Westminster, 1963.

———. *The Word of God and the Word of Man*. Translated by Douglas Horton. New York: Harper, 1928.

Bartlett, Billy Vick. "George Whitefield—Gospel Rover." *Fundamentalist Journal* 4 (1985) 45–47.

Bartlett, Gene E. "The Preaching and Pastoral Roles." *Pastoral Psychology* 3 (1952) 21–28.

Bartow, Charles L. *God's Human Speech: A Practical Theology of Preaching*. Grand Rapids: Eerdmans, 1997.

Baxter, Richard. *The Poetical Fragments of Richard Baxter*. 4th ed. London: Pickering, 1821.

Bickell, R. Bruce. *Light and Heat: The Puritan View of the Pulpit*. Morgan: Soli Deo Gloria Ministries, 1999.

Bond, Edward L. *Damned Souls in a Tobacco Colony: Religion in Seventeenth-Century Virginia*. Macon, GA: Mercer University Press, 2000.

Bonomi, Patricia U. *Under the Cope of Heaven: Religion, Society, and Politics in Colonial America*. New York: Oxford University Press, 1986.

Bost, George Henry. "Samuel Davies, Colonial Revivalist and Champion of Religious Toleration." PhD diss., University of Chicago, 1942.

Braaten, Carl E. "The Interdependence of Theology and Preaching." *Dialog* 3 (1964) 12–20.

Broadus, John A. *Lectures on the History of Preaching*. New ed. New York: Armstrong and Son, 1907.

Brockway, Robert W. "The Significance of James Davenport in the Great Awakening." *Journal of Religious Thought* 24 (1967–1968) 86–94.

Brown, H. C., Jr. *A Quest for Reformation in Preaching*. Waco: Word, 1968.

Brydon, George MacLaren. *Virginia's Mother Church and the Political Conditions Under Which It Grew*. Vol. 2. Philadelphia: Church Historical Society, 1952.

Brynestad, Lawrence E. "The Relation of Gilbert Tennent to the Religious Development of the Middle Colonies." PhD diss., Biblical Seminary of New York, 1931.

Bumsted, J. M. *The Pilgrim's Progress: The Ecclesiastical History of the Old Colony, 1620–1775*. New York: Garland, 1989.

Bumsted, J. M., and John E. Van de Wetering. *What Must I Do to Be Saved? The Great Awakening in Colonial America*. Hinsdale, IL: Dryden, 1976.

Bushman, Richard L., ed. *The Great Awakening: Documents on the Revival of Religion, 1740–1745*. New York: Atheneum, 1970.

Butler, Jon. *Awash in a Sea of Faith: Christianizing the American People*. Cambridge: Harvard University Press, 1990.

———. "Enthusiasm Described and Decried: The Great Awakening as Interpretative Fiction." *Journal of American History* 69 (1982) 305–25.

———. *Religion in Colonial America*. New York: Oxford University Press, 2000.

Buttrick, David. *The Mystery and the Passion*. Minneapolis: Fortress, 1992.

Byrd, Christopher. "Controversies of the Great Awakening in the Middle Colonies." *Reformation and Revival* 8 (1999) 85–101.

Byrne, James M. *Religion and the Enlightenment*. Louisville: Westminster John Knox, 1996.

Carrick, John. *The Imperative of Preaching: A Theology of Sacred Rhetoric*. Carlisle, PA: Banner of Truth Trust, 2016.

Carse, James. *Jonathan Edwards and the Visibility of God*. New York: Charles Scribner's Sons, 1967.

Cassirer, Ernst. *The Philosophy of the Enlightenment*. Princeton: Princeton University Press, 1951.

Chamberlain, Ava. "Self-Deception as a Theological Problem in Jonathan Edwards' Treatise Concerning Religious Affections." *Church History* 63 (1994) 540–49.

Chapell, Bryan. *Christ-Centered Preaching: Redeeming the Expository Sermon*. Grand Rapids: Baker, 1994.

Chapell, F. L. *The Great Awakening of 1740*. Philadelphia: American Baptist Publication Society, 1903.

Coalter, Milton J., Jr. *Gilbert Tennent, Son of Thunder: A Case Study of Continental Pietism's Impact on the First Great Awakening in the Middle Colonies*. New York: Greenwood, 1986.

Cobban, Alfred. *In Search of Humanity: The Role of the Enlightenment in Modern History*. New York: George Braziller, 1960.

Coleman, Robert E. "Jonathan Edwards: A Man Swallowed Up in God." *Christian Education Journal* 11 (1990) 87–94.

Collins, Edward M., Jr. "The Rhetoric of Sensation Challenges the Rhetoric of the Intellect: An Eighteenth-Century Controversy." In *Preaching in American History: Selected Issues in the American Pulpit, 1630–1967*, edited by Dewitte Holland, 98–117. Nashville: Abingdon, 1969.

Colman, Benjamin, et al. *Three Letters to the Reverend Mr. George Whitefield*. Philadelphia: Bradford, 1739.

Conforti, Joseph A. *Jonathan Edwards, Religious Tradition, and American Culture*. Chapel Hill: University of North Carolina Press, 1995.

Conrad, Leslie, Jr. "The Importance of Preaching in the Great Awakening." *Lutheran Quarterly* 12 (1960) 111–20.

———. "Jonathan Edwards' Pattern for Preaching." *Church Management* 33 (1957) 45–47.

Cooke, Jacob Ernest, et al., eds. *Encyclopedia of the North American Colonies*. 3 vols. New York: Scribner, 1993.

Cowing, Cedric B. *The Great Awakening and the American Revolution: Colonial Thought in the Eighteenth Century*. The Rand McNally Series on the History of American Thought and Culture. Chicago: Rand McNally, 1971.

Craddock, Fred B. *As One Without Authority: Revised and with New Sermons*. St. Louis: Chalice, 2001.

———. *Overhearing the Gospel*. Nashville: Abingdon, 1978.

Cragg, Gerald R. *The Church and the Age of Reason: 1648–1789*. Grand Rapids: Eerdmans, 1960.

Crawford, Michael J. *Seasons of Grace: Colonial New England's Revival Tradition in Its British Context*. New York: Oxford University Press, 1991.

Dallimore, Arnold A. *George Whitefield: The Life and Times of the Great Awakening of the Eighteenth-Century Revival*. 2 vols. Edinburgh: Banner of Truth Trust, 1979.

Dargan, Edwin Charles. *The Art of Preaching in the Light of Its History*. New York: Doran, 1922.

———. *From the Close of the Reformation Period to the End of the Nineteenth Century, 1572–1900*. Vol. 2 of *A History of Preaching*. Grand Rapids: Baker Book House, 1954.

Davies, Samuel. "Dissent in Virginia: Samuel Davies, Letter to the Bishop of London, 1752." In *The Great Awakening: Documents on the Revival of Religion, 1740–1745*, edited by Richard L. Bushman, 162–66. New York: Atheneum, 1970.

———. "Letter to Bellamy, 4 July 1751." In *Presbyterian Magazine* 4 (1854) 513.

———. "Letter to Mr. Bellamy of Bethlehem, in New England, 28 June 1751." In *Biographical Sketches of the Founder and Principal Alumni of the Log College*, by Archibald Alexander, 220–21. Philadelphia: Presbyterian Board, 1851.

———. *The Reverend Samuel Davies Abroad: The Diary of a Journey to England and Scotland, 1753–55*. Edited by George William Pilcher. Urbana: University of Illinois Press, 1967.

———. *Sermons*. 3 vols. Philadelphia: Presbyterian Board, 1864.

———. *Sermons on Important Subjects*. Edited by Albert Barnes. Vol. 2. New York: Robert Carter, 1845.

———. *The State of Religion Among the Protestant Dissenters in Virginia*. In *The Great Awakening: Event and Exegesis*, edited by Darrett B. Rutman, 46–51. Huntington: Krieger, 1977.

Demaray, Donald E. *Pulpit Giants: What Made Them Great*. Chicago: Moody, 1973.

Doddridge, Philip. *Lectures on Preaching and the Several Branches of the Ministerial Office*. Boston: Manning and Loring, 1808.

Downey, James. *The Eighteenth Century Pulpit: A Study of the Sermons of Butler, Berkeley, Secker, Sterne, Whitefield, and Wesley*. Oxford: Clarendon, 1969.

Edwards, Jonathan. "The Distinguishing Marks." In *The Great Awakening*, edited by C. C. Goen, 213–79. Vol. 4 of *The Works of Jonathan Edwards*. New Haven: Yale University Press, 1972.

———. *The Great Awakening*. Edited by C. C. Goen. Vol. 4 of *The Works of Jonathan Edwards*. New Haven: Yale University Press, 1972.

———. *An Humble Attempt to Promote Explicit Agreement*. In *Apocalyptic Writings*, edited by Stephen J. Stein, 307–436. Vol. 5 of *The Works of Jonathan Edwards*. New Haven: Yale University Press, 1977.

———. *Letters and Personal Writings*. Edited by George S. Claghorn. Vol. 16 of *The Works of Jonathan Edwards*. New Haven: Yale University Press, 1998.

———. *Notes on Scripture*. Edited by Stephen J. Stein. Vol. 15 of *The Works of Jonathan Edwards*. New Haven: Yale University Press, 1998.

———. *The Puritan Pulpit: Jonathan Edwards, Containing 16 Sermons Unpublished in Edwards' Lifetime*. Edited by Don Kistler. Morgan: Soli Deo Gloria, 2004.

———. *Sermons and Discourses, 1720–1723*. Edited by Wilson H. Kimnach. Vol. 10 of *The Works of Jonathan Edwards*. New Haven: Yale University Press, 1992.

———. *Sermons and Discourses, 1723–1729*. Edited by Kenneth P. Minkema. Vol. 14 of *The Works of Jonathan Edwards*. New Haven: Yale University Press, 1997.

———. *Sermons and Discourses, 1730–1733*. Edited by Mark Valeri. Vol. 17 of *The Works of Jonathan Edwards*. New Haven: Yale University Press, 1999.

———. *Sermons and Discourses, 1739–1742*. Edited by Harry S. Stout and Nathan O. Hatch. Vol. 22 of *The Works of Jonathan Edwards*. New Haven: Yale University Press, 2003.

———. *Sermons and Discourses, 1743–1758*. Edited by Wilson H. Kimnach. Vol. 25 of *The Works of Jonathan Edwards*. New Haven: Yale University Press, 2006.

———. *Some Thoughts Concerning the Revival*. In *The Great Awakening*, edited by C. C. Goen, 289–515. Vol. 4 of *The Works of Jonathan Edwards*. New Haven: Yale University Press, 1972.

———. *Thoughts on the Revival of Religion in New England, 1740*. New York: American Tract Society, 1800.

———. *To the Rising Generation*. Orlando: Soli Deo Gloria, 2005.

Ellis, Thomas Talbot. "Samuel Davies: Characteristics of His Life and Message." *The Banner of Truth Magazine* 236 (1983). https://web.archive.org/web/20070414182107/http://www.puritansermons.com/banner/sdavies2.htm.

English, Donald. *An Evangelical Theology of Preaching*. Nashville: Abingdon, 1996.

Erickson, Millard. *Christian Theology*. 2d ed. Grand Rapids: Baker, 1998.

Erskine, Ebenezer. *The Whole Works of the Rev. Ebenezer Erskine*. 3 vols. Philadelphia: Young, 1836.

Fant, Clyde E. *Preaching for Today*. New York: Harper and Row, 1975.

Fant, Clyde E., and William M. Pinson Jr. *Wesley to Finney, 1703–1875*. Vol. 3 of *Twenty Centuries of Great Preaching: An Encyclopedia of Preaching*. Waco: Word, 1971.

Finley, Samuel. "Christ Triumphing and Satan Raging: A Sermon on Matthew 12:26 Wherein It Is Proven That the Kingdom of God Is Come Unto Us at This Day." In *The Great Awakening: Event and Exegesis*, edited by Darrett B. Rutman, 70–79. Huntington: Krieger, 1977.

Forsyth, Peter Taylor. *Positive Preaching and the Modern Mind*. 3d ed. Cumbria, Can.: Paternoster, 1949.

Garraty, John A., and Mark C. Carnes, eds. *American National Biography*. New York: Oxford University Press, 1999.

Garvie, Alfred Ernest. *The Christian Preacher*. New York: Charles Scribner's Sons, 1921.

Gaustad, Edwin Scott. *The Great Awakening in New England*. New York: Harper and Brothers, 1957.

———. *Records of the Presbyterian Church in the United States of America, 1706–1788*. New York: Arno and The New York Times, 1969.

———. *A Religious History of America*. Rev. ed. San Francisco: Harper, 1990.

Gaustad, Edwin Scott, et al. *New Historical Atlas of Religion in America*. Rev. ed. New York: Oxford University Press, 2001.

Gay, Peter. *Age of Enlightenment*. New York: Time, 1966.

———, ed. *The Enlightenment: A Comprehensive Anthology*. New York: Simon and Schuster, 1973.

Gewehr, Wesley M. *The Great Awakening in Virginia, 1740–1790*. Durham: Duke University Press, 1930.

Gewehr, Wesley M., et al., eds. *American Civilization: A History of the United States*. McGraw-Hill Series in History. New York: McGraw-Hill, 1957.

Gibb, Nancy. "How Much Does the Preaching Matter." *Time* 158 (2001) 62–63.

Gilborn, Craig A. "The Literary Work of the Reverend Samuel Davies." MA Thesis, University of Delaware, 1961.

Gildrie, Richard P. *The Profane, the Civil, and the Godly: The Reformation of Manners in Orthodox New England, 1679–1749*. University Park: Pennsylvania University, 1994.

Goff, Phillip. "Revivals and Revolution: Historiographic Turns Since Alan Heimert's Religion and the American Mind." *Church History* 67 (1998) 695–721.

Goldsworthy, Graeme. *Preaching the Whole Bible as Christian Scripture: The Application of Biblical Theology to Expository Preaching*. Grand Rapids: Eerdmans, 2000.

———. "What Is Preaching?" *Preaching* 17 (2001) 46–53.

Gonzalez, Justo L. *The Reformation to the Present Day*. Vol. 2 of *The Story of Christianity*. San Francisco: Harper, 1985.

Goodwin, Gerald J. "The Anglican Reaction to the Great Awakening." *Historical Magazine of the Protestant Episcopal Church* 35 (1966) 343–71.

Grasso, Domenico. *Proclaiming God's Message: A Study in the Theology of Preaching*. Notre Dame, IN: University of Notre Dame Press, 1965.

Greene, Jack P., and William G. McLoughlin. *Preachers and Politicians: Two Essays on the Origins of the American Revolution*. Worcester: American Antiquarian Society, 1977.

Greenhaw, David M. "Theology of Preaching." In *Concise Encyclopedia of Preaching*, edited by William H. Willimon and Richard Lischer, 477–82. Louisville: Westminster John Knox, 1995.

Greidanus, Sidney. *The Modern Preacher and the Ancient Text.* Grand Rapids: Eerdmans, 1989.

Gura, Philip F. *Jonathan Edwards: America's Evangelical.* New York: Hill and Wang, 2005.

Hall, E. Eugene, and James Heflin. *Proclaim the Word!* Nashville: Broadman, 1985.

Hambrick-Stowe, Charles E. "The Spirit of the Old Writers: Print Media, the Great Awakening, and Continuity in New England." In *Communication and Change in American Religious History*, edited by Leonard I. Sweet, 126–40. Grand Rapids: Eerdmans, 1993.

Hardman, Keith J., ed. *Issues in American Christianity: Primary Sources with Introductions.* Grand Rapids: Baker, 1993.

Harlan, David. *The Clergy and the Great Awakening in New England.* Ann Arbor: University Microfilms International, 1980.

Hatch, Nathan O. *The Democratization of American Christianity.* New Haven: Yale University Press, 1989.

Heimert, Alan. *Religion and the American Mind: From the Great Awakening to the Revolution.* Cambridge: Harvard University Press, 1966.

Heimert, Alan, and Perry Miller, eds. *The Great Awakening: Documents Illustrating the Crisis and Its Consequences.* Indianapolis: Bobbs-Merrill, 1967.

Heisler, Greg. *Spirit-Led Preaching: The Holy Spirit's Role in Sermon Preparation and Delivery.* Nashville: Broadman and Holman, 2007.

Heyrman, Christine Leigh. *Southern Cross: The Beginnings of the Bible Belt.* Chapel Hill: University of North Carolina Press, 1997.

Hill, Jonathan. *Faith in the Age of Reason: The Enlightenment from Galileo to Kant.* Downers Grove, IL: InterVarsity, 2004.

Hinson, E. Glenn. "The Baptist Experience in America." *One in Christ* 17 (1981) 190–204.

Hodge, Charles. *The Constitutional History of the Presbyterian Church in the United States of America, 1705–1741.* Philadelphia: Presbyterian Board of Publication and Sabbath-School Work, 1851.

Holifield, E. Brooks. *God's Ambassadors: A History of the Christian Clergy in America.* Grand Rapids: Eerdmans, 2007.

Holland, Dewitte, ed. *Preaching in American History: Selected Issues in the America Pulpit, 1630–1967.* Nashville: Abingdon, 1969.

———. *The Preaching Tradition: A Brief History.* Nashville: Abingdon, 1980.

Hopkins, Samuel. *The Life and Character of the Late Reverend, Learned, and Pious Mr. Jonathan Edwards.* In *Jonathan Edwards, a Profile*, edited by David Levin, 1–86. American Profiles. New York: Hill and Wang, 1969.

Howard, Leon. *"The Mind" of Jonathan Edwards: A Reconstructed Text.* Los Angeles: University of California Press, 1963.

Howe, Reuel. *Partners in Preaching.* New York: Seabury, 1967.

Hudson, Winthrop S., and John Corrigan. *Religion in America: An Historical Account of the Development of American Religion Life.* 5th ed. New York: MacMillan, 1992.

Hyland, Paul, ed. *The Enlightenment: A Sourcebook and Reader.* London: Routledge, 2003.

Isaac, Rhys. *The Transformation of Virginia, 1740–1790.* Chapel Hill: University of North Carolina Press, 1982.

Jamison, Wallace N. *Religion in New Jersey: A Brief History*. Princeton: Van Nostrand, 1964.

Jarratt, Devereux. *The Life of the Reverend Devereux Jarratt: An Autobiography*. Cleveland: Pilgrim, 1995.

Jensen, Richard A. *Telling a Story: Variety and Imagination in Preaching*. Minneapolis: Augsburg, 1980.

Jenson, Robert W. *America's Theologian: A Recommendation of Jonathan Edwards*. Oxford: Oxford University Press, 1988.

Johnson, Curtis D. *Redeeming America: Evangelicals and the Road to Civil War*. Chicago: Dee, 1993.

Johnston, Graham. *Preaching to a Postmodern World: A Guide to Reaching Twenty-First Century Listeners*. Grand Rapids: Baker Academic, 2001.

Jones, Hugh. The Present State of Virginia. New York: Sabin, 1865. Produced by Julia Miller et al., Project Gutenberg, 2009. https://www.gutenberg.org/files/29055/29055-h/29055-h.htm.

Jones, Philip. *Assessing the Nation's Religious Composition*. North American Mission Board, accessed March 18, 2008. http://media2.sbhla.org.s3.amazonaws.com/collections/hmb_namb_reports/hmb-namb-report_169.pdf.

Keck, Leander. *The Bible in the Pulpit: The Renewal of Biblical Preaching*. Nashville: Abingdon, 1978.

Keevil, Philip W. *Preaching in Revival: Preaching and a Theology of Awakening*. Lanham: University Press of America, 1999.

Kidd, Thomas S. *The Great Awakening: The Roots of Evangelical Christianity in Colonial America*. New Haven: Yale University Press, 2007.

Kimball, Dan. *The Emerging Church*. Grand Rapids: Zondervan, 2003.

Kuklick, Bruce. *Churchmen and Philosophers: From Jonathan Edwards to John Dewey*. London: Yale University Press, 1985.

Lambert, Frank. "The Great Awakening as Artifact." *Church History* 60 (1991) 223–46.

———. *Inventing the "Great Awakening."* Princeton: Princeton University Press, 1999.

———. *"Peddlar in Divinity": George Whitefield and the Transatlantic Revivals, 1737–1770*. Princeton: Princeton University Press, 1994.

Larsen, David L. *The Company of Preachers: A History of Biblical Preaching from the Old Testament to the Modern Era*. Grand Rapids: Kregel, 1998.

Larson, Barbara Ann. "A Rhetorical Study of the Preaching of the Reverend Samuel Davies in the Colony of Virginia from 1747–1759." PhD Thesis, University of Minnesota, 1969.

Lee, Sang Hyun, and Allen C. Guelzo, eds. *Edwards in Our Time: Jonathan Edwards and the Shaping of American Religion*. Grand Rapids: Eerdmans, 1999.

Lescelius, Robert H. "The Great Awakening: A Pattern Revival." *Reformation and Revival* 4 (1995) 25–38.

Lessenich, Rolf P. *Elements of Pulpit Oratory in Eighteenth-Century England (1660–1800)*. Cologne: Böhlau, 1972

Library of Congress. "The Eliot Indian Bible: First Bible Printed in America." https://web.archive.org/web/20130526165750/http://www.myloc.gov/Exhibitions/Bibles/OtherBibles/ExhibitObjects/TheEliotIndianBibleFirstBiblePrintedinAmerica.aspx?ImageId=886c5b91-a9b5-4fbf-a7e2-776c45f18484%3A8275982c-7354-4f46-af30-5948c4102449%3A321.

Lim, Johnson T. K. *Power in Preaching*. Lanham: University Press of America, 2002.

Lippy, Charles H., and Peter W. Williams, eds. *Encyclopedia of the American Religious Experience: Studies of Traditions and Movements*. 3 vols. New York: Scribner's, 1988.
Lischer, Richard, ed. *The Company of Preachers: Wisdom on Preaching, Augustine to the Present*. Grand Rapids: Eerdmans, 2002.
———. *A Theology of Preaching: the Dynamics of the Gospel*. Nashville: Abingdon, 1981.
Lloyd-Jones, D. Martyn. *The Puritans: Their Origins and Successors*. Carlisle: Banner of Truth Trust, 1987.
Lodge, Martin Ellsworth. "The Great Awakening in the Middle Colonies." PhD diss., University of California, Berkeley, 1965.
Long, Thomas G. *Preaching and the Literary Forms of the Bible*. Philadelphia: Fortress, 1989.
Loscalzo, Craig A. *Apologetic Preaching: Proclaiming Christ to a Postmodern World*. Downers Grove, IL: InterVarsity, 2000.
Lovejoy, David S., ed. *Religious Enthusiasm and the Great Awakening*. New Jersey: Prentice-Hall, 1969.
Lovelace, Richard. "The Surprising Works of God." *Christianity Today* 39 (1995) 28–32.
Lowry, Eugene. *The Homiletical Plot: The Sermon as Narrative Art Form*. Louisville: Westminster, 1980.
Macartney, Clarence Edward. *Sons of Thunder: Pulpit Power of the Past*. New York: Revell, 1929.
Manuel, Frank E. *The Enlightenment*. Englewood Cliffs, NJ: Prentice Hall, 1965.
Marsden, George M. "Edwards, Jonathan." In *Concise Encyclopedia of Preaching*, edited by William H. Willimon and Richard Lischer, 113–15. Louisville: Westminster John Knox, 1995.
———. *Jonathan Edwards: A Life*. New Haven: Yale University Press, 2003.
Maxson, Charles Hartshorn. *The Great Awakening in the Middle Colonies*. Chicago: University of Chicago Press, 1920.
May, Henry F. *The Enlightenment in America*. New York: Oxford University Press, 1976.
McDow, Malcolm, and Alvin L. Reid. *Firefall: How God Has Shaped History Through Revivals*. Nashville: Broadman and Holman, 1997.
Merriam-Webster. "Occupation." Last updated January 13, 2026. https://www.merriam-webster.com/dictionary/occupation.
———. "Vocation." Last updated January 21, 2026. https://www.merriam-webster.com/dictionary/vocation.
Miller, Howard. *The Revolutionary College: American Presbyterian Higher Education, 1707–1837*. New York: New York University Press, 1976.
Mulder, Philip N. *A Controversial Spirit: Evangelical Awakenings in the South*. Religion in America. Oxford: Oxford University Press, 2002.
Muncy, W. L., Jr. *A History of Evangelism in the United States*. Kansas City: Central Seminary Press, 1945.
Murphy, Thomas. *The Presbytery of the Log College*. Philadelphia: Presbyterian Board of Publication and Sabbath-School Work, 1989.
Murray, Iain H. *Jonathan Edwards: A New Biography*. Edinburgh: Banner of Truth Trust, 1987.
———. *Revival and Revivalism: The Making and Marring of American Evangelicalism, 1750–1858*. Carlisle: Banner of Truth Trust, 1994.
Nichols, Stephen J. *Jonathan Edwards: A Guided Tour of His Life and Thought*. Phillipsburg, NJ: P&R, 2001.

Noll, Mark A. "From the Great Awakening to the War of Independence." *Christian Scholar's Review* 12 (1983) 99–110.

———. *A History of Christianity in the United States and Canada*. Grand Rapids: Eerdmans, 1992.

———. *The Rise of Evangelicalism: The Age of Edwards, Whitefield, and the Wesleys*. Downers Grove, IL: InterVarsity, 2003.

Noll, Mark A., et al., eds. *Eerdman's Handbook to Christianity in America*. Grand Rapids: Eerdmans, 1983.

Northcutt, Jesse J. "Proclamation: The Theological Imperative." *Southwestern Journal of Theology* 8 (1966) 7–14.

Oberg, Barbara B., and Harry S. Stout. *Benjamin Franklin, Jonathan Edwards, and the Representation of American Culture*. New York: Oxford University Press, 1993.

O'Brien, Susan. "A Transatlantic Community of Saints: The Great Awakening and the First Evangelical Network, 1735–1755." *American Historical Review* 91 (1986) 811–32.

Old, Hughes Oliphant. "Gilbert Tennent and the Preaching of Piety in Colonial America: Newly Discovered Tennent Manuscripts in Speer Library." *Princeton Seminary Bulletin* 10 (1989) 132–37. https://archive.org/details/princetonseminar1021prin/page/n3/mode/2up.

———. *Moderatism, Pietism, and Awakening*. Vol. 5 of *The Reading and Preaching of the Scriptures in the Worship of the Christian Church*. Grand Rapids: Eerdmans, 2004.

Olsen, Kirstin. *Daily Life in 18th-Century England*. Westport: Greenwood, 1999.

Ong, Walter J. *Orality and Literacy: The Technologizing of the Word*. London: Routledge, 1982.

Packer, J. I. *Among God's Giants: The Puritan Vision for the Christian Life*. Eastbourne, UK: Kingsway, 1991.

Pagitt, Doug. *Preaching Re-Imagined*. Grand Rapids: Zondervan, 2005.

Pang, Patrick. "The Pastoral Preaching of Jonathan Edwards." *Preaching* 7 (1992) 56–62.

Pattison, T. Harwood. *The History of Christian Preaching*. Philadelphia: American Baptist Publication Society, 1903.

Perkins, William. "The Arte of Prophesying." In *The Work of William Perkins*, edited by Ian Breward, 325–50. Foxton, UK: Burlington, 1970.

Pilcher, George William. *Samuel Davies: Apostle of Dissent in Colonial Virginia*. Knoxville: University of Tennessee Press, 1971.

Piney.com. "Cause and Effect: The First Great American Awakening." https://web.archive.org/web/20031002215825/http://www.piney.com/ColAwkEffect.html.

Piper, John. *The Supremacy of God in Preaching*. Rev. ed. Grand Rapids: Baker, 2004.

Prince, Thomas. *An Account of the Revival of Religion in Boston, in the Years 1740–1743*. Boston: Armstrong, Crocker, & Brewster, 1823.

———, ed. *The Christian History*. Saskatoon: HardPress, 2018.

Quicke, Michael J. *360-Degree Preaching: Hearing, Speaking, and Living the Word*. Grand Rapids: Baker Academic, 2003.

Richard, Ramesh. *Preparing Expository Sermons: A Seven-Step Method for Biblical Preaching*. Grand Rapids: Baker, 2001.

Ritschl, Dietrich. *A Theology of Proclamation*. Richmond: John Knox, 1960.

Roberts, Richard Owen. *Revival*. Wheaton, IL: Richard Owen Roberts, 1997.

———. *Revival Literature: An Annotated Bibliography with Biographical and Historical Notices*. Wheaton, IL: Richard Owen Roberts, 1987.

Robinson, Haddon. *Biblical Preaching: The Development and Delivery of Expository Messages*. 2d ed. Grand Rapids: Baker Academic, 2001.

Robinson, Haddon, and Craig Brian Larson, eds. *The Art and Craft of Biblical Preaching: A Comprehensive Resource for Today's Communicators*. Grand Rapids: Zondervan, 2005.

Rudé, George. "Philosophers of the Enlightenment." In *Headlines in History: The 1700s*, edited by Stuart A. Kallen, 101–4. San Diego: Greenhaven, 2001.

Rust, Eric C. *The Word and Words: Towards a Theology of Preaching*. Macon, GA: Mercer University Press, 1982.

Rutman, Darrett B., ed. *The Great Awakening: Event and Exegesis*. Huntington: Krieger, 1977.

The SAGE Digital Library. Vol. 1–4. Albany: SAGE Software, 1996. CD-ROM.

Scharpff, Paulus. *History of Evangelism*. Translated by Helga Bender Henry. Grand Rapids: Eerdmans, 1966.

Schmitt, Dale J. "Preparation for the Great Awakening in Connecticut." *Religion in Life* 47 (1978) 430–40.

Scott, Donald M. *From Office to Profession: The New England Ministry, 1750–1850*. Pittsburgh: University of Pennsylvania Press, 1978.

Secretary of the Commonwealth of Massachusetts. "The History of the Arms and Great Seal of the Commonwealth of Massachusetts." https://www.sec.state.ma.us/divisions/public-records/history-of-seal.htm.

Semmelroth, Otto. *The Preaching Word: On the Theology of Proclamation*. New York: Herder and Herder, 1965.

Shaw, Mark R. "The Spirit of 1740." *Christianity Today* 20 (1976) 7–8.

Shelley, Bruce. *Church History in Plain Language*. Dallas: Word, 1982.

Sherman, David. *Sketches of New England Divines*. New York: Carlton and Porter, 1860.

Simonson, Harold P. *Jonathan Edwards: Theologian of the Heart*. Grand Rapids: Eerdmans, 1974.

Sleeth, Ronald E. "The Office of Preaching: A Theological Appraisal." *Perkins School of Theology Journal* 19 (1965) 38–44.

Smith, Elwyn Allen. *The Presbyterian Ministry in American Culture*. Philadelphia: Westminster, 1957.

Smith, H. Shelton, et al. *American Christianity: An Historical Interpretation with Representative Documents*. 2 vols. New York: Charles Scribner's Sons, 1960.

Smith, John E. *Jonathan Edwards: Puritan, Preacher, Philosopher*. Notre Dame, IN: University of Notre Dame Press, 1992.

———. "A Treatise Concerning Religious Affections." *American Presbyterians* 66 (1988) 219–22.

Sprague, William B. *Annals of the American Pulpit*. New York: Carter and Brothers, 1857.

Spener, Philipp Jacob. *Pia Desideria*. Translated and edited by Theodore G. Tappert. Philadelphia: Fortress, 1964.

Stearns, Monroe. *The Great Awakening, 1720–1760: Religious Revival Rouses Americans' Sense of Individual Liberties*. New York: Watts, 1970.

Steimle, Edmund A. "Preaching as the Word Made Relevant." *Lutheran Quarterly* 6 (1954) 11–22.

Steimle, Edmund A., et al. *Preaching the Story*. Philadelphia: Fortress, 1980.

Stevenson, Dwight T. "The Word of God Through the Words of Men." *Lexington Theological Quarterly* 7 (1972) 1–10.

Stoddard, Solomon. *The Defects of Preachers Reproved, in a Sermon Preached at Northampton, May 19th, 1723*. 2nd ed. Boston: Kneeland and Green, 1747. https://archive.org/details/bim_eighteenth-century_the-defects-of-preachers_stoddard-solomon-minis_1747/page/n1/mode/2up.

Stott, John R. W. *Between Two Worlds: The Art of Preaching in the Twentieth Century*. Grand Rapids: Eerdmans, 1982.

Stout, Harry S. *The Divine Dramatist: George Whitefield and the Rise of Modern Evangelicalism*. Grand Rapids: Eerdmans, 1991.

———. "Heavenly Comet." *Christian History* 38 (1993). https://web.archive.org/web/20041104191836/http://ctlibrary.com/3948.

———. *The New England Soul: Preaching and Religious Culture in Colonial New England*. New York: Oxford University Press, 1986.

———. "The Transforming Effects of the Great Awakening." In *Eerdman's Handbook to Christianity in America*, edited by Mark A. Noll et al., 127–30. Grand Rapids: Eerdmans, 1983.

Sweet, Leonard I., ed. *Communication and Change in American Religious History*. Grand Rapids: Eerdmans, 1993.

Sweet, William Warren. *Religion in Colonial America*. New York: Charles Scribner's Sons, 1942.

———. *Revivalism in America: Its Origin, Growth, and Decline*. New York: Charles Scribner's Sons, 1944.

———. *The Story of Religion in America*. New York: Harper and Brothers, 1939.

Tanis, James. *Dutch Calvinistic Pietism in the Middle Colonies: A Study in the Life and Theology of Theodorus Jacobus Frelinghuysen*. The Hague: Nijhoff, 1967.

———. "Frelinghuysen, The Dutch Clergy, and The Great Awakening in the Middle Colonies." *Reformed and Review* 38 (1985) 109–18.

Taylor, Thomas Templeton. "The Spirit of the Awakening: The Pneumatology of New England's Great Awakening in Historical and Theological Context." PhD diss., University of Illinois, 1988.

Tennent, Gilbert. "The Danger of an Unconverted Ministry." In *The Great Awakening: Documents Illustrating the Crisis and Its Consequences*, edited by Alan Heimert and Perry Miller, 71–99. Indianapolis: Bobbs-Merrill, 1967.

———. *Discourses on Several Important Subjects*. Philadelphia: Bradford, 1745.

———. *The Divinity of the Sacred Scriptures Considered*. Boston: 1739.

———. *The Gilbert Tennent Manuscript Collection*. Princeton: Princeton Theological Seminary Library, 1994.

———. *The Necessity of Holding Fast the Truth Represented in Three Sermons*. Boston: Kneeland and Green, 1743.

———. *The Preciousness of Christ to Believers*. Boston: 1739.

———. *A Sermon Upon Justification*. Philadelphia: Franklin, 1741.

———. *Sermons on Important Subjects*. Philadelphia: Chattin, 1758.

———. *Thoughts on Extempore Preaching*. 1762.

———. *Twenty-Three Sermons Upon the Chief End of Man*. Philadelphia: Bradford, 1744.

———. *The Unsearchable Riches of Christ*. Boston: Draper, 1737.

Tennent, Gilbert, and Samuel Davies. *To the Worthy and Generous Friends of Religion and Learning; The Petition of G. Tennent and S. Davies, in the Name of the Trustees of the Infant College of New Jersey*. 1754.

Thompson, Ernest Trice. *1607–1865*. Vol. 1 of *Presbyterians in the South*. Richmond: John Knox, 1963.

Thornbury, John F. "Another Look at the First Great Awakening." *Reformation and Revival* 4 (1995) 15–23.

Tracy, Joseph. *The Great Awakening: A History of the Revival of Religion in the Time of Edwards and Whitefield*. Edinburgh: Banner of Truth Trust, 1976.

Tracy, Patricia J. *Jonathan Edwards, Pastor: Religion and Society in Eighteenth Century Northampton*. New York: Hill and Wang, 1980.

Trinterud, Leonard J. *The Forming of an American Tradition*. Philadelphia: Westminster, 1949.

Turnbull, Ralph G. *From the Close of the Nineteenth Century to the Middle of the Twentieth Century*. Vol. 3 of *A History of Preaching*. Grand Rapids: Baker, 1974.

———. *Jonathan Edwards: The Preacher*. Grand Rapids: Baker, 1958.

Van de Wetering, John E. "The 'Christian History' of the Great Awakening." *Journal of Presbyterian History* 44 (1966) 122–29.

Vos, Howard Frederic. "The Great Awakening in Connecticut." PhD diss., Northwestern University, 1967.

Watts, Isaac. *An Humble Attempt Toward the Revival of Practical Religion Among Christians*. London: Matthews, 1731.

Webber, F. R. *A History of Preaching in Britain and America*. 3 vols. Milwaukee: Northwestern, 1952–57.

Weis, Frederick Lewis. *The Colonial Clergy and the Colonial Churches of New England*. Baltimore: Genealogical, 1977.

———. *The Colonial Clergy of the Middle Colonies: New York, New Jersey, and Pennsylvania, 1628–1776*. Worcester: Society, 1957.

Westerkamp, Marilyn. "Division, Dissension, and Compromise: The Presbyterian Church During the Great Awakening." *Journal of Presbyterian History* 78 (2000) 3–18.

Whitefield, George. *George Whitefield's Journals*. London: Banner of Truth Trust, 1960.

———. *Letters of George Whitefield*. Edited by S. M. Houghton. Edinburgh: Banner of Truth Trust, 1976.

Wigglesworth, Samuel. "An Essay for Reviving Religion." In *The Great Awakening: Documents Illustrating the Crisis and Its Consequences*, edited by Alan Heimert and Perry Miller, 3–7. Indianapolis: Bobbs-Merrill, 1967.

Willimon, William H., and Richard Lischer, eds. *Concise Encyclopedia of Preaching*. Louisville: Westminster John Knox, 1995.

Wilson, Paul Scott. *Preaching and Homiletical Theory*. St. Louis: Chalice, 2004.

Wilson-Kastner, Patricia. *Coherence in a Fragmented World: Jonathan Edwards' Theology of the Holy Spirit*. Washington: University of America, 1978.

Winslow, Ola Elizabeth. *Jonathan Edwards, 1703–1758: A Biography*. New York: Macmillan, 1940.

Witham, Larry. *A City Upon a Hill: How Sermons Changed the Course of American History*. New York: Harper Collins, 2007.

Woodfin, Yandall. "The Theology of Preaching: A Search for the Authentic." *Scottish Journal of Theology* 23 (1970) 408–19.

Woolverton, John Frederick. *Colonial Anglicanism in North America*. Detroit: Wayne State University Press, 1984.

Wright, Henry Alexander. *Southern Presbyterian Leaders, 1683–1911*. Edinburgh: Banner of Truth, 2000.

Young, Ed, Jr. “Communicating with Creativity.” *Preaching* 20 (2005) 9–13.

Young, Ed, Jr., and Andy Stanley. *Can We Do That? 24 Innovative Practices That Will Change the Way You Do Church*. New York: Howard, 2002.

www.ingramcontent.com/pod-product-compliance
Lightning Source LLC
LaVergne TN
LVHW050638100826
845148LV00011B/1903

* 9 7 8 1 6 6 6 7 0 7 0 0 7 *